W9-CIP-929

The
Basset Hound

Front Cover: Ch Brackenacre Navan. Photo: Michael M Trafford
Above: (left to rignt) Badgerbrook Bonn of Brushdew,
Ch Badgerbrook Dirty Harry and Badgerbrook Berlin of Brushdew.
Overleaf: Ch Pointgrey Suss's Folly.

© 1999 Kingdom Books, PO Box 15, Waterlooville PO7 6BQ, England.

The Basset Hound
Contents

DEDICATION

This book is dedicated to my husband, Jim, who also is devoted to the Basset Hound.

ACKNOWLEDGEMENTS

I should like to thank the following for their help with this book:

The Kennel Club
for allowing Breed Standard and the definitions of various classes at dog shows to be printed;

Mr George Johnston (Sykemoor Bassets)
for all his help and advice and for the use of his Basset memorabilia;

Mr Bob Wine (Freway Chow Chows)
who has spent so much time typing my manuscript onto the computer;

Mr Robert Lusk BVMS MRCVS
who checked the chapter on Health Care
and has taken such good care of the Brackenacre Bassets for so many years;

Mrs Margaret Rawle (Barnspark Bassets)
who has advised me about the Bassets of yesteryear and allowed me to use her Basset memorabilia;

Mr Michael Errey,
who so kindly wrote the chapter on the hunting Basset;

Mr Frederiksen (Ambrican)
who me gave so much information about the Basset Hound in North America.

I am most grateful to all who have sent me details of their kennels and given me permission to use photographs of their hounds.

FOREWORD

As a lifelong devotee of Basset hounds and an eager student of their history I am always delighted when a new book about the breed appears. The author and I have been friends since her debut with Bassets in 1962. Since that year Marianne Nixon has produced 17 British champions and become a Hound Group judge with an international reputation. The hounds emerging from the Brackenacre kennels (a partnership concern with her husband, Jim) have impressed many with their type, sensible size, good temperaments and tri-colour hue. Perseverance and a conviction to produce the same style of Basset, regardless of fashion changes within the breed, have been the hallmarks of her West Country kennel. These credentials provide Marianne with more than adequate qualifications to pen this book.

Much has changed since Marianne's introduction to Basset Hounds. The Kennel Club Breed Standard has been revised, importations of hounds from Europe and the United States of America have been made, new breed societies have been formed and old records and photographs have come to light. These changes have taken place since the last book by a British Basset Hound breeder was written. The most important works in recent years have been the meticulously researched volumes by Mlle Berton and Messrs Leblanc and Miller – both published in French. An up-to-date work in English and of equal depth was essential, and Marianne's book will certainly do much to redress the balance. Access to the recently-discovered breed records enables her to present new material to those who revel in the Basset's past, while her chapters on breeding, rearing and feeding these dwarf hounds will be closely scrutinised by those wishing to produce sound, healthy hounds, be they for exhibition, sport or companionship.

Authors have served the breed well in the past, their work, time and effort making their books 'labours of love'. This book is timely, taking Basset literature one step further, and Marianne's commonsense approach to text, content and provision of illustrations gives us a volume which will be frequently used for reference, help and – above all – pleasure.

George Johnston
Wigton, Cumbria

Chapter 2

INTRODUCTION

I have been surrounded by dogs all my life. My parents bred Pekingese under the Budemoor prefix and I handled them at shows. My brother and his wife bred Cavalier King Charles Spaniels and had a Staffordshire Bull Terrier. So how did I start with Basset Hounds?

Before our marriage, Jim accompanied my mother and me to Crufts. Not wanting to stay with the Pekingese all day, he wandered off to look at other breeds. Hours later, he came back to say he had found a marvellous hound. It was a Basset, of course.

When we had been married a couple of years, I bought Jim a tri-coloured bitch from Mrs Goldie, of the Kierhill Bassets, as a surprise birthday present. This was our first Basset: Kierhill Oonagh (Ch Crochmaid Bold Turpin of Blackheath ex Grims Flimsy), otherwise known as Bijou. When that happy, self-possessed little 10-week-old puppy trotted out of her travelling crate after a 500-mile train journey, little did I know that, 30 years later, we would have bred 17 United Kingdom

The author with two Brackenacre Bassets, April and Daisy.

champions and countless overseas champions in direct line from her.

Because we liked the dark tri-colours, Bijou was mated in 1964 to Hardacre Sungarth Eager. In her only litter she produced Ch Brackenacre Annabella. Annabella had two litters, the first to Ch Wingjays Ptolemy and the second to Ch Fredwell Varon Vandal. From Vandal she produced Ch Brackenacre Daisy Belle and from Ptolemy the bi-colour Brackenacre Chime of Bells who, when mated to Ch Fredwell Ideal, produced Ch Brackenacre Fino de Paris, owned by Mrs May Bews and winner of 14 Challenge Certificates (CCs) and Best Of Breed (BOB) at Crufts in 1973 and 1974. When mated to Brackenacre Emma Peel, a daughter of Ch Ballymaconnel Forester, Fino sired Ch Brackenacre James Bond. When put with Witchacre Magpie of Brackenacre (Bezel Action Man ex Ch Brackenacre Jingle Bell), Ch Brackenacre James Bond produced what was, to my mind, the best Basset we had ever bred: the black-blanket Ch Brackenacre The Viking, who won 30 CCs, 30 Reserve CCs, BOB Crufts, many Best In Show (BIS) awards at breed championship shows and Reserve BIS at Southern Counties All-Breed Championship Show. He sired several champions and is the great-great-grandsire of Ch Brackenacre Navan, BOB at Crufts 1996 and herself a championship show hound group winner.

The Bassets created a different life style for us: most week-ends were spent travelling to different shows, making new friends, and enjoying all the good times. We became involved in judging Bassets and various other breeds. I now judge 14 breeds of hound at championship show level and hound group, and Jim also judges several breeds at championship show level.

With all the enjoyment the Bassets have given us, I can only hope our breeding will be a foundation for future Basset enthusiasts of sound, healthy hounds with all the breed characteristics and happy temperaments.

Marianne R Nixon
Plymouth, Devon

It is known that all dogs evolve from *Tomarctos*, who lived 15 million years ago. This animal was ancestor of *Canis familiaris leinieri*, the forerunner of the sighthound breeds, Afghan Hounds, Greyhounds and Saluki, continuing down to the St Hubert type scenthounds and their descendants, including *basset*-sized hounds.

All modern, straight-legged scenthounds have St Hubert ancestry, and most of the French hound breeds had a dwarfed or *basset* version with crooked and shortened limbs. The generally accepted view is that the first basset-sized hound appeared in litters from normal *(Grand chien)* parents. These hounds are found in several versions: the blue-mottled Gascogne, the rough-coated *(griffon)* Vendéen and Bretagne and the ancestors of the present-day Basset Hound: Basset d'Artois and Basset Normand. The names indicate the areas of France where each of these breeds originated. Apart from their obvious lack of height, the little hounds are identical in every way to the parent breed.

Basset means *dwarf*, or *low structure*, and the reduction in height is not confined to canines; its occurrence is well recorded in other species. Although we have no authenticated history of early Basset Hound development, it is fairly safe to assume that curiosity prompted breeders to breed basset to basset, thus establishing a type of hound that proved invaluable for slow, musical and diligent hunting. Artists and authors working in the Middle Ages have provided evidence of the little hounds and the work they did. To all intents and purposes, the Basset is an accident of nature, a freak perpetuated by breeding like to like. Centuries of such breeding has not entirely eliminated the occurrence of normal-sized hounds in Basset litters, although this is rare, the last recorded instance in Great Britain being in the mid-1930s.

A diagram by Leon Verrier (L'Eleveur 1939), showing how the basset is a reduction of the *Grandchien*.

French Origins

There is a charming story regarding Hubert, a nobleman in the sixth century, son of the Duc de Guienne, who was very fond of breeding and hunting hounds. One day whilst hunting in a forest in the Ardennes he came upon a magnificent stag. Between the antlers of the stag was a shining cross. Taking this to be a sign from heaven, Hubert dedicated the rest of his life to God. He became the Abbot of a large monastery, The Abbey of St Hubert in the Ardennes. He was subsequently canonised and became the patron saint of hunting.

St Hubert bred his hounds in two varieties of colour: black-and-tan and white. The black-and-tan hunted boar and wolf and were probably the originators of Bloodhounds as we know them today. The white hounds were used for stag hunting.

George Turbeville wrote in his book *Art of Venerie* (1576): *the St Hubert are mighty of body, legs low and short, not swift, but very good on scent, they come in all colours*. The definition in an French-English dictionary dated 1632 is: *Chien de St Hubert: a kind of strong short-legged hound, and deep mouthed*.

The St Hubert Hounds were vastly superior to most other hounds of the period and much sought after. They were given to or obtained by the aristocracy over a wide area of France. Because of this wide distribution, the St Hubert played a leading role in developing the numerous French hound breeds. By mating the St Hubert to their own native breeds and culling undesirable colours and types, the noblemen established stag hunting dogs *(chiens courants)* of distinct breeds, but with the genes of the low-set St Hubert behind them. These hounds occasionally threw back to their ancestors and produced low-set hounds. In the early days, each French hound breed was found in these versions, regulated only by size:

- *Chiens d'ordre:* full-sized hounds standing upwards of 60cm (23in), hunting such quarry as stag and boar.
- *Chiens briquets:* hounds standing 38–55cm (15–22in), hunting small game such as the hare.
- *Chiens bassets:* low hounds, under 38cm (15in) in height, hunting small game and used as terriers.

The last of these groups was sub-divided by the degree of crook of the forelegs:

- *Bassets à jambes droites:* straight-legged bassets.
- *Bassets à jambes torses:* full-crooked forelegs.
- *Bassets à jambes demi torses:* half-crooked forelegs.

The straight-legged hounds were used as running hounds for hunting hares and rabbits and the two crooked-legged varieties were used underground as terriers and truffle-hunting dogs.

Petit Basset Griffon Vendéen:
Ch Kasani Jofflu, owned by Mrs Bews. Photo: Gibbs

Basset Fauve de Bretagne: Vanity v Gellrichs Hoekje of Houndsline, owned by Mr and Mrs R Johnson.

Basset Artésien-Normand:
Fin Ch Billhill Elan, owned by Mrs Marita Massingberd.

Basset Petit Bleu de Gascogne.
Faileuse de la Petite Gloriette, owned by Mme Dupont.

France possesses several varieties of hounds, of which six have a basset variety. Although this book is about the Basset Hound, I cannot fail to mention these distant relations. No doubt all derived from a common ancestor many centuries ago, but evolved to hunt the particular terrain they lived in. They include:

- Basset Griffon Vendéen (rough-coated)
- Basset Fauve de Bretagne (rough-coated)
- Basset Bleu de Gascogne (smooth-coated)
- Basset Artésien-Normand (smooth-coated)
- Vosges/Forêt Noire Basset (smooth-coated)
- Basset Saintongeois

Hounds in Britain

Meanwhile, the British had their own hunting dogs, and the exchange across the Channel did not end with the exchange of local produce. The Cornish and Bretons held wrestling competitions, the fishermen intermingled, and there were marriages between English and French aristocracy. Can we assume the French arrivals brought hounds, including Bassets, with them? I like to think so.

Centuries ago, Cornwall was home of a breed of short, crooked-legged hounds. Several places in Devon and Cornwall contain wood carvings depicting a pack of hounds with their Master. The hounds are very similar, with short legs, long bodies and ears, and sterns carried gaily. One such carving is on a Welsh oak bedstead in Cothele House at St Dominicks in Cornwall. The bed was part of the furniture when a certain Katherine married Sir Piers Edgcumbe in 1532. There are other scenes carved on this bedstead, but it is interesting to note the English Heraldic Lions, the Tudor Arms and the French Fleurs-de-Lis. Another piece of carving, on the fireplace in the great hall at The Manor, Lewtrenchard, Lewdown, near Okehampton, Devon, which was built about 1600, depicts a pack of hounds very similar in type to what we now know as Basset Hounds.

In all probability, the St Hubert breed was brought over by William The Conqueror. His hounds were described as having long ears, often crook-fronted and with heavy dewlaps. Could these hounds have been what eventually became known as *Talbots* – an anglicised version of *Taillebois*, and also possibly an ancestor of the old Southern Hound? This breed was known in England for centuries and figures prominently in the literature of English fox hunting. It would seem this hound varied in size and colouring from county to county. In a painting of 'The Southern Hound' in 1803 by P Reinagle RA, from *The Sportsman*, the hound appeared more like a Harrier, with plenty of white about its body, but a much heavier head, deep lips and long ears. When writing about Harriers, The Lady Gifford, Master of Hounds in 1907, remarked, *some masters have a great fancy for the dark colouring of the old Southern Hound,* leading one to believe they were more Bloodhound in colouring.

Basset History in England

Stonehenge (Mr J H Walsh) when writing about the Basset in 1859, quoted: *The earliest French authority Du Fouilloux described them as Bassets d'Artois,* and explains the title by saying that the breed originally came from that province and nearby Flanders. He divided them into varieties: the Artésien, with full-crooked forelegs, smooth coats, brave, and having teeth like wolves, and the Flemish, straight-legged, rough-coated, black, and sterns curled like a horn. This division was confirmed by two later authors, Selincourt and Leverrier de la Contèrie. The latter expressed his preference for the Flemish, as being faster, but said they gave tongue noisily, and were babblers. He found the Artésiens *courageous in going to earth, long in body, and with noble heads.* The descendants of the Flemish type still exist in the Forêt Noire and in the Vosges and possibly in the German Dachshund.

Basset d'Artois à jambes droites.

The Artésien type is that with which English dog show habitués are now familiar. After the ravages of war, many of that hound breed had disappeared or were dispersed either singly or in small groups in various areas. Comte Couteulx de Canteleu spared neither trouble nor expense to obtain and preserve the smooth-coated tri-colour Basset d'Artois in its purity. It was the Couteulx strain that was sought after by English breeders when Bassets began to be popular and fashionable in the 19th Century.

It was interesting to read how useful the Basset was to French sportsmen. Two or three would be used to drive small quarry, such as hare, rabbits, and roebuck out of covert. They would drive the quarry slowly, giving the guns ample time to prepare for a shot at the game. This type of hunting *(Chasse au tir)* is still widely practised in France. The Basset was not familiar to British sportsmen prior to 1863, when some were exhibited at the first exhibition of dogs held in Paris. Many English visitors

Briquets d'Artois.

expressed great admiration for this quaint little hound. Two were imported by Lord Galway in the autumn of 1866.

The Basset in Britain in the 19th Century

Lord Galway wrote a letter to Major C Heseltine (Walhampton Bassets) dated 26 August 1925:

> In July 1866, I was staying at Royat, Puy de Dome, France where I met the Marquis de Tournon and his son the Comte de Tournon. The latter promised me a couple of Basset Hounds from his pack which duly arrived in the autumn at Selby. They were a dog and a bitch and I called them Basset and Belle. They were long low hounds shaped much like a Dachshund with crooked fore legs at the knees with much more bone and longer heads than on a Beagle. They were not the dark tan colour of Dachshunds but the colour of Foxhounds with a certain amount of white about them. They had deep heavy tongues more like Foxhounds than Beagles. I mated these two in 1867 and had a litter of five all of which survived. I remember I called one Bellman. I sold these three and a half couples to the late Lord Onslow, in I think 1872 but I am not quite sure of the date.
>
> Galway

The hounds from the Comte de Tournon's were of the Couteulx strain. Lord Onslow continued breeding, and obtained more Bassets direct from the kennels of the Comte de Couteulx.

In 1874 Mr (later Sir) Everett Millais purchased a hound called Model from the Jardin d'Acclimatation in Paris. Model was standing at stud at the Jardin, along with another hound called Fino de Paris. It is to Sir Everett Millais that we are indebted for his enthusiasm and foresight in the evolution of the Basset as it is known today.

Model was exhibited at the Wolverhampton Show of 1875 and won a prize in a variety class, inspiring Millais to increase his hounds. At this time the paths of Millais and Lord Galway had not crossed, so he resorted to using a Beagle bitch and had a litter of two females, Dina and Flo. Flo was Beagle in appearance, but Dina was mated back to Model to produce Waddle and Ravanger, both resembling pure-bred Bassets, who were exhibited with success. This pair went to Mr Alfred Baret and Mr Percival de Caster. Regretfully, no records appear of any breeding from this pair. They could have been lost in the same outbreak of distemper that killed Dina and Flo.

Bassets imported from France and owned by Mr G Krehl: Jupiter, Fino de Paris and Pallas.

Between 1873 and 1875, Lord Onslow imported Fino, Nestor, Finette and, at a later date, Juno. Lord Onslow sent Finette to Model, and the mating produced Proctor, a lemon-and-white male – the first Basset of this colour to be seen in England – and a tri-colour bitch, Garenne, whom Millais had in lieu of a stud fee. Garenne was mated back to her sire six times, but only reared three pups: Isabel, Model II and Vesta. Isabel was mated to Lord Onslow's Fino and, in 1879, produced Bratias, Ulfius, Kathleen, Niniche and Marie. Millais then mated two pairs of brothers and sisters (Ulfius to Kathleen and Bratias to Niniche). Regretfully, during 1880, Millais had to dispose of his hounds and go to Australia, because of ill health. It was unfortunate that Lord Onslow disbanded his pack at approximately the same time.

During the 19th century M Louis Lane of Château de Frangueville, near Rouen, was successfully breeding and exhibiting quality Bassets. As the Le Couteulx hounds found favour in England, so the Lane hounds were popular in France. The Lane hounds were predominantly lemon-and-white or grey-and-white – generally bi-coloured. They were heavy, with good bone, and very low to the ground, the front legs usually full-crooked or half-crooked, with a tendency to knuckle over. The heads were finely sculptured with superb ears, set low, curling, and ending in points.

In 1882, Mr Krehl and Mr Louis Clement imported two Lane-type Bassets: Blanchette and Oriflamme. In 1880, Mr Krehl had already imported a large quantity from France, including Fino de Paris, Jupiter and Guineviere. Mr Krehl exhibited his hounds extensively, and the breed became more widely recognised.

Several bitches were inbred to Fino de Paris in the hope that he would stamp his type but, unfortunately, this did not happen. The bitch Vivienne looked like her grandsire Termino. Nothing of the breeding of Termino seems to be recorded, and it is assumed that Le Couteulx used one of the French breeds to outcross and bring in new blood, possibly to counteract the inbreeding of Fino de Paris. At this period people spoke learnedly on the Couteulx type, the Fino de Paris type, the Lane type or the Termino type.

Sir Everett Millais returned from Australia in 1884, his health restored, and was re-united with his old hound Model, now in his 13th year. Model was mated to his great-granddaughter, Finette II, and produced three puppies. With the return of Millais, many Basset Hound breeders felt it was time to form a Basset Hound club to protect the welfare of the breed. In February 1883, at 25 Downing Street, the Basset Hound Club (BHC) was formed to encourage the breeding of Basset Hounds for exhibition and hunting. Count Le Couteulx de Canteleu was elected President, with Vice Presidents Lord Onslow and Mr G R Krehl, Secretary H W Carter, and Treasurer G R Krehl. Shortly after the inauguration of the BHC, Mr Krehl presented two Basset puppies to HRH The Prince of Wales. The Prince was so delighted with this addition to his kennel that he gave Mr Krehl a scarf-pin in the design of the Prince of Wales Plumes. Several eminent people became members of the BHC, including HRH Princess Alexandra, Lord Galway, Sir Everett Millais, Mmes Ellis, Tottie, Lubbock, Walsh and Wimbuush, and Messrs Musson, Heseltine and Wooton.

The breed flourished in the show ring, but interest was also growing among the British sporting fraternity, who knew of the breed's reputation in the field. By 1886, a few packs of Bassets had been established to hunt the hare. Mrs Ellis, one of the breed's greatest enthusiasts, mated her first bitch Venus II (a granddaughter of Fino de Paris) to Fino VI (a grandson of Fino de Paris), and Venus II produced Ch Psyche, who became a champion before her second birthday. Several good Bassets were winning at this period, most of them descended from Fino de Paris, among them Ch Forester, Ch Paris, Ch Psyche II, Ch Queen of the Geisha, Ch Louis le Beau and Ch Lurine.

The Bloodhound Influence

After several years of inbreeding to Fino de Paris, evidence could be seen of some deterioration in the Basset; infertility and nervousness were creeping in. Millais decided to bring in an outcross, knowing from his trials with Beagles that it could be bred out within a few generations. He used the Bloodhound bitch Innoculation (Chorister ex Artemis), a reasonable specimen of the breed, and the Basset sire Nicholas, a hound very inbred to Fino de Paris. The Bloodhound bitch was artificially inseminated. One may wonder why Millais did not return to France for fresh blood, but he said (and I quote): *I may state at once that when we imported our Bassets from France we imported the best that France possessed and that, not withstanding deterioration, what we have in England is better than France can now offer us.* Twelve puppies were born from Nicholas and Innoculation but, unfortunately, the mother and, later, five of the puppies died.

When half-cross dog hounds were mated to Basset bitches, the litters contained more black-and-tan puppies. When quarter-cross hounds were mated back to Bassets, all the offspring were pure Basset in appearance. Mr Croxton-Smith noted that, with the Bloodhound/Basset cross, in the first generation there were black-and-tan puppies of more or less Basset shape, but heavier and clumsier. In the next generation, bred back to a Basset, the progeny were Basset tri-colour of more correct shape. He reckoned that it took four generations to remove traces of alien blood. Mr Croxton-Smith was given a hound of the fourth generation from the Bloodhound cross, who produced a champion Basset.

More French imports arrived. In 1895, M Puissant sent 11½ couples to England for sale at a show, and most were bought and retained by British breeders. They preferred the heavier bone and size and, with the Bloodhound influence, they retained the size required.

HM Queen Alexandra with her rough and smooth Bassets.

The Basset from 1900

By the turn of the century, the Basset had been established in Great Britain for 34 years. Although by far the most enthusiasts were for the smooth-coated Artésien-Normand, a few rough-coated Bassets were being shown. Although the smooth-coated were known as 'Artésien-Normand' they were not strictly the same as their counterparts in France, having the Beagle and

Every one a beauty: the Walhampton pack, 1912.

Miss Keevil and Mr Alex McDonald with some of the Grims.

Bloodhound crosses in their background. One cannot be sure whether the Beagle cross was continued to any great extent, but the Bloodhound cross certainly was. British breeders continued to breed for the lower, heavier, Bloodhound type, and drew up a standard to meet their requirements.

The Basset was enjoying great popularity in the hands of prominent breeders whose hounds were winning well in the show ring. These breeders included such persons as Queen Alexandra, Mrs Tottie, who also owned Petits Bassets Griffons Vendéens (PBGVs), Mrs Walsh, Mrs Lubbock, Mrs Proctor and Mr A Croxton-Smith. Mrs Proctor's tri-colour Ch Queen of the Geisha (Paris ex Fair Star) won 18 CCs between 1899 and 1905, setting a record which remained unequalled for 50 years.

Despite the enthusiasm of the breeders in the early 1900s the Basset Hound began to decline in quality and stamina. Mr Godfrey Heseltine and his brother Major C Heseltine, owners of the Walhampton Bassets, considered it to be due to lack of knowledge on the breeders' part. Up to that time, the brothers had concentrated on upgrading their pack. The Walhampton hounds had great quality, and the Heseltines were so incensed at the poor quality and unsoundness of the show hound that they resigned from the Basset Hound Club and, shortly afterwards, were instrumental in forming the Master of Basset Hound Association (MBHA). Show-minded exhibitors were not allowed to exhibit at MBHA events.

During the 1914–1918 war, most Basset Hound packs were disbanded. The Walhamptons absorbed several. The show hound declined even further and, after the war, the numbers being exhibited dropped dramatically. In 1920, only two were registered with The Kennel Club. The Basset Hound Club was wound up in 1921, but Major Heseltine started to show his hounds again. He imported Meteor and Pampeute, two litter brothers, from M Mallart of Barly. These were just the new influx of blood the breed needed and can be found behind nearly all the Walhampton champions.

Walhampton Lymington, 1926.

From 1925–1938 the Walhampton were dominant in the ring but, regrettably, Major Heseltine died in 1932 and his widow sold most of the hounds. Mrs Grew bought Grazier and Mrs Elms Ch

Lynnewood and Nightshade, Gravity, Waspish and Graechus. Some were purchased by French breeders.

In 1935 Miss Keevil bought her first Basset from Mrs Elms, a bitch called Dulcamara of Reynalton. This bitch was soon joined by Walhampton Medway and Marquis of Labran (two hounds from the Westerby kennels) and Wick Welcome. Dulcamara was mated to Walhampton Medway and produced Grims Daisy.

In 1939 Mr G Johnston Sr purchased two Reynalton Bassets from Mrs Elms, but these were returned at the breeder's request when World War II began. At this time most Basset Hound packs were disbanded. In fact, only two survived: the Scalford Hall pack belonging to Colonel Coleman and Lt-Col Morrison's Westerby Pack, which had taken over several of the Walhamptons. These two packs absorbed many of the disbanded packs.

Through the war years very little breeding was accomplished, although in 1940 Miss Keevil mated Marquis to Wick Welcome, the ensuing litter producing Ch Grims Wishful and Grims Worship. Grims Worship was mated to his niece Grims Waspish to produce Ch Grims Warlock.

Basset Exhibitors 1900–1950

Well-known exhibitors between 1900–1950 and their most famous exhibits:

Exhibitor	Exhibit	Parents
Mr Croxton Smith	Ch Wantage	Ch Louis Le Beau ex Witch
	Ch Welbeck	As above
	Ch Wensum	As above
Mrs Tottie	Ch Louis Le Beau	Ch Paris ex Fair Star
	Ch Lurline	As above
	Ch Loo Loo Loo	Ch Louis Le Beau ex Bibella
HRH Queen Alexandra	Ch Waverer	Major ex Daisy
J W Proctor	Ch Queen of the Geisha	Ch Paris ex Fairstar
J P and W Roberts	Ch Mentor	Ch Waverer ex Ch Melanie
	Ch Melanie	Ch Loo Loo Loo ex Mirette
Mrs E Grew	Ch Patience	Walhampton Lingerer ex Walhampton Pardon
	Ch Walhampton Ambassador	Walhampton Lymington ex Walhampton Amber
Major C Heseltine	Ch Walhampton Andrew	Walhampton Ferryman ex Walhampton Actress
	Ch Walhampton Gratitude	Walhampton Linguist ex Walhampton Grizel
	Ch Walhampton Lynewood	Walhampton Musket ex Walhampton Lyric
Mrs N Elms	Ch Walhampton Nightshade	Walhampton Grazier ex Walhampton Nicknack
	Ch Orpheus of Reynalton	Ch Walhampton Lynnewood ex Ch Walhampton Nightshade
	Ch Venus of Reynalton	As above
	Ch Minerva of Reynalton	As above
	Ch Narcissus of Reynalton	As above
Mrs Grew	Ch Pigeon	Walhampton Grazier ex Walhampton Nicknack
Mrs Roberts	Ch Plover	As above

The Advent of Ulema de Barly

Despite obvious difficulties, Miss Keevil managed to maintain her Grims pack throughout the war years (1939–1944). Certainly, without her efforts the Basset Hound in Great Britain would have died out, and all current breed enthusiasts owe her an enormous debt. By 1949 she was becoming increasingly disturbed regarding certain factors creeping into the breed. Nervousness and long coats were appearing. After years of inbreeding it was acknowledged that an infusion of fresh blood was required.

Miss Keevil travelled to France and managed to find and import two Bassets Artésiens-Normands. The magnificent stallion hound Ulema de Barly (Sans Souci de Bourcevillex ex Querelle de Barly) was bred by M Mallart, one of the oldest established breeders in the Somme.

Ulema had a tremendous influence on the breed, and probably most of today's champions are directly or indirectly descended from him. The second hound was a bitch, Cornemuse de Blendecques (Taiaux ex Vistule), usually referred to as U Cornemuse. She was bred by M Paul Leduc of Blendecques, Pas de Calais. With two successful French imports in her kennel, Miss Keevil decided to visit France again and this time obtained the tri-colour Aiglon des Mariettes (Taiaut de la Chée ex Soupirante de Bourceville) bred by Mme Raulin of Chermizy, in Aisne. Ulema de Barly was a dominant dark-blanketed tri-

Grims Ulema de Barly,
an Artésien-Normand imported by Miss P Keevil.

colour with the traditional Artésien-Normand markings: he only ever sired tri-colours. He sired Ch Grims Useful, Grims Wideawake, Grims Willow, Ch Grims Whirlwind and Ch Grims Westward.

Basset Hounds 1950–1960

Between 1950 and 1960 the breed underwent a remarkable revival due to the indefatigable work of a small group of dedicated fanciers.

The Basset Hound Club was re-formed, the founder members being Miss Keevil (Grims), Mr Johnston Sr and Mr G Johnston (Sykemoor), Mr and Mrs Baynes (Breightmet), Mrs Grew (Maybush), Mrs Hodson (Rossingham), Mr L Woolner (West Lodge Hounds), Mr E Allen of the Kimblewick Hounds, F Beckwith of Allercoats, Dr Beer, Lord and Lady Chelmsford, Miss Brown, Mrs Candy, Mrs Cane, D Egremont, Dr Harrison-Sleap, Miss Hind, Mrs Hurst, Sir Jocelyn Lucas, Mr A McDonald (Wickwell), J Martyn, G Mossman, Mrs Scott-Plumner, Miss D Still and Mrs Tarry.

Many of today's Bassets can be traced back within a few generations to these famous affixes. Of the founder members of the Basset Hound Club only Mr George Johnston (Sykemoor) is still actively engaged with the breed. The registrations at The Kennel Club were steadily increasing, as can be seen from the table on page 24. In 1954 four sets of CCs were on offer, and 26 sets were available in 1996. The breed is indebted to Miss Keevil for her dedication and knowledge of the Basset. Her stock was the foundation in the 1950s on which several kennels were founded.

Mrs Angela Hodson acquired Grims Willow and started the Rossingham Bassets. Willow, mated to Ch Grims Warlock, produced the sisters Ch Rossingham Amber and Anxious. Amber was purchased by Mr Johnston (Sykemoor) and gained her championship in 1957. Amber was mated to Ch Grims Whirlwind and produced in her litter Ch Sungarth Sykemoor Aimwell. Rossingham Ambassador was acquired by Mr

Mr G Johnston Sr with Ch Rossingham Amber.

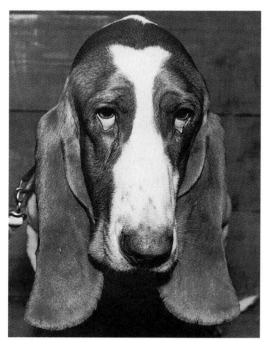

Ch Sungarth Sykemoor Aimwell.

and Mrs Appleton (Appeline). The next time Mrs Hodson mated Willow she used Ch Grims Doughnut as a sire. This litter produced Ch Rossingham Badger, Blessing and Barrister. She repeated this mating and produced Ch Rossingham Cosy who was purchased by the late Lt Col Amyas Biss (Potwalloper).

Mr and Mrs Appleton, known for their Beagles, owned Ch Appeline Rochester. They also bred Mrs Minto's beautiful lemon-and-white bitch Ch Dreymin Appeline Coral. In 1960 Mr Appleton wrote *The Basset Hound Handbook*.

In 1954 Mrs Elms made up Ch Songster of Reynalton, and then retired from the show ring. His litter brother, Mrs Jaggers' Trumpeter of Reynalton, became the last hound bearing that famous affix to figure in Basset breeding when he mated Mr Johnston's Ch Rossingham Amber in 1955, producing nine puppies – his only litter.

The same year saw the birth of the two excellent tri-colour dogs who subsequently became Ch Grims Whirlwind and Ch Grims Westward (Grims Ulema de Barly ex Grims Wanda). This pair sired eight champions between them. Ch Grims Whirlwind was owned by Wendy Jagger (Fochno) and he sired Ch Fochno Trooper, owned by Gerald Dakin MRCVS (Brockhampton), and his sister, Ch Fochno Trinket, as well as Ch Sungarth Sykemoor Aimwell. Ch Grims Westward sired Int Ch Mariseni Breightmet Wessex, Ch Appeline Rochester, Ch Barnspark Vanity, Ch Brockhampton Solomon and Ch Barnspark Rakish.

At the time Westward and Whirlwind were battling it out in the show ring, Miss Keevil was campaigning another tri-colour, a Basset with very little French breeding in him. This dog, Grims Emblem, sired two champions: Ch Grims Vapid and Ch Kelperland Baneful.

In 1956 Mrs Margaret Rawle (Barnspark) saw a Basset Hound, and it was love at first sight. She managed to obtain from Miss Keevil, on breeding terms, the bitch Grims Garrulous. Mated to Ch Grims Wideawake, Garrulous produced Ch Grims Gracious, the dam of Ch Barnspark Rakish, owned by Mmes MacArthur and Kewley. When mated to Ch Breightmet Chimer, Gracious produced Mrs Wendy Benge-Abbot's Ch Barnspark Clarion. Swe Ch Grims Rambler and Rollick arrived in that same litter. Rollick, owned by Mr Evans Roberts (Varon), was mated to Ch Fochno Trooper and produced Ch Fredwell Varon Vandal. Barnspark Rustic was another from this litter, and she in turn produced Ch Mariseni Rarnee.

Ch Grims Vapid. Photo: C M Cooke

Ch Fredwell Varon Vandal (22 CCs). Photo: Thomas Fall

Mrs Rawle then obtained Ch Grims Useful from Miss Keevil, again on breeding terms. Useful, mated to Emblem, produced Ch Grims Vapid, and Vapid, mated to Ch Grims Westward, produced Ch Barnspark Vanity. Vanity was the first champion other than Miss Keevil's to win a working certificate. Mrs Rawle also proved that Bassets can be obedience trained and I saw her give a demonstration with two Bassets simultaneously carrying out a variety of obedience exercises.

In 1957 Mrs Rawle was elected Secretary of the BHC on the resignation of Mrs Hodson. Miss Mary Povey issued the Club's first newsletter, and Mr Dakin edited the yearbook. The Earl of Northesk was President, Mr Lionel Woolner Chairman, Dr S Beer Vice Chairman, Mrs C Baynes Treasurer, and the Committee consisted of Miss Keevil, Mr Townson MRCVS, Mr Dakin MRVCS, Mr MacDonald and Mr Johnston.

Mr Townson MRCVS, well known for his Kelperland Bloodhounds, bought Rossingham Badger, who quickly gained his title. Badger had the distinction of winning the highest award a Basset had ever attained at that time: Reserve Best in Show at Windsor Championship Show 1958.

Mrs Beryl Prior (Sungarth) had been breeding Bulldogs for several years before deciding to try Basset Hounds. She bought Rossingham Artful from Mrs Hodson. Artful was mated to Grims Vigil, a Basset who had Bloodhound breeding behind him. A bitch called Gipsy from this litter, mated to Kelperland Adrian, produced Sungarth Jasmine. Mrs Rowett-Johns (Wingjays) bought

Jasmine, her first Basset, as a present for her son. Jasmine, mated to Ch Sungarth Sykemoor Aimwell, who was now owned by Mrs Prior, produced Ch Wingjays Fanciful, who won BOB at Crufts, thus bonding the Wingjays into the Basset fraternity for life.

Mrs Prior bred several Basset litters but her most famous must surely have been the litter of eight bred from Ch Sungarth Sykemoor Aimwell ex Aesops Able. This included two males called Plunder and Paris. Paris was obtained by Mrs May Bews in Plymouth, who later became the Treasurer of the BHC. The bitch Plover became a cornerstone of Mrs Anne Matthews' Hardacre Bassets. Placid was obtained by Mrs Bridgham in Northern Ireland. Provocative was owned by Mrs Wallis in Cornwall, and then there was Primula, Peewit and Mrs Jeanne Rowett-Johns' Ch Sungarth Phoebe.

During the 1950s Mr George Johnston Sr, with his son, also George, was rebuilding his kennel of Sykemoor Bassets alongside his Dandie Dinmont Terriers. Sykemoor Aimwell was born and sold to Mrs Prior (Sungarth), who campaigned him and quickly achieved his championship. Aimwell became a dominant sire, imparting his beautiful head to his offspring, who included Ch Sungarth Phoebe, Ch Hooksway Cheeky Checkmate and Ch Wingjays Fanciful. On the death of George Sr in 1958, his son George decided, reluctantly, to disband the Dandies and concentrate on the hounds. He and his wife Cynthia had a good grounding in dog breeding and hunting. George's great-grandfather bred black Pomeranians and was a keen follower of the Carlisle Otterhounds. His grandfather was a Whippet and coursing enthusiast. His aunts, uncles and cousins all kept dogs of various breeds, including Bassets and Dandie Dinmont Terriers, but it was his father who was the real fanatic, particularly drawn to the long and low breeds: hence Bassets and Dandies. He served on the committees of both breed societies and also bred Shetland Ponies and Old English Game Fowl. His first Bassets were obtained from Mrs Nina Elms of Reynalton fame. George's maternal grandfather had Fox Terriers and an uncle had Dandies.

George Jr's wife Cynthia grew up next door to the Cumberland Foxhound Kennels at Westward and was responsible for the rearing of the Border Collies used on her father's large sheep

Ch Sykemoor Ruby. Photo: Frank Garwood

farm. She awards CCs in Basset Hounds and has also judged Otterhounds at championship show level. George awards CCs in Bassets, Beagles, Bloodhounds, Otterhounds, Petits Bassets Griffons Vendéens (PBGVs) and Dandie Dinmonts. He also judges the French Hound breeds in Group VI under Fédération Cynologique Internationale (FCI) rules and has officiated at the Special Venerie Hound Show in France. He has also judged the Westward Foxhound Show, Oulton Lurcher and Trail Hound Show, was co-judge with Lionel Woolner at the Albany Basset Hound Show and judged Basset Hounds at the World Show in Amsterdam in 1985. His Crufts judging appointments have been for Bassets, Otterhounds, PBGVs and Dandie Dinmont Terriers.

For many years, George was 'Breed Note' contributor to *Dog World* and he has contributed Basset Hound and French Hound chapters to several canine encyclopedias. He is the author of *The Basset Hound* 1968 and *Hounds of France* 1979. When the breed's rejuvenation was undertaken, George favoured the French outcross. Hercule de L'Ombrée and Q'Château de L'Ombrée were imported from Pierre Leparoux of Maine-et-Loire, and Hercule especially figures in the pedigrees of most Sykemoor hounds. Champion Basset Hounds carrying the Sykemoor affix have been: Aimwell, Emma, Wiza, Rosamund and Gilder, but perhaps this distinguished kennel's proudest achievement was the litter sired by Ch Balleroy Luther out of Sykemoor Urfa in 1977 that contained the 'three Rs' champions: Ruby, Ruthie and Rosebud. A repeat mating in 1978 produced Ch Bugle-Ann and Birdsong. Ch Rosamund and Ch Gilder were both *Dog World* Spillers Pup of the Year qualifiers in 1983 and 1985. As well as the show champions, George and Cynthia are proud of American Field Trial (FT) Champion Sykemoor Nestor and French *Brevet de Chasse* holder Sykemoor Quintonine.

George has served on the Committee of the Basset Hound Club and is a former President of the Hadrian Basset Hound Club, representing that Club when all the breed societies discussed the revised Breed Standard at The Kennel Club in 1985. He is a keen collector of Basset memorabilia and inherited Mrs Edith Grew's Maybush kennel records. He also has a massive collection of documents, pedigrees and photographs sent to him by Carl Smith, the pioneer American breeder.

Bassets from the 1960s Onwards

From the early 1960s, the Basset's popularity increased dramatically. Media coverage included the breed being featured in advertisements, films and a cartoon strip and, with the Hush Puppy advertisement, the general public clamoured for the sad-looking hound on short legs. Regretfully, many back-street traders (one cannot call them breeders) jumped on the band wagon, ever eager to sell a puppy at quick profit, regardless of its future welfare. I saw some strange looking so-called Basset Hounds in that period (see table on page 24). During the years 1962–1972, registrations jumped from 839 to 3173 – thankfully, this was the peak! They then dropped dramatically in the following five years: in 1977 only 337 were registered at The Kennel Club. Once again, the Basset was safe in the hands of dedicated breeders, who had watched with incredulity their beloved breed rise to such a peak of popularity.

In the show ring during this period, several quality Bassets were winning top honours. These hounds carried the Chantinghall, Barnspark, Sykemoor, Fredwell, Wingjays, Rowynan, Hardacre, Dreymin and Maycombe affixes. Miss Keevil had a very strong team of stud dogs in the early 1960s, including Ch Grims Westward, Ch Fochno Trooper, Ch Breightmet Chimer and Lyn-Mar Acres Dauntless.

More up-and-coming breeders were beginning to come to the fore to make up champions in the 1970s: Akerwood, Balleroy, Beacontree, Bassbar, Brackenacre, Blaby, Charford, Harecroft, Jeffrone, Langpool, Ledline, Rollinhills, Saxonspring, Tintally, Verwood and Turbeville were kennels to be reckoned with.

In the last 25 years many Basset kennels have bred good hounds. These are too numerous to mention all, but the names which come readily to mind are: Andyne, Barrenger, Balmacara,

Carresmar, Dahenol, Gladsomes, Helmsdown, Islwyn, Kortina, Siouxline, Switherland and Viness Vinell.

The Basset Hound Clubs

The Basset Hound Club

The story of how the first Bassets were imported into Great Britain by Lord Galway has been told earlier in the chapter, and the formation of the Basset Hound Club (BHC) – the first specialist club to be registered with The Kennel Club – in 1891 and its closure in 1921 is also described.

By 1954 the necessary numbers required to reform the club were assembled, and in that year the present Basset Hound Club was founded. The President was The Earl of Northesk and the Secretary Mrs A Hodson. Mr Hodson was succeeded by Mrs M Rawle in 1958, by Mrs M Seiffert in 1962, by Mrs A Charman in 1975 and by Mrs S Hipkins in 1979. The current Secretary is Mrs S Ergis, who took up the post in 1992.

In 1956 the BHC decided to import a stud dog, as new blood in the breed was desirable. Lyn-Mar Acres Dauntless was bought from Mrs Peg Walton's famous American kennel. Dauntless stood at stud at Miss Keevil's kennels and she eventually bought him.

Since 1960 a championship show has been held annually, as well as an open show. As membership grew and the Basset became increasingly popular the formation of regional branches of the BHC were encouraged. At present there are seven: East Anglian, London and Northern Home Counties, Thames Estuary, South East, South West, Midland, and North-West. Each branch holds social events and guarantees Basset classes at certain open shows in their area.

The working branch of the BHC was organised in the early days of the club, for those interested in hunting. Miss Keevil helped a great deal and lent her own Bassets as a nucleus for a pack. Later Mr John Evans (Stalwart) built kennels on his land at Arkley, near Barnet, to house the Basset Hound Club Pack, of which he became Master. History was made when the BHC became the only breed club with its own hunting pack to be recognised by The Kennel Club. In 1973 the pack was invited to apply for membership of the Masters of Basset Hound Association. Mr Tim Thomas negotiated the acquisition of registered country in Rutland and Lincolnshire and the pack was registered and became known as The Albany.

Basset Hound Rescue is a rescue and welfare service run under the auspices of the Basset Hound Club. The object is the resettlement of unwanted Basset Hounds and the counselling of owners having difficulties with their hounds. The aim is to provide loving and permanent homes for those Bassets whose owners, for whatever reason, can no longer keep them. Those – the dispossessed – will need patience, love and security. The National Co-ordinator is Mrs Pat Green (see **Useful Addresses**).

With the increasing interest in the Basset Hound, further clubs have been registered with The Kennel Club:

The Basset Hound Club of Scotland

This Club was formed in 1966 and held its first open show in 1968. This show gained championship status in 1969. The Club has held a championship show each year except on two occasions. In the mid-1990s, when The Kennel Club reduced the allocation of CCs for Basset Hounds, the Club had to suspend the CCs for one year. The only other time this happened was when The Kennel Club stated that all championship shows must have benching, and the Club could not afford it immediately.

An open show is still run in addition to the championship show and there are also annual fun days and other social events. The Hon Secretary is Mr D Sharpe, the Chairman Colin Gillanders and the President Mrs Pat Moncur.

The Midlands Basset Hound Club
This Club was registered with The Kennel Club, with 42 founder members, in 1973. It was given permission to hold a championship show in 1975, and this has been an annual event ever since.The Club holds an open show and various other events during the year and also issues a very good newsletter to its members. The Hon Secretary is Mrs J Horsley, the Chairperson Mrs B White and the President Mr L Pagliero OBE.

The Hadrian Basset Hound Club
This Club was approved by The Kennel Club in 1975 and held its first open show in April 1976.

Liz Frazer, who is President of the Lancashire, Yorkshire and Cheshire Basset Hound Club, with Brackenacre Bracken. Photo: Evening Argus, Brighton

It received championship status in 1978, since when the championship show has been held every year.

The club strives to ensure equality between all aspects of Basset promotion, welfare and interest. Walks and social events are held and a newsletter is issued to all members. The charity walks organised with members and hounds have raised over £1000 for Cancer Research and Guide Dogs for the Blind. The Hon Secretary is Mr Tony Coddington, the Chairperson Mrs Betty Johnson and the post of President is currently vacant. Much credit for the excellent reputation of this North Country club must go to the late Billy Wells (Cornmeade), who pioneered its foundation.

The Lancashire, Yorkshire and Cheshire Basset Hound Club

This Club was given Kennel Club approval in 1979. It was awarded championship status in 1982 and has held this show annually. The club organises social events, giving donations to various charities, and issues a very good newsletter to all its members. The Hon Secretary is Mrs M Ledward, the Chairman Mr D Ledward and the Presidents are Mrs W Graham and Mrs Liz Fraser.

The South of England Basset Hound Club

This Club was formed on 1 April 1989 and registered with The Kennel Club on 2 August 1990. It started with 70 founder members and at the end of 1996 has a membership of over 300. As yet the Club has not been granted permission to hold championship shows but it holds two open shows a year and organises walks, an annual garden party and Christmas lunch, and seminars. The Club takes a keen interest in the health of the Basset and is proud to have been associated with Dr Ross

Members of the Basset Hound Club of Northern Ireland, 1968.

Bond of the Royal Veterinary College in investigating the yeast skin problem, Malassezia Pachydermats, that affects some Bassets. The Club's Hon Secretary is Ms S Thexton and the Chairperson Mrs J Laurie. Sadly the President, Jeanne Rowett-Johns, died in 1996, so the post is currently vacant.

The Basset Hound Club of Wales

Bassets have been strong in the Principality since the 1950s but, apart from a short-lived BHC Welsh branch in the 1970s, no national club had emerged on the lines of those in Scotland and Northern Ireland. Its origin, at the 1990 West of England Ladies Kennel Society (WELKS) Championship Show, is perhaps unusual in that the impetus came in the form of an article about Welsh puppy farms in a *Daily Telegraph* colour supplement. The half-page picture of a forlorn Basset bitch, used twice yearly and housed seemingly in a damp tip, so incensed three Basset exhibitors (Jeff Savory, Ann Roberts and Marion Brown) that they set about forming a national organisation in Wales to promote all aspects of Basset welfare, which was the foundation of the Basset Hound Club of Wales.

The Basset Hound Club of Wales received Kennel Club recognition in 1992. It has since grown in strength and holds two open shows a year. It also promotes educational seminars and is active in rescue. Newsletters, walks and social activities promote its Code of Ethics and provide a support network for pet Basset owners. The Hon Secretary is Mrs Ann Roberts, the Chairperson Mr S Roberts and the President Mrs M Nixon.

The Basset Hound Club of Northern Ireland

This became a Club in its own right in November 1973, having been a branch of the BHC since 1965. The membership numbered 30–40, and is about the same today. The first open show was in 1974, and championship show status was granted in 1976. A championship show is held every year. The Hon Secretary is Mr Phil McGarry Arthur.

The Basset Hound Club of Ireland

This Club was formed in 1966 and has been affiliated to the Irish Kennel Club ever since, running a championship show each year. At the end of 1996 there were 145 members and 279 Bassets registered in Ireland. The Hon Secretary is Mrs Gill McDowell.

Basset Hound Kennel Club Registrations

This is a list of the registrations of Basset Hounds with The Kennel Club from 1917–1996. As has already been indicated, the sharp rise and fall in the 1960–1970s tells its own rather alarming story!

Year	Reg	Year	Reg	Year	Reg	Year	Reg
1917	0	1937	10	1957	145	1977	337
1918	0	1938	41	1958	249	1978	678
1919	0	1939	13	1959	237	1979	922
1920	2	1940	7	1960	441	1980	816
1921	3	1941	3	1961	552	1981	713
1922	4	1942	17	1962	839	1982	655
1923	9	1943	11	1963	922	1983	626
1924	20	1944	13	1964	1523	1984	609
1925	23	1945	0	1965	1687	1985	736
1926	51	1946	10	1966	1955	1986	641
1927	32	1947	20	1967	2246	1987	657
1928	2	1948	23	1968	2510	1988	585
1929	27	1949	20	1969	2679	1989	1152
1930	13	1950	25	1970	2642	1990	1031
1931	31	1951	24	1971	2837	1991	1118
1932	29	1952	34	1972	3173	1992	1008
1933	27	1953	20	1973	2875	1993	1551
1934	20	1954	64	1974	2379	1994	1158
1935	39	1955	81	1975	1721	1995	1202
1936	20	1956	131	1976	641	1996	1240

I have divided this chapter into two parts. The first part consists of Basset kennels of yesteryear. These Basset Hounds are probably behind most of today's winning hounds. It is interesting to see how the various lines have been intermingled to produce quality Bassets. The second part is concerned with some well-known contemporary breeders and their hounds. It is interesting when reading the various résumés to note the different breeding techniques, with the occasional judicious use of an outcross.

Basset Hound Kennels of Yesteryear

Badgerbrook

Joe Williamson obtained her first Basset in 1974 from Frankie Shaw: Franshaw Rosie of Badgerbrook. In 1976, her second Basset was purchased from Marjorie Travis: Gaymel Miss Smartypants of Badgerbrook. Miss Smartypants was mated in 1979 to Ch Harecroft Magnus of Balleroy and produced Ch Badgerbrook Tokyo Joe and his sister Ch Badgerbrook Casablanca. Ch Tokyo Joe was mated to Rosie, producing Ch Badgerbrook Dirty Harry. Ch Badgerbrook Tokyo Joe won Best in Show (BIS) at the Border Counties Hound Championship Show 1984.

Ch Badgerbrook Tokyo Joe. Photo: Diane Pearce

Barnspark Rowynan Magic, showing that Bassets can be obedience trained.

Barnspark

Mrs Margaret Rawle bred her first champion in 1957: Ch Barnspark Rakish (Ch Grims Westward ex Ch Grims Gracious). Margaret had obtained Gracious as a youngster and campaigned her to championship, and she did the same with Ch Grims Vapid. The second home-bred champion was Ch Barnspark Clarion (Ch Breightmet Chimer ex Ch Grims Gracious). Then came Ch Barnspark Vanity (Ch Grims Westward ex Ch Grims Vapid), followed by Ch Barnspark Frolic (Ch Pointgrey ex Barnspark Charity), who was sold to and campaigned by Miss Wendy Thomas and her friend Miss Biddy Basset. In 1968 she obtained Maycombe Victoria and campaigned her to her championship. Margaret also obedience-trained several of her Bassets to a high standard and bred champion Bloodhounds.

Margaret was Secretary of the Basset Hound Club (BHC) for a period, and she was also a championship judge in the breed for many years and judged Crufts in 1977.

Chantinghall

Jim and Rosemary McKnight registered their affix in 1959, and another extremely successful kennel was started, based on two Sykemoor bitches – Sykemoor Anabel (Ch Grims Whirlwind ex Ch Rossingham Amber) and Sykemoor Brigit (Sykemoor Garnet ex Sykemoor Jealousy) – and Appleline Serious (Rossingham Ambassador ex Appleline Come Here). A later addition was Mariseni Goodness Gracious.

Jim and Rosemary obviously had the knack of breeding and picking Bassets because, before emigrating to Canada, they had bred Ch Chantinghall Ancestor, Ch Chantinghall Harmony and Ch Chantinghall Jemima of Maycombe. Three other champions bore the Chantinghall affix: Ch Chantinghall Fredwell Amber, Ch Chantinghall Kitebrook Barley and Ch Chantinghall Beatrice. The McKnights continued breeding successfully under the Chantinghall affix in Canada.

Ch Cwmdale Kyaston of Aberthin, BOB Crufts 1975. Photo: Diane Pearce

Cwmdale

Jean Elliott-Jones' first Basset was Saddleheath Samantha (Chantinghall Hannibal ex Garbo); not a show hound but she had terrific personality. When Jean and Martin moved to Shropshire, their veterinary surgeon was Frank Jagger (Fochno). In 1967, on the advice of Wendy Jagger, Jean visited Peggy Keevil (Grims) and came away with two puppies: Grims Tinsel (Wingjays Perseus ex Grims Telltale) and Grims Banjo (Wingjays Perseus ex Grims Resolute). These were the foundation bitches of the Cwmdales. Tinsel was mated to Ch Fredwell Varon Vandal and had a litter of nine. Banjo was mated to Vandal but tragically died after a caesarean; Jean hand reared the litter on powdered pigs' milk with a little help from June Hallett (Aberthin). Badger and Bon Bon were kept, and the affix Cwmdale registered. Both Badger and Bon Bon won well at championship shows. In 1970, Badger of Cwmdale was mated to Monklow Aphrodite of Aberthin, and this union produced Kynaston, whom June gave to Jean. What a wonderful gift! He became Ch Cwmdale Kynaston of Aberthin, winning his first CC at seven months and continuing in his winning ways. He was Best of Breed (BOB) at Crufts in 1975 and 1976. Badger meanwhile sired other champions, including Alda Hainsworth's Hobcote Portrait. In 1981, Jean purchased Karipat Winter Breeze, who won a Reserve CC. In 1982, Mary Powell (Bascor) let Jean have Bascor Royal Nugget, who won a CC when quite young, along with three Reserve CCs. Unfortunately, benching collapsed on him at a show and frightened him for the show ring. He made his reputation by siring champions. Jean judged her first championship show in 1977 and culminated by judging Bassets at Crufts in 1997. Thirty-four years on, Jean and Martin have Cwmdale Victoria, a granddaughter of Nugget, directly descended from Saddleheath Samantha.

Dahenol

Val and Jeff Savory obtained their first Basset in 1977 as a pet for their son, Jonathan, and started to show the dog in local shows. In 1980, a dog was purchased from Dr Elizabeth Andrews: Wenceslas of Langpool (Remraf Monsieur Maurice ex Linda of Langpool). In 1981, the bitch Bascor Ola of Dahenol (Ch Langpool Carries Lad of Islwyn ex Langpool Dolly Daydream) was

purchased from Mary Powell, and went on to win a Junior Warrant and a Reserve CC. In 1985, Wenceslas was mated to Ola, producing the dog Dahenol Sovereign, winner of a Junior Warrant and five Reserve CCs, and two bitches, Dahenol Sapphire (Junior Warrant and five Reserve CCs) and Ch Dahenol Diamond. Diamond was the star of the litter, winning her Junior Warrant, thirteen CCs (six with BOB) and five Reserve CCs. She won the Bitch CC at Crufts in 1987, in 1988

Ch Dahenol Diamond. Photo: Gibbs

with BOB, and again 1989. In 1990, both Sapphire and Diamond were mated and, to Val and Jeff's everlasting sorrow, both bitches died on the operating table having caesarean sections. From these matings, Dahenol Florentine Diamond, Dahenol Hope Diamond and Dahenol Ceylon Sapphire were kept. The only one to excel in the ring was Dahenol Florentine Diamond, who won a Reserve CC, but she was not shown to her full potential because of business and family commitments. Jeff has been a championship judge in the breed for several years.

Fredwell

Prior to acquiring a Basset Hound in 1956, Mrs Joan Wells had been extremely successful in showing and training gundogs. Joan bought her first Basset, Barnspark Rollick, from Mr and Mrs Robert Towsown. Rollick was mated to Ch Rossingham Badger, and three bitches were kept from this litter, while one was sold to Mr Evan Roberts but kennelled with Joan. The three bitches in time were mated to three different stud dogs, and then Joan did not go outside her kennel for studs for several years, using her own stock to line breed. This proved a very successful policy, as in the next few years Joan bred the champions Fredwell Ideal, Fredwell Charmer, Fredwell Maitri, Fredwell Perfect, Fredwell Symon and Chantinghall Fredwell Amber. Mr Evan Roberts was the official breeder of the following three champions, although they remained with Joan, who kennelled and campaigned them: Ch Fredwell Varon Vandal (see page 17), Ch Fredwell Varon Fawkes and Ch Fredwell Varon Fichle. Joan's skill at breeding is shown by the number of champions she has bred; apart from the above these are Ch Fredwell Tolly, Ch Fredwell Flick, Ch Fredwell Finesse, Ch Fredwell Freebie and, in partnership with Mr Nicholas Frost, Ch Fredwell Fiasco.

Apart from being skilled in breeding, Joan is a highly sought-after judge, awarding CCs in many gundog and hound breeds. With fellow Basset enthusiast Mrs Mildred Seiffert, Joan was instrumental in reintroducing the Petit Basset Griffon Vendéen (PBGV), the first of which arrived in 1969. Since that time the breed has attracted many admirers and now holds championship status. Joan is President of the Petit Basset Griffon Vendéen Club.

Helmsdown

Colin Gillander's first Basset Hound was Kierhill Whisper (Int Ch Crochmaid Bold Turpin of Blackheath ex Cotlands Charmian), bred by Sheila Goldie. Whisper had two litters. One was to Sykemoor Gilpin, bred by George Johnston, and from this litter Aust Ch Kierhill Donald was to become arguably the most important Basset Hound dog in the development of the breed in Australia. The other litter was to Houndslease Edward.

In 1970, Colin acquired the Helmsdown affix and in the same year he purchased a lovely tri-colour bitch from Jeanne Rowett-Johns: Wingjays Petulant (Wingjays Prometheus ex Wingjays Petunia), who was to win two CCs and a Reserve CC. Petulant's only litter, to Ch Balleroy Fiddler, produced Helmsdown Belinda, who did not always enjoy showing and did not produce any puppies. Colin had to find another Basset, and he chose a beautiful red-blanket-and-white bitch from Rod and Jan Price. This bitch joined Colin's kennel in 1980 and went on to become Ch Harecroft Regina of Helmsdown, also winning her Junior Warrant. Regina produced three litters. The first was to Langpool Lodestar. The second was to Ch Lodway Lancer of Islwyn, and from this litter Colin kept a bitch who became Ch Helmsdown Daphne (seven CCs, five Reserve CCs, including CC and BIS at the BHC Championship Show 1987 and the Bitch CC the following year). Daphne's brother Helmsdown Dragoon was also retained. He won his Junior Warrant and three Reserve CCs and sired Lowaters Lottery, who in turn sired a number of champions; another dog became Ir Ch Helmsdown Daniel. Regina's third litter was to Ch Brackenacre The Viking, and from this litter Helmsdown Fenella (Reserve CC) was retained. Daphne's only litter, to Ch Balmacara Gunfire, produced Ch Helmsdown Gertrude who, in 1991, won BIS at the BHC Championship Show.

Ch Helmsdown Gertrude.

Due to family commitments and pressure of work, Colin no longer exhibits, but retains an interest in the breed. He is Chairman of the Basset Hound Club of Scotland, and chaired the meeting of Breed Club Representatives when The Kennel Club Breed Standard was revised. Colin is a championship judge of Basset Hounds and PBGVs.

Langpool

Dr Liz Andrews founded her kennel in 1965. Her first champion, Ch Langpool Miss America Pie (Am Ch Long View Acres Bonzax ex Balleroy Barshaw Caprice), was made up in 1973, followed by her full sister Ch Langpool Carrie Anne and brother Ch Langpool William, who won the Dog CC at Crufts in 1978. Ch Langpool Miss America Pie was mated to Ch Stormfield Hugo and produced Am Ch Langpool Song of Sixpence. Ch Langpool Carrie Anne had three litters. The first, by Ch Langpool William, produced Dutch/Lux Ch Langpool Lancelot, BOB at the Winners Show, Amsterdam. The second, to Verwood Wabash, produced Ch Langpool Carries Lad of Islwyn, sire of Ch Lodway Lancer of Islwyn. The third, by Ch Rollinhills Sailing By, produced Ch Langpool Scrumpy, who won 14 CCs. Scrumpy was BOB at Crufts at 17 months. Between them, William and Scrumpy won the dog CC at the BHC Championship Show five years running. William sired many winners, including Ch Langpool Wishing Star, Ch Langpool Wandering Star (sire of Ch Locket White Sweet Inspiration of Kharabay), Ch Norends Amazing Grace, Ch Barnspark Annie, Swedish Show and Hunting Ch Langpool New Moon and Ch Mayflower of Langpool (dam of Ch Lancer). Aust Ch Langpool Lasseter (Ch Lancer ex Meddgoed Moonbeam of Langpool) has been successful 'down-under'.

The kennel moved to Sweden in 1987, and since then only five litters have been bred. However, in 1995 Swe Ch Langpool Cherry Blossom, the eighth generation of Langpool, was the Swedish Basset Club's top winning bitch. The year 1996 saw the arrival of Islwyn Simply Red for Langpool, who became a Swedish champion in three consecutive shows. She is line bred to Lancer, and Liz's hope for the future.

Ch Langpool William, BOB Crufts 1978.

Maycombe

Mrs Mildred Seiffert has been involved with Basset Hounds for many years. She owned Ch Chantinghall Ancestor (Ch Pointgrey Suss's Folly ex Chantinghall Harmony), who sired five champions: Ch Balleroy Chestnut, Ch/Ir Ch Ballymaconnel Forester, Ch Maycombe Merryman, Ch Fredwell Ballroy Faithful and Ch Langstone Pearl. A youngster Mildred bought from the Wingjays kennel was to become Ch Wingjays Polygamy of Maycombe, and he was awarded the Basset Hound Club title Dog Hound of the Year 1967 and 1968. Mildred also had Ch Chantinghall Jemima of Maycombe and Ch Galants Etcetera of Maycombe. The Bassets bred at Maycombe were Ch Maycombe Victoria, Ch Maycombe Vaisya, Ch Maycombe Mignon, Ch Maycombe Merryman, Ch Maycombe Mirontine and Ch Maycombe Ali Baba.

In partnership with Mrs Joan Wells, Mildred reintroduced the Petit Basset Griffon Vendéen into Great Britain. She was also the Secretary of the Basset Hound Club from 1962–1975 and Chairman from 1985–1995. She awards CCs in Bassets and PBGVs.

Meddgoed

Arthur Reed and his Belgian-born wife were living in Hengoed when they acquired their first Basset: Meddlesome Monty of Hengoed. Monty was an extrovert showman and had an amazing career at open shows, and through Monty the Reeds developed a deep interest in the breed. Several Aberthin bitches were bought from June Hallett, of whom none was more successful than the lovely, substantial Ch Meddgoed Sensation of Aberthin (Ch Coastal Weaver of Aberthin ex Minerva of Aberthin) (see page 34). Arthur and Julia bought Meddgoed Cedarglen Diomed and mated her to Ch Trevayler Thomas John, producing their prolific winner Ch Meddgoed Mary Poppins. Meddgoed Moonsmead Thomasine subsequently joined the kennel and, mated to Ch Langpool Scrumpy, produced two Reserve CC winners: Meddgoed Moonmaid of Langpool and Meddgoed Moonlight, who was later exported to Australia in whelp to Ch Langpool William.

The Reeds no longer show, but Arthur, a sprightly octogenarian, and Julie are regularly to be seen stewarding at all-breed championship shows, which they have always enjoyed.

Rollinhills

The Rollinhills Kennels, owned by Betty and Ron White, were started in 1963. Their nine champions were made up in the following order:

1   Ch/Ir Ch Bactona Jupiter (Ch Fredwell Varon Vandal ex Narrabri Andromeda), BOB Crufts 1966.
2   Ch Rollinhills Wingjays Fabric (Ch Wingjays Ptolemy ex Ch Wingjays Fabulous). Fabric tragically died at 13 months of pyometra.
3   Ch Rollinhills Wingjays Phoebe (Ch Wingjays Ptolemy ex Wingjays Vanilla), BOB Crufts 1971.
4   Ch Rollinhills Camilline Cuckoo (Ch Wingjays Prometheus ex Bargriff Camille), owned jointly with Mrs J Lawther. Past record holder with 13 CCs and Basset Hound of the Year 1971.
5   Ch Rollinhills The Swan (Ch Wingjays Prometheus ex Rollinhills Rolick), bred in partnership with Mrs J Lawther.
6   Ch Rollinhills Sailing By (Ch Rollinhills The Swan ex Rollinhills Peppermint).
7   Ch Rollinhills Silver Wings (Ch Rollinhills The Swan ex Rollinhills Peppermint). Past bitch record holder with 16 CCs.
8   Ch Knockfin Isabel of Rollinhills (Ch Rollinhills The Swan ex Ir Ch Cillfoyle Francheska).
9   Ch Rollinhills Bascor Quarrel (Bascor Royal Nugget ex Bascor Dolly Daybream).

Ch Rollinhills Silver Wings. Photo: Diane Pearce

Since Ron has had health problems they have not exhibited but continue to take an active interest in the breed. Betty was made Chairman of the Midland Basset Hound Club in 1986 and Ron is now Vice-Chairman. Both Betty and Ron were founder members, and both are championship show judges. Betty judged the breed at Crufts in 1988.

Tancegems

Tanya Dovey and her Tancegems Basset were highly successful from the late 1970s to the early 1990s, which is particularly commendable considering that she owned only a small number of Bassets and Tancegems was located in the West of Cornwall. The handsome red-blanket Brackenacre Magnificent (Ch Brackenacre James Bond ex Brackenacre Kind of Bell) was the first to make his mark. He amassed enough points for a double Junior Warrant at championship shows. Sadly, the dreaded parvovirus struck when he was two years old, damaging his heart. Tanya's next hound was Brackenacre Primrose (Witchacre Jim Lad ex Brackenacre Diamond Lil), a tri-colour who loved the show ring. She soon attained her championship title. Primrose was mated to Ch Brackenacre The Viking and produced the multiple championship show first prize winner Tancegems Morvoren. In 1985 the extrovert black-blanket bitch Brackenacre Fancy and Free of Tancegems (Ch Brackenacre The Viking ex Brackenacre Zero Zero) made her debut. She gained her Junior Warrant at 11 months and her first CC at 12 months under breed expert Mrs Alda Hainsworth and two more CCs under breed experts Mrs A Matthews and Mr George Johnston, so another Champion was kennelled at Tancegems. She was awarded another CC and two Reserve CCs. Fancy was mated to Ch Vinell Dapper Dandy, but Tanya's health by this time did not allow

Ch Brackenacre Fancy and Free of Tancegems.
Photo: Lionel Young

her to campaign another Basset. Prior to Fancy's litter, Tancegems Morvoren was mated to Ch Lodway Lancer of Islwyn, producing the lovely bitch Tancegems Hoodwink, who won multiple groups and BISs at open shows and several championship show first prizes.

Unfortunately, Tanya had a bad fall, severely injuring her spine, which took a long time to improve. However, in 1990 she attained her Judging Diploma and then took the Canine/Human Interface Course. Tanya now runs her own Canine Behavioural Consultancy with Veterinary Reference. Over the last few years her physical condition has improved and remains steady enough to judge dogs at BIS level all breeds at open shows. Tanya has been the Basset Hound rescue representative for Devon and Cornwall since 1984.

Turbeville

Denise Shemeld purchased her first Basset in 1954 from Mr Mossman, a founder of the BHC. In 1956, Rossingham Blissful arrived, litter sister to Ch Rossingham Badger. Turbeville remained a small kennel, never numbering more than four or five hounds.

Denise started showing in 1965 with the purchase of Kelperland Necessity from Mr and Mrs Townson, as she carried a line back to Badger. Mated to Ch Wingjays Ptolemy, Necessity produced Ch Turbeville Amaryllis and Turbeville Acanthus, who won one Reserve CC. Acanthus, mated to Akerwood Garland, produced Ch Turbeville Akerwood Jester. Amaryllis' daughter, Turbeville Duchess, was mated to Ch Tamsmorna Heinekin to produce

Ch Turbeville Easter Rose.

Ch Turbeville Easter Rose, who won BOB at Crufts. Ch Turbeville Easter Rose, mated to Ch Mayacre Mr Magoo, produced Turbeville Lady Rose Pearl (one CC and one Reserve CC), Turbeville Lady Lily (one Reserve CC) and Ch Waldo of Akerwood, who was campaigned by Mrs Joan Walker. Denise also bred Ch Turbeville Woodpecker, exported as a puppy to Rob and Jan Albon in Canada, who campaigned him to his Canadian title.

As well as breeding winners, Denise served as a committee member of the BHC and as a championship show judge of Basset Hounds for many years.

Wingjays

Mrs Jeanne Rowett-Johns bred her first champion in 1961: Ch Wingjays Fanciful (Ch Sungarth

Wingjays Chanter, with Crysalis (dam) and Caterpillar (sire). Photo: Diane Pearce

Sykemoor Aimwell ex Sungarth Jasmin). It was to Aimwell that Jeanne attributed the deep chestnut-and-white colouring and good heads her hounds always carried. After Fanciful, a stream of champions were produced, including Ch Wingjays Fabulous, Ch Wingjays Ptolemy, Ch Wingjays Polygamy of Maycombe, Ch Wingjays Polonaise, Ch Wingjays Parthenon, Ch Wingjays Pippin, Ch Wingjays Polygon, Ch Wingjays Opinion, Ch Wingjays Pania, Ch Rollinhills Wingjays Phoebe and Ch Rollinhills Wingjays Fabric. Apart from the champions, Jeanne bred stud dogs who produced many champions. One of her best-loved Bassets was one she bought in the early 1960s and made a champion: Ch Sungarth Phoebe. Phoebe held a birthday party every year at The Red Lion, and all Basset folk and their hounds were invited.

Jeanne was Breed Correspondent for *Dog World* for many years, and also wrote the book *All About The Basset Hound*, published in 1973. Even when finished with breeding, Jeanne still held a lively interest in everything to do with the breed. She was the President of The South of England Basset Hound Club up to her demise in late 1996.

Others

I feel I cannot close this part of the chapter without mentioning a few more breeders of yesteryear, as several of their champions will no doubt be in the background of many of today's winning hounds.

- Mr Albert Wood bred Ch Lymewoods Finesse and Ch Lymewoods Howard, one of the first Bassets to be BIS at an all-breed championship show.
- Mr John Evans bred Ch Stalwart Debbie and for several years was Master of The Albany Basset Hound Pack.
- Steve and Maureen Ashton bred Ch Avenwood Dulcis, one of the youngest champions made up.
- Mrs Rosemary Goodyear, who had a large kennel of Bassets in the 1960s, bred Ch Rowynan Lark and Ch Rowynan Taro. Several of her Bassets were sent to Italy to become champions.

32

- Mrs Anne Matthews had a large kennel of Bassets before changing to Lhasa Apsos. She bred Ch Hardacre Valorous.
- Mr and Mrs Hall Parlby bred Ch Huckworthy Leader and Ch Huckworthy Lyric and also had their own private pack of Bassets.
- Mrs Josephine Thompson bred Ch Langstone Pearl.
- Mrs Sheila Blackler bred the two lovely bi-colour sisters, Ch Tintally Deborah and Ch Tintally Dubonnet; when one didn't win, the other did! She also bred Ch Tintally D'Arcy.
- Mrs Minnie Williams bred Ch Trevalyer Thomas John and

Ch Lymewoods Howard; from a painting by Tom Green.

campaigned Ch Foyewyn Stroller, another lovely bitch. Trevalyer Tambourine went to Italy and soon became a champion.
- Mrs Sally Goodwin bred Ch Foyewyn Stroller and Ch Foyewyn Berenice. She also bred the two lovely sisters Foyewyn Flirtie and Flapper, who won two CCs each.
- Mrs Alda Hainsworth bred Ch Hobcote Portrait and Ch Hobcote Folly.
- Mrs M Travis bred Ch Gaymel Gay Tamarisk and Ch Gaymel Saffron Dehazebury.
- Mr and Mrs Wood bred Ch Eastville King of Swing.
- Mrs Rosemary Leaf bred Ch Yeldersley Geminesse.
- Mrs C Freeman bred Ch Boarfield Cassius.
- Mr F Shaw bred Ch Franshaw War Cry.
- Mr P Rooney bred Ch Biscovey Robert-E-Lee and Ch Biscovey Sweet Caroline.
- Mrs Barbara Golding bred the champions Beacontree Vanessa and Teazel, and campaigned Beacontree Gelarista Gold Blend to his championship. Barbara also exported several Bassets, who became champions in their respective countries.
- Mrs Margaret Thorley bred Ch Bezel Sweety Pie, Ch Bezel Genevive of Tamsmorna, Ch Bezel Isabella, Ch Bezel Jolly Gollyman and Ch Bezel Lorna Doon. Bezel Action Man was a very dominant sire, although he did not become a champion. Most of the Bezel hounds were tri-colours, with plenty of substance and beautiful, dark eyes.

Contemporary Breeders

Abbeyacres

Mrs C Montizambert bought her first Basset, sired by Janvrins Destry, in 1967. In 1970, Foyewyn Erica (Ch Fredwell Varon Vandal ex Foyewyn Diamond) was obtained from Mrs Sally Goodwin. In 1972, Erica was mated to Fredwell Destrie and produced three lovely lemon-and-white sisters Ch Abbeyacres Pippa, who was made BOB at Crufts in 1977, Abbeyacres

Ch O' Hara v Hollandeim.

33

Puddleduck (one CC and one Reserve CC) and Abbeyacres Peggotty. Future litters produced Crufts and championship show winners Abbeyacres Amos, Augusta, Amelia, Becassine, Beau, Sadie and Benedict.

Aberthin

Mrs June Hallett's Bassets won extremely well in the 1960s and 1970s. They were the first Welsh-bred Bassets to win CCs while residing in Wales. June's first hound was Rodney of Aberthin (Lyn-Mar Acres Dauntless ex Gambol), who won one CC and four Reserve CCs. Rodney was a prepotent stud whose progeny were easily recognisable, with classical heads and colouring. The second hound to arrive was Coastal Alice (Ch Fredwell Ideal ex Ch Barnspark Frolic), bred by Wendy Thomas.

Ch Meddgoed Sensation of Aberthin.

Rodney and Alice were the foundation of the Aberthin kennels. In 1967 they produced Miniver of Aberthin, who won a CC at six months, Murlyn, who won a CC at Crufts in 1974, Montague (one CC) and Dutch/Lux Ch Meddlesome of Aberthin. Ch Cwmdale Kynaston of Aberthin was also bred by June.

In 1968 Montague of Aberthin was mated to Miss Wendy Thomas' Coastal Agnes, and produced Ch Coastal Weaver of Aberthin, Ch Coastal Winston, Coastal Welshman (Reserve CC) and Coastal Walnut, who won a CC in Ireland. Ch Weaver, mated to Miniver of Aberthin, produced Ch Meddgoed Sensation of Aberthin and Dutch/Continental Ch De Neers Buffalo Bill. The mating of Montague of Aberthin to Bazalgette Dulcimara produced Bazalgette Sabot of Aberthin (one CC, two Reserve CCs).

June reluctantly retired from showing when she went to live in Minorca, although she is seen occasionally at some British shows. She is Patron of the Basset Hound Club of Wales.

Akerwood

Joan Walker founded her kennel in 1965, based on Wyebank Butterscot, Ch Fredwell Rosemarine and Fredwell Mink. Joan bred low-set, substantial hounds with excellent temperaments that were eagerly sought after by European Basset breeders. Akerwood champions were made up in Germany (Akerwood Fabian, Akerwood Pims and Akerwood Hello Dolly) and in Sweden (Akerwood Oliver Twist). Joan used mainly her own stud dogs, but acquired Tamsmorna Heinekin (Crowolla John Peel ex Tamsmorna Cleopatra), whom she quickly campaigned to a champion. Heinekin combined well with Akerwood bitches and, when mated to Akerwood Echelle, produced Ch Akerwood Tweedledum. Another bitch, Akerwood Elsa, was exported to Canada and became foundation bitch of the then Verulams. Bezel Genevieve of Tamsmorna joined the kennel and soon achieved her championship, as did Ch Mayacre Mr Magoo who, when mated to Mrs Denise Shemeld's Ch Turbeville Easter Rose, produced Ch Waldo of Akerwood. Magoo also sired Can Ch Charford Corn Marigold, bred by Audrey Charman and owned in Canada by her daughter, Penny Frederiksen. Waldo was used by several breeders and is behind a number of Basset Hounds. Joan also bred Ch Turbeville Akerwood Jester and campaigned Bassbarr Dutch Bonnet to her title. Although Akerwood studs were not widely used in the United Kingdom, they have proved very influential in Europe, and descendants of Akerwood exports are now back in this country with the recent import from Holland, Ch O'Hara van Hollandheim (see page 33).

Joan was a committee member of the BHC for 18 years. She was involved in importing two of the first PBGVs into this country: the dog Windsor von Schloss Isabella can be found in most pedigrees of the breed today. Joan is a British and international judge of both Bassets and PBGVs at championship show level.

Albanium

Jan and Rob Albon obtained their first Basset, Fredwell Merry Boy, in May 1972. He came as a pet and fired their enthusiasm to purchase one for show. They booked a pup from Neda Adams: Nedajays Homer (Ch Tamsmorna Heinekin ex Nedajays Damsel), who joined them in 1974 while they were living in Canada. Homer became a Canadian champion and was successfully field trialled. In 1976 their affix Verulam was registered and they obtained a bitch from Joan Walker: Akerwood Elsa (Ch Tamsmorna Heinekin ex Akerwood Orchid). Elsa was mated to Am Ch

Ch Verulan Morgan Le Fay.

Linpets Argus and raised one pup. In a repeat mating she produced four puppies and two were retained: Can Ch Verulam Halinka and Can Ch Verulam Hopkins (owned by Penny Frederiksen). In 1982, Turbeville Woodpecker was imported from Denise Shemeld and mated to Halinka, producing Can Ch Verulam Harriet. In 1987, Harriet was mated to Can Ch San-Dells Sanko, an extrovert tri-colour dog from the Sandell kennel who provided much of the foundation stock in Canada. From this came nine puppies, of whom three were retained: Gawaine, Blasine and Morgan Le Fay.

In 1989, Jan and Rob returned to England, bringing seven of their Bassets with them. These took quarantine in their stride, possibly because they were together. Morgan Le Fay became a champion, winning three CCs and three Reserve CCs. Unfortunately, someone had registered the Verulam affix in Great Britain, so they chose Albanium as the new affix. Ch Morgan Le Fay was mated to Lugano and raised four pups after a caesarean. Beguiling and Batwing won well for their new owner (Mrs A Dyne), who later exported them to Holland. Bellman won his stud book number and is winning well, and Bewitched has a Reserve CC. One British and six Canadian champions have been bred from this kennel, which is still producing quality hounds.

Rob Albon is on the committee of the Basset Hound Club and Jan has been passed to award CCs in the breed.

Andyne

Mrs Andy Dyne campaigned White Gold of Andyne (Balleroy of Jazzman ex Freckles Golden Sunset), bred by Mrs Jerram, to his championship. White Gold is the sire of four champions: Bassbarr O'Sullivan, Locketwhite Magic Merle, Bassbarr O'Shea and Bassbarr O'Clare. Andy also campaigned Andyne Milky Way to her championship. She also owns Bassbarr on Parade at Andyne, who has sired Ch Switherland Sage, Ch Switherland Surprise, Switherland Strudel and her own Milky Way.

Balleroy

In 1964, Pat Moncur purchased her first Basset Hound, Aline Foxglove, who proved to be no show dog but excelled at obedience. Pat's love of Bassets led her to obtain from Rosemary McKnight Chantinghall Beatrice (Ch Wingjays Fanciful ex Chantinghall Airs and Graces), bred by Jeanne Rowett-Johns. Chantinghall Airs and Graces was a daughter of Am Ch Crochmaid Bold Turpin of Blackheath. Beatrice was campaigned to her championship. Chantinghall Linnet also joined the kennels, winning one CC and three RCCs. Balleroy Chantinghall Ballad

Ch Harecroft Magnus of Balleroy. Photo: Diane Pearce

(one CC) joined the expanding kennels. Ch Beatrice produced Ch Balleroy Chestnut (nine CCs) and Ch Fredwell Balleroy Faithful.

Ch Balleroy Chestnut sired Ch Balleroy Nero, Ch Balleroy Yasmin, Aust Ch Balleroy Karl and Balleroy Barshaw Caprice (one CC), who produced three champions for Liz Andrews. Karl, who won one Reserve CC before leaving this country, sired Balleroy Bacchus, who won one CC prior to going to Sweden. Bacchus also sired Ch Balleroy Luther (12 CCs), who sired several champions, the most notable being Ch Harecroft Magnus of Balleroy, winner of 26 CCs, one-time breed record holder and sire of several champions. Interestingly, Chestnut, Karl, Bacchus and Luther were red-blankets.

Other champions have been Ch Balleroy Elegant, Ch Balleroy Fiddler and Ch Harecroft Lucretia of Balleroy, as well as a champion Bloodhound and Beagle.

Pat was a founder member of the Basset Hound Club of Scotland and was on the initial committee, serving as its Secretary for several years prior to moving south of the Border. She now holds the position of President.

Pat judged her first championship show at the age of 24, at Dumfries, which no longer has championship status. She was probably the youngest person in Great Britain at that time to award CCs in Basset Hounds. She has judged regularly ever since, including Crufts in 1979.

Balmacara

Mr and Mrs Meredith obtained their first Basset and started to show in 1969. This was Harratons Hoya. Soon two more Bassets joined the kennel: Fredwell Floozey and Maycombe Lemon Drop. Floozey was mated by Ch Wingjays Polygamy of Maycombe, and a male, Balmacara Foghorn, was retained from this litter and went on to win a Reserve CC. Floozey was then mated to Barabooka Far to Go, and two bitches were retained from the ensuing litter: Balmacara Cocoa and Balmacara Crumpet. Cocoa went to the Barabooka kennels and won a Reserve CC. Both bitches won well at championship shows. In 1971, after a move to Wiltshire, Balmacara Crumpet was mated to Ch Stormfield Hugo, and from this litter came Balmacara Dewdrop, Balmacara Dougal, Balmacara Droopy Drawers and Balmacara Dounbeg. Jim and Norah Green of the Noredo Bassets had Balmacara Dounbeg, who won two CCs and two Reserve CCs and gained her Irish title. From a repeat mating, Balmacara Love-in-May was retained and, when they moved to Germany, she was mated to Ch Endeavour von Bengalon, sired by Akerwood Chorister. From this litter was kept the dog Ch Balmacara Puddles (CACIB.CAC.RCC). The Balmacaras were in Germany for several

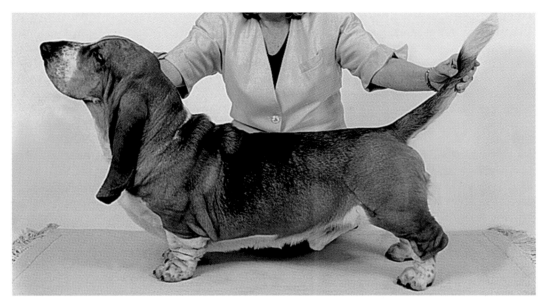

Ch Morkebergs It's Now or Never at Balmacara (Danish import).

years and, on their return to England, Puddles was mated to Ch Stormfield Russet of Merreybeech. From this litter Merreybeech Wellington of Balmacara was purchased; he gained one CC and many championship firsts. A bitch, Balleroy Buxom, was purchased from Pat Moncur and later, when mated to Wellington, produced the two outstanding red-and-white males, Ch Balmacara Gunfire and Ch Balmacara Gunshot (owned by S Johnston). Late in 1996, a Basset from Denmark was imported and, within three-and-a-half months of showing, he became Ch Morkebergs It's Now or Never at Balmacara (Am/Dk Ch Scheels Excalibur ex Dk Ch Morkebergs Ophelia).

Ch/Ir Ch Barrenger Devil's Snuffbox, Ch Barrenger Demon King and Barrenger Devil May Care. Photo: John Hartley

Barrenger

Sandra Thexton and Margaret Martin's Barrenger affix was granted in 1970. Fredwell Tampo was their first show dog but, on the death of Sandra's father, showing became a casual hobby for approximately 10 years, becoming serious with the purchase of Verwood Brimstone (Ch Langpool William ex Ch Zondas I'm a Muddy Girl of Verwood) from Veronica Ross. Brimstone, mated to her half-brother Verwood Royal Swede, produced a lemon-and-white bitch, who became Ch Barrenger Queens Indian.

Queens Indian produced two litters of 13, the first to Ch Vinell Dapper Dandy, from which came Barrenger Indian Summer (three Green Stars), and the second to Siouxline Reuben, from which came Ch/Ir Ch Barrenger Demon King. Demon King was owned in partnership with Margaret Martin, who now shares the Barrenger affix, and he has won 10 CCs and 10 Reserve CCs, Junior Warrant, four BISs at open shows and runner up PRO dog of the year in 1992. A great character! A mating to his half-sister, Indian Summer, produced a third-generation champion: Ch Barrenger Devils Snuffbox, owned in partnership with Enid Smith. From the same litter came Barrenger Devil May Care, winner of one CC, and Barrenger Red Devil. Other winners are Barrenger Figaro (Junior Warrant), Barrenger Hooray It's Summer (Reserve CC) and the young dog Barrenger Double Demon, from a father/daughter mating (Demon King ex Devils Snuffbox). The Barrengers have based their success on close line breeding, and are not afraid to inbreed, this having produced two of their champions.

Barratini

Carol Daykin obtained her first Basset, Barrabooka Georgia Brown, in 1979. Georgia Brown was mated to Margaret Thorley's Bezel Bannerman – and Carol's first litter was born. Judy Wilson (Barabooka) and Margaret Thorley (Bezel) proved valuable friends, and Barabooka Jolly Good joined the team. Bezel Genevieve was also there for a short time, gaining her crown with Joan Walker. In 1988, Brandydale Evita and her brother, Brandydale Equerry for Barratini, were purchased. Brandydale Equerry gained his title in six weeks, aged 21 months, and then went to Holland, where he gained his Dutch title in eleven weeks. He came back to England with his son, The Third Kind Presented Dutch, who produced a ticket winner in his only litter. Equerry was then sold to a breeder in Norway, where he gained his Norwegian and Swedish titles. Evita produced one litter, whose members have gone on to produce three champions: Dereheath Cuddles, Siouxline Doyle of Dereheath and Siouxline Daniella. In recent years Carol has campaigned Bassbarr Fame and Fortune, who won two CCs and three Reserve CCs. Unfortunately, Fame and Fortune suffered gastric bloat and was unable to continue her show career. Barratini Strawberry Blonde (one CC and two Reserve CCs) and Ch O'Hara van Hollandheim now enjoy each other's company on the show circuit. O'Hara is now in veteran classes and won first at Crufts in 1997.

Bassbarr

Mr Bill O'Loughlin's first Basset was born in 1964: Bassbar Gertrude of Reddicap. She was mated to Foxmere Cheyenne and produced It/Int Ch Bassbarr Gretel. Returning from Italy to Great Britain in 1971, Bill bought Temerloh Sundays Child, a granddaughter of Gertrude. Sunday's Child gained two CCs and, when mated to Ch Hardacre Valorous, produced Ch Bassbarr Victoria Plumb. Flareout Contralto was obtained from Fae Morgan and, mated to Chesterfield Simon, she produced Ch Red Baron of Ide, who became Basset Hound of the year before being exported to Sweden. He also sired Ch Franshaw War Cry. Ch Bassbarr Dutch Bonnet (Dutch Ch Beacontree Whynot ex Bassbarr Chanteuse) was owned and campaigned by Mrs Joan Walker (Akerwood). Bill returned to Italy for several years and, while there, he bred It Ch Bassbarr David, who is the sire of the re-imported It Ch Bassbarr Fred Astaire, who in turn sired Ch Viness Vinell Yum Yum.

Lancashire, Yorkshire and Cheshire Championship Show 1995: (left to right) Dog CC – Ch Bassbarr O'Sullivan; Bitch CC – Ch White Mischief of Moragden; Best Puppy – Bassbarr Queen of Diamonds (later Ch). Photo: Harold Corney

Up to the end of the 1980s, the Bassbarrs had been a blend of Fredwell, Wingjays, Beacontree, Hardacre and Langpool. The most important era for the Bassbarrs began when O'Hara van Hollandheim (Dutch/Int/Belg Ch Lonesome Lover van Hollandheim ex Dutch/Int Ch Sensation van Hollandheim) was purchased from Mrs Carla Gerber (Holland). O'Hara's sire and dam were out of Ch Phoebe van Hollandheim, a daughter of Beacontree Calender. Sensation was sired by Am/Int Ch Tal-E-Ho's Top Gun. Apart from the Tal-E-Hos, most of O'Hara's ancestors stemmed from some wonderful Akerwood hounds exported by Mrs Walker and the Beacontree line. O'Hara's great-great-grandmother was Beacontree Emotion, a granddaughter of Ch Sungarth Sykemoor Aimwell. O'Hara was mated to White Gold of Andyne (Balleroy Jazzman at Andyne ex Freckles Golden Sunset), later a champion. He had corresponding ancestors to O'Hara: on his sire's side Endeavour von Bengalen and Beacontree Emotion, on his dam's side a line to Ch Lodway Lancer of Islwyn and back to Lyn-Mar Acres M'Lord Batuff. The litter of eight born to O'Hara included Ch Bassbarr O'Sullivan, Ch Bassbarr O'Clare, Ch Bassbarr O'Shea, Bassbarr on Parade at Andyne (two Reserve CCs), Bassbarr Only Scarlet for Andyne and Bassbarr O'Toole.

Ch Bassbarr O'Sullivan's (Gilbert's) show career has been outstanding. He is current breed record holder and, in 1993, he achieved the unique distinction of winning Top Dog All Breeds in the United Kingdom. He followed this with Runner-up Top Dog in 1994 and 1995. Gilbert has won 64 CCs, 29 Hound Groups and nine BISs at all-breed championship shows. He has sired Ch Bassbarr Queen of Diamonds, Ch Bassbarr Obsession with Bronia, Ch/Ir Ch Faburn Gypsy and three overseas champions. Several of his offspring have won CCs. O'Shea produced CC winners in her litter and On Parade is proving an important stud.

Ch Maghefeld Defender of Bassbarr (Verwood Hyper Hyper ex Lady Emma of Maghefeld) was obtained as a puppy and made his mark prior to being exported to Sweden, where he gained his Swedish, Danish and Norwegian titles.

Belvere

The Belvere affix is owned by Jim and Maggie Gray. Their first Basset, obtained in 1968, was Coastal Winston (Montague of Aberthin ex Coastal Agnes), bred by Mrs Wendy Thomas. With her guidance, Winston attained his title. Another Coastal Basset was obtained to keep Winston company but, unfortunately, the two dogs hated each other. A third Basset therefore arrived and lived for 16^{1}/$_{2}$ years. The pastimes previously loved by Maggie had by now 'gone to the dogs', as she says. There had been a move from town to country, and a transition from saloon car to estate. Fingernails were broken rather than manicured, and fun on the sea had given way to mopping up wee!

Having served their apprenticeship, Maggie and Jim decided to obtain a bitch to breed and acquired Barrabooka I'm Lovely (Ch Wellshim Cruiser ex Ch Barrabooka Apple Pie), bred by Mrs Judy Wilson. Thus emerged the Belvere Bassets, producing a litter usually every two years.

In 1981 Kuntree Rhodes at Belvere (Ch Langpool Carries Lad of Islwyn ex Belvere Gemima) was purchased from Mrs A Ventrella. He gained his title in 1983 and, in 1984 under Mr G Johnston (Sykemoor), the breed specialist, won the Reserve CC at Crufts, his daughter winning the Reserve Bitch CC and 10 of his offspring being placed first, second or third.

The hounds that Maggie has shown have all had their moments of glory, several winning CCs or Reserve CCs. Her winners include Goodness Gracious, Bella, Clarion, Candida, Hallmark, Tiffany, Artemis and Saffron.

Bewmay

Mrs May Bews had her first Basset in 1960. This was Sungarth Paris, full litter brother to Ch Sungarth Phoebe (owned by Mrs J Jowett-Johns). Soon two more joined the household, Bayard and Blondin. When Paris died, May purchased two litter brothers from us: Brackenacre Fino de Paris and Brackenacre Fidus Achates (Ch Fredwell Ideal ex Brackenacre Chime of Bells). At five months of age, neither would walk on a lead. In desperation, she rang for help and was advised to take them to the local dog training class. When we saw Paris we realised he was a winner. May allowed Jim to show him and, at Crufts in 1973, aged 16 months, he won CC and BOB under John Evans. This was followed by CC and BOB in 1974 under judge Mrs Joan Wells-Meacham and 1975 Reserve CC under judge Amyas Biss in 1975. Paris won many CCs, one BIS all breeds and sired Ch Brackenacre Jessica, Ch Brackenacre Jingle Bell, Ch Tintally D'Arcy, Ch Brackenacre James Bond, and many more CC winners.

May became the Treasurer of The Basset Hound Club in 1975 and retired in 1994.

Blaby

Doreen Gilberthorpe purchased her first Basset, Sharon of Snowthorpe, in 1966. In September 1968, Sharon was mated to Ch Fredwell Ideal, and from the resulting litter two bitches were retained: Blaby Biddy and Blaby Bess. Blaby Biddy gained her stud book number and Reserve CCs in 1974 and her second litter was born to Ch Lymewoods Howard. Sadly she died after a caesarean. The puppies were hand reared and two were retained: Blaby Hesta, who won one CC, and Blaby Hal. Hal became a champion, winning 15 CCs and 13 Reserve CCs. Throughout his show career he was hunting with the Albany. His Hunt Certificate was the first to be awarded to a show champion since his grandfather Ch Breightmet Chimer. He was declared Champion Dog Hound of the Pack in 1978, so he became a

Ch Blaby Marrygolde, Bitch CC record holder.
Photo: Diane Pearce

legend in his lifetime. Other CC winners were born at Blaby and Blady Bramble (Ch Fredwell Varon Fawkes ex Sharron of Snowthorpe) was another to gain a Hunt Certificate.

In 1980 another star was born. Jusland Fancy and Free, Hal's daughter, bred by Una Golland, was mated to Ch Harecroft Magnus of Balleroy and, from a litter of eight, two bitches were kept: Blaby Melody (one CC, four Reserve CCs) and Ch Blaby Marrygolde, the bitch CC record holder, with 26 CCs, 15 Reserve CCs, two Hound Group wins and many BISs at championship breed shows.

Balleroy Jazzman at Andyne, whose dam was Blaby Camilla, produced Blaby Jolly Conqueror, who was exported to Sheila Tarr (Greystones) in South Africa, where he became a champion and was Top Dog of all breeds.

Doreen awards CCs in Bassets and judged at Crufts in 1987. She has judged in many countries and also awards CCs in five of the Dachshund breeds, having owned them since 1946. In Doreen's own words: 'Thirty years of honour, heartbreak and much joy in the world of Dachshunds and Bassets.'

Mr J Nixon with (left to right) Brackenacre Chime of Bells, Ch Brackenacre Annabella, Brackenacre Kierhill Oonagh and Grims Flimsy

Brackenacre

In partnership with my husband Jim, I have bred Ch Brackenacre Annabella (Hardacre Sungarth Eager ex Brackenacre Kierhill Oonagh), Ch Brackenacre Daisy Bell (Ch Fredwell Varon Vandal ex Ch Brackenacre Annabella), Ch Brackenacre Fino de Paris (Ch Fredwell Ideal ex Brackenacre Chime of Bells), Ch Brackenacre Jessica (Ch Brackenacre Fino de Paris ex Ch Brackenacre Daisy Bell), Ch Brackenacre Jingle Bell (Ch Brackenacre Fino de Paris ex Ch Brackenacre Daisy Bell), Ch Brackenacre James Bond (Ch Brackenacre Fino de Paris ex Brackenacre Emma Peel), Ch Brackenacre The Viking (Ch Brackenacre James Bond ex Witchacre Magpie of Brackenacre),

Ch Brackenacre Primrose (Witchacre Jim Lad ex Brackenacre Diamond Lil), Ch Brackenacre The Witch (Ch Brackenacre James Bond ex Pendlewitch of Brackenacre), Ch Brackenacre The Challenger (Ch Brackenacre The Viking ex Pendlewitch of Brackenacre), Ch Brackenacre Jasmine (Ch Brackenacre The Viking ex Brackenacre Zero Zero), Ch Brackenacre Katie Mia (Ch Brackenacre The Viking ex Brackenacre Zinnia), Ch Brackenacre Top Class (Brackenacre Black Knight ex Brackenacre Mary Rose),

Ch Brackenacre The Viking. Photo: Diane Pearce

Ch Brackenacre Fancy and Free of Tancegems (Ch Brackenacre The Viking ex Brackenacre Zero Zero), Ch Brackenacre My April Fool (Ch Hollysend Ghostbuster ex Ch Brackenacre Top Class), Ch Brackenacre Navan (Ch Hollysend Glostbuster ex Brackenacre Victoria) and Ch Brackenacre Mary Anne (Ch Hollysend Ghostbuster ex Ch Brackenacre Top Class).

Jim and I are both championship show judges of several breeds of hound. I award CCs in 13 breeds and am passed by The Kennel Club to judge the hound group at championship show level. We have bred Bassets for more than 30 years, with a preference for the traditional tri-colours. We both have judged overseas on several occasions.

Burnvale

Sandra and Tommy Johnston's first show Basset, Rittyrig Sergeant Pepper (Langpool Lodestar ex Balleroy Negress), was obtained in 1978 from Mrs D Campbell. An early litter sired by Ch Carresmar Legend produced Burnvale Blueberry and Bilberry. Bilberry, mated to Helmsdown Caper (Langpool Lodestar ex Ch Harecroft Regina of Helmsdown), produced a bitch who was subsequently mated to their first champion, Balmacara Gunshot, and produced Burnvale Impatiens (one CC and one Reserve CC). Balmacara Gunshot was obtained from Mrs Francis Meredith and campaigned to his title. A bitch obtained from Mrs V Ness, Viness Vinell Xciting for Burnvale (Ch White Gold of Andyne ex Ch Viness Vinell Vice Versa) was mated to Gunshot and produced Burnvale Komfrey. Both Komfrey and Impatiens were mated to Ch Bassbarr O'Sullivan and produced several quality offspring: Burnvale Quatergill, Burnvale Orange Blossom and Burnvale Origano (three Reserve CCs). Orange Lily (O'Sullivan ex Impatiens) has been exported to Siegfried Peter (Germany) and Quintessential (O'Sullivan ex Komfrey) has been exported to Australia and become an Australian champion. Burnvale Quicksilver was mated to Ch Switherland Blue Jeans, which produced a very promising litter. Although still quite young, one of these has quickly established himself in Eire and is one of the top dogs all breeds.

With the demise of the Helmsdown and Rittyrig Basset Hounds, Burnvale has been the most consistent winning Basset Hound kennel in Scotland in recent years.

Carresmar

Mrs Elizabeth Watson showed her first Basset in 1975: Birchacre Laurel of Carresmar (Langpool Friar Tuck U the Beacontree ex Birchacre M'Lady), bred by Mrs Pearl Laing. Laurel was mated

Ch Carresmar Legend.

to Ch Mayacre Mr Magoo and from this mating came Carresmar Laurelyne (Reserve CCs), Carresmar Laurustinus (Junior Warrant, one CC, and one Reserve CC), Carresmar Lauris, owned by Mrs S Waskett (one Reserve CC) and the well-known Ch Carresmar Legend (six CCs, two Reserve CCs and BOB at Crufts in 1985). Legend died before he was seven years old and, although sparingly used at stud, he sired Mrs A Charman's Ch Charford Ceilidh and other winners including Carresmar Look at Me (Junior Warrant and two Reserve CCs). When mated to Ch Lodway Lancer of Islwyn, Look At Me produced Ch Carresmar Lindsay (nine CCs and four Reserve CCs), who won BIS at breed club shows. Lindsay, mated to Charford Cariad, sired Ch Charford Claudia at Puckaman, bred by Mrs A Charman and owned by Mrs M Clements. Another winner was Lodway Lyric By Carresmar (two CCs and one Reserve CC), bred by Mr and Mrs Tranter out of Lodway Carmel By The Sea. Lindsay's sister, Carresmar Lemma, when mated to Ch White Gold of Andyne, produced Carresmar Lady of Louvaine, who was mated to Ch Lindsay to produce the current youngsters, Carresmar Lonesome and Carresmar Libby.

Elizabeth is a championship show judge of Basset Hounds, and takes great pleasure in breeding her predominantly tri-colour Bassets.

Charford

Mrs Audrey Charman has bred Basset Hounds for several years. In 1985, Leirum Chrysanthemum was mated to Ch Carresmar Legend, and produced Ch Charford Ceilidh. Charford Cariad, paired with Ch Carresmar Lindsay, produced Ch Charford Claudia at Puckaman, owned and campaigned by Mandy Clements. Audrey's daughter Penny emigrated to Canada and then America (see chapter 3). Over the years, Charford Bassets exported to Penny have won well and become champions.

Audrey was Secretary of the BHC for a period, and she awards CCs in Basset Hounds.

Coastal

Wendy Thomas obtained her first Basset in 1960. She wanted a hound to accompany her on horseback on her poultry farm in Dorset. Candid Cruiser, mainly Grims breeding, bred by Mrs Coombes, was her choice. Although not shown very frequently, he won the Wickwell Collar for Best Veteran at the BHC show at the age of 12. Cruiser was a natural hunter and qualified for his BHC working certificate.

In 1964 Barnspark Frolic (Ch Pointgrey Suss's Folly ex Barnspark Charity) was purchased in partnership with Miss Biddy Basset. Frolic became a champion, also gaining her working certificate. Mated to Ch Fredwell Ideal, she produced the foundation of many Coastal winning hounds. Coastal Agnes was kept and, when mated to Montague of Aberthin, produced Ch Coastal Winston (owned by Mrs Gray), Ch Coastal Weaver (owned by June Hallett), Coastal Welshman, winner of Reserve CC at Crufts (owner John Roberts), Coastal Wrinkle and Coastal Walnut, winner of one CC. Over the following decades, many winning hounds were produced, including

Coastal Farthing, Bramble, Olga, Gumboots and Soloman. Sue Ergis (Siouxline) started with a Coastal hound, and now Wendy has two Siouxline Bassets, related back to her own line.

Wendy's first love is hunting with her hounds, and she regularly joins the local Beagle Pack in the Purbeck area. She has awarded CCs in Basset Hounds since 1979.

Dereheath

Heather and Derek Storton obtained Verwood Dolly Catch from Veronica Ross in 1979 and Lelaurin Kerfuffle of Vinell from

Coastal Bramble. Photo: Astley Colour Laboratories

Malcolm and Debbie Ellrich in 1986. In 1989 and 1990 Malrich Dignity and Siouxline Clarence were being shown. Two Bassets from Carol Daykin were obtained: Barratini Pickles (Ch Bassbarr O'Sullivan ex Brandydale Peony at Barratini) and Barratini Almond (Ch White Gold of Andyne ex Brandydale Evita). Sue Ergis kindly gave them Siouxline Doyle (Barratini Ambassador to Siouxline ex Ch Suzanna of Siouxline). All of these were successfully shown. Barratini Pickles was mated to The Third Kind Presented Dutch and a bitch from the ensuing litter, Dereheath Dark Desdemona, was awarded a CC while still a puppy. In the next letter, Barratini Almond, a Reserve CC winner, was mated to Karipat Dicken, and a dog and bitch were retained. Of these, Dereheath Claret won a Reserve CC while a puppy and Dereheath Cuddles became a champion in 1996, the same year as Ch Siouxline Doyle of Dereheath. More youngsters are in the wings awaiting their debut in 1997: Dereheath Sinatra, Dereheath Love Me Tender and Dereheath Viva Las Vegas.

Drawdell

Margaret and Dennis Ledward obtained their first Basset in the mid-1960s. Later a Gaymel-bred Basset was purchased and the dog showing started. Gaymel Gay Tamarisk entered the household at eight weeks and was in time campaigned to her championship. Tamarisk's sister Tamerlane was purchased to use the bloodline for breeding and, mated to Verwood Zigzag, she produced Annapurna and Karakoram. Annapurna, mated to Ch Lymewoods Howard, produced Ch Cillfoyle Franchesca. Tamerlane was mated to Gaymel Indigo Pipkin, and Drawdell Betsy Trotwood was kept. Betsy gained two CCs and a Reserve CC prior to being exported at 18 months to Italy, where she became an Italian champion and won numerous awards. Drawdell Rembrandt was also exported and became an Italian Champion. Drawdell Karakorum was mated to Gaymel Indigo Pipkin and produced Kalamity Kate and Kansas Kid. Kate won a CC and Kansas a Reserve CC. Kate eventually became the foundation bitch for Ron Parker's Rossfell kennels. Mated to Drawdell San Sebastian, she produced Drawdell Weeping Willow, who was purchased by Mr R Parker (Rossfell). Drawdell Magnolia Blossom was purchased by Mr and Mrs Rooney (Biscovey). Silver Maple was tragically killed on her way to Crufts. Mellow Mahogany was purchased by Mr and Mrs Hankinson. Drawdell Weeping Willow, mated to Ch Harecroft Magnus of Balleroy, produced Mr and Mrs Parker's Ch Rossfell Crazy Horse. Drawdell Magnolia Blossom, mated to Magnus, produced Ch Biscovey Robert-E-Lee and litter sister Ch Biscovey Sweet Caroline. Ch Caroline was mated to Ch Gladsome Harvest Gold, and Drawdell Inca Gold was the result. He was shown successfully until the tragic accident of his owner, when he was returned to Drawdell. Margaret and Dennis are now showing two young bitches (Inca Gold ex Rossfell Bilberry of Drawdell): Drawdell Tammy Wynette and Crystal Gale.

Margaret and Dennis have served on various committees. At present they are both serving on the Lancashire, Yorkshire and Cheshire BHC Committee.

Eastport

John and Eileen Mayne obtained Langpool Bizzie Lizzie (Ch Langpool William ex Ch Langpool Carie-Anne) as their foundation bitch in 1976. Previously they had owned a Basset with a lot of Grims breeding, but it was not their intention to breed from this one. From their first litter by Ch Stormfield Hugo they retained a bitch, Eastport Penelope Pit Stop, who won very well. In 1986, a home-bred bitch, Eastport Paper Lace, was mated to Ch Beacontree Gelarista Gold Blend, and whelped eight puppies. Normally they only kept bitches, but two very nice dog puppies caught their eye, so they kept the black blanket puppy and Miss Wendy Fairbrother, who had been looking for a puppy, had the lemon-and-white. These two males became Ch Eastport Black Coffee and Ch Eastport Classic Gold Lace. Both dogs won extensively. Unfortunately, Black Coffee has died, but his son, Ch Hollysend Ghost Buster, has sired several champions. Gold Lace has won a string of top honours, including a Hound Group at a general championship show, and is still enjoying life in his eleventh year. John and Eileen strive to breed sound and typey Bassets of (most importantly) excellent temperament.

Ch Eastport Classic Gold Lace.

Fivevalleys

Sandra Allen studied Bassets back in 1972, when she was living in St Albans. With the Basset kennels belonging to Denise Shemeld (Turbeville), Joan Wells-Meacham (Fredwell) and Michael Browne within easy reach, Sandra had a good grounding. Eventually she obtained a handsome red-and-white male from Africandawns kennel. When Sandra decided to start to breed she obtained a bitch, Kortinas Madonna, from Tina Cornell. When mated to Kortina Patrolman, Madonna produced the bitch Ch Fivevalleys Aurora (see overleaf) and the dog Fivevalleys Locomotion (one CC) and, when mated to Bentley van Hollandheim (imported), she produced Fivevalleys Evening Star. Mated to Patrolman, Evening Star produced Fivevalleys Grenadier, who gained a Reserve CC at seven months and became a champion by two years of age. His litter sister, Fivevalleys Shooting Star, not to be outdone, gained a Reserve CC as a puppy and is a champion at twenty months.

Gladsomes

Don and Gladys registered their affix in 1979. Their foundation stock was bred by Mrs Margaret Hadock and included the male Hadders Bouncer (Ch Bezel Action Man ex Hadders Cynnie) and his litter sister Hadders Derbyshire Lass. Another bitch was added: Windwell Hanky Panky (Cedarglen Quemby ex Lingross Debonair) bred by Pat Baggot. This bitch did a lot of winning and was awarded the Midland Points Trophy. Hadders Bouncer was also very successful. Bouncer was mated to

Ch Fivevalleys Aurora. Photo: Jan Ralph

Hanky Panky and from the resulting litter, born in 1980, a tri-colour dog was retained. This was Gladsomes Miguel, who won his Junior Warrant, a CC and three Reserve CCs. Bassbarr Dutch Courage of Jeffrone was mated to Derbyshire Lass, and two bitches were kept: Gladsomes Davina and Gladsomes Dolores. Davina won well, gained her Junior Warrant, a CC and three Reserve CCs. Ch Biscovey Robert-E-Lee was chosen to mate Hanky Panky, but unfortunately she died giving birth to 11 puppies, 10 of which were hand reared. Out of this litter a lemon-and-white dog

Ch Gladsomes Harvest Gold. Photo: Diane Pearce

and a tri-colour bitch were retained. These became Ch Gladsomes Harvest Gold and Ch Gladsomes Hisper. Harvest Gold won 21 CCs and 17 Reserve CCs, BIS at the Scottish Kennel Club Championship Show and Reserve BIS at the Border Hound Championship Show in 1985, Basset Hound of the Year in 1985 and runner-up 1986 and 1987. Not only was he a good show dog – he sired five champions. Mated to Davina, he produced the lemon-and-white dog Gold Ransome, who quickly became a champion, winning nine CCs and four Reserve CCs. In October 1990, Gold Ransome won Reserve BIS at the Driffield Championship Show. Hisper won 10 CCs and one Reserve CC.

Gladsomes Tycoon (Ch Bassbarr O'Sullivan ex Gladsomes Trinket) won the CC at the LKA.

A champion tri-colour bitch, Bassbarr Obsession with Bronia (Ch Bassbarr O'Sullian ex Andyne Chanel for Bassbar) was added to the kennel and mated to Ch Morkebegs It's Now or Never. She produced a litter of 12 tri-colours. A dog from this litter may be run on but, because of Gladys' ill-health, this may not be possible.

Both Don and Gladys are championship show judges.

Harecroft

Janis and Rodney Price registered their affix in 1974, although interest in the breed had been maintained since 1962 through friends who owned the Harraton kennel. Their first hound was a Harraton, followed by Candis Poacher. In the early 1970s Gaymel Sinbad and Gaymel Moray were bought from Mrs Travis. Both were shown successfully, winning CCs. In 1976 Moray was mated to Ch Balleroy Luther and produced the one-time breed record holder Harecroft Magnus of Balleroy (26 CCs). A repeat mating produced the champion sisters Harecroft Lydia and Harecroft Lucretia. Magnus went on to sire six champions. Although they had only a small kennel, Janis and Rodney became Breeders of the Year in 1978 and 1979. Success has been maintained over the years, with several CC and Reserve CC winners bred, including Mr C Gillander's Ch Harecroft Regina of Helmsdown. In 1994 it was felt that new blood was needed, so the blanket-tri-colour puppy Brackenacre Mairwenna of Harecroft was bought in and shown successfully. When she was mated to Brackenacre Huguenot she produced the kennel's latest young CC winner: Harecroft Soloman.

Hartlake

Maggie and Mike Bursey bought their first Basset in 1969, travelling to Somerset to choose the puppy, little knowing Glastonbury was to be their home in the future. Realising that Bassets are gregarious, they obtained another in 1970, a dark tri-colour bitch by Beacontree Ebonite. This triggered their love for black-blanket hounds. Barbara Golding (Beacontree) befriended them and introduced them to the Basset Hound world. In 1974, Beacontree Virgil (Ch Hardacre Valorous ex Beacontree Emotion) was added to their kennel. He was litter brother of Ch Beacontree Vanessa. Virgil was used at limited stud but can be found behind many successful kennels of today. His acquisition as part of the foundation stock at Hartlake consolidated the type of hound required. Virgil is behind Hartlake Vanity, Verity and Black Magic. Hartlake Black Magic was mated to Ledline Why Not Me and produced Ch Hartlake Twilight. In 1980, parvovirus hit the kennel hard, and it has taken several years to re-establish the black-blanketed Bassets so loved at Hartlake.

Ch Hollysend Ghostbuster.

Hollysend

Mrs June Bartley has bred dogs for several years. Dachshunds and Dobermanns were her first interest – then came the Basset Hounds. June had one of her bitches, Fieldsman Mistletoe, mated to Ch Eastport Black Coffee, and produced the handsome bi-colour Ch Hollysend Ghostbuster, who in turn has sired the litter sisters Ch Brackenacre My April Fool and Brackenacre Mary Anne and the 1996 Crufts BOB Ch Brackenacre Navan.

Islwyn

While at training class at Poole with their first Basset, Gardencity Vanguard, Ann and John Roberts met Wendy Thomas (Coastal), who encouraged them to show. Soon John was hooked, and he bought Coastal Welshman, who gained a Reserve CC and two firsts at Crufts. In 1975 they acquired their affix 'Islwyn', borrowed from the Welsh bard of that name who is buried in the chapel near them. The first litter with Islwyn affix was Beagles; John continued showing the

Ch Lodway Lancer of Islwyn. Photo: Collin Davies

Bassets and Ann the Beagles. In 1976 they purchased Langpool Carries Lad (Verwood Wabash ex Ch Langpool Carrie Anne) from Dr E Andrews. Carries Lad won nine CCs and seven Reserve CCs, including Dog CC Crufts 1983. His first litter to Ch Mayflower of Langpool (bred by Mrs Patsy Flyn, now Tranter) produced the one-time breed record holder Ch Lodway Lancer of Islwyn, who won 52 CCs and 27 Reserve CCs, including Crufts BOB 1987, six Groups, two Reserve Groups, and Reserve BIS at Belfast Championship Show under Mrs Joan Wells-Meacham. In 1988 he was Reserve in the Contest of Champions, beaten only by the Crufts BIS English Setter. He won his last group at eight-and-a-half years and last Reserve CC at nine. Lancer sired six British champions, two Australian champions, one New Zealand champion and two Irish champions, and is behind many top show winners today.

Ann and John waited until their children were grown up before breeding their first litter of Bassets. They mated Lancer to Lillie of Langpool, retaining Islwyn Pluto. In 1989, Triple Bar B Cleopatra at Islwyn, bred by Fred and Leny van der Velden, was imported from Holland. Mated to Lancer, she produced the brother and sister Islwyn Centurion and Islwyn Myfanwy. In 1983 Myfanwy was mated to Lancer's son, Mooroolbark, from the Master at Islwyn, and from that litter emerged the first home-bred champion, Islwyn Sophinee, with litter sister Swe Ch Islwyn Simply Red and litter brother Islwyn Crusader of Blackvein.

Both Anne and John award CCs in Basset Hounds and Ann is the Secretary of the Basset Hound Club of Wales.

Kortina

Tina Cornell has owned Bassets for over 30 years but it wasn't until the 1980s that she was bitten by the show bug. She progressed through limit and open shows to the prestigious championship events. Some of her well-known hounds include Lodway Private Benjamin and Kortina's Dark Crystal, both regular winners, who between them produced a black-blanket giant of some 36.3kg

Ch Kortina's Big Bad Dom. Photo: Jan Ralph

(80lb), Ch Kortina's Big Bad Dom. Dom, an outstanding stallion hound with a temperament second to none, attained eight CCs

Another excellent stud dog is Kortina's Patrolman, a red-and-white who gained his Junior Warrant and Reserve CC. Patrolman clearly did not like showing, so was withdrawn. His outstanding conformation was to prove a great asset to the breed, and some of his progeny have won high honours, including Kortina's Del Boy, who to date has in excess of 100 wins at all levels, including two CCs, Ch Fivealleys Aurora (see page 46) and, more recently, the brother and sister Ch Fivevalleys Grendier and Ch Fivevalleys Shooting Star at Kortina. The dam of this pair was Fivevalleys Evening Star. Not to be left out is Kortina's Crystal Queen of Furlongs, a bitch with numerous wins at championship shows.

Kortina's Del Boy.

Tina has always believed that temperament is as important as conformation and the other physical qualities required of a show Basset. The litters she has occasionally bred reflect this. Tina is deeply committed to Basset Hound Welfare and Rescue.

Ledline

In 1976, Trevor Ledbury and Pam Ledbury (now White) started the Ledline Kennel from Tonegar ex Beacontree stock obtained from Barbara Golding. Their first champion, Ledline White Apache (Inov the Red at Beacontree ex Tonegar Warbler), was born 21 February 1978, and their next champion, Ledline Lady Chatterley (Ch Waldo of Akerwood ex Ch Ledline White Apache), was born in 1982. From Tonegar Warbler's litter sister, Calamity of Ledline, came Ledline Foolish Maid who, when mated to Beacontree

Wigeon, produced Ch Ledline Drucilla Penny, born in 1984. Ch Ledline Drucilla Penny, mated to Ch Lelaurin Lennox, produced Ch Ledline Rosie Glow at Castlebrook, owned by Mr and Mrs J Carter.

Trevor Ledbury now lives in America. Pam White returned to Bassets in 1997 with the Houndstone affix after some time with Old English Mastiffs. She awards CCs in Basset Hounds.

Moragden

Terry and Pat Tryhorn obtained their first Basset in 1981, a Siouxline bitch who was later mated to Ch Kuntree Rhodes at Belvere. From this litter was retained a bitch, Moragden Morgana Magic Maiden, who gained her stud book number in the show ring. She in turn was put to Ch Vinell Dapper Dandy, and another bitch was retained and mated to Ch Eastport Black Coffee. This produced Moragden Maxim (five Reserve CCs). Magic Maiden, mated to Siouxline Reuben, produced Moragden Madeline. Maxim and Madeline were paired, producing Moragden Malandra (Reserve CC) and Moragden Magnolia, owned by Phillip Carter and Maggie Gray. Magnolia, mated to Lowaters Lottery, produced Ch White Mischief at Moragden, who won her first CC at 10 months and her title at 13 months. She has six CCs and six Reserve CCs.

Rittyrig

Mr and Mrs Campbell bought their first Basset in 1974. This was followed by two more Balleroy bitches and a Langpool dog from Dr E Andrews. These were the foundation of the Rittyrigs. Their first litter was born and their affix registered in 1976. Rittyrig Hazel (Langpool Lodestar ex Balleroy Quarto) won two CCs and one Reserve CC, plus many other awards. Hazel produced Rittyrig Harriette, who won a CC, and Harriette produced Rittyrig Hazy and Henrietta, who gained Reserve CCs. Balleroy Gee (Ch Balleroy Luther ex Balleroy Rapture) mated to Balleroy Export (Ch Langpool Scrumpy ex Ch Harecroft Lucretia of Balleroy) produced Rittyrig Xitta and Rittyrig Xena, both of whom won well, gaining many BISs at breed shows also three Reserve CCs. Xitta, mated to Merreybeech Wellington of Balmacara, produced Ch Rittyrig Wallis (six CCs and five Reserve CCs, BHC top winning Bitch 1988, top winning bitch in Scotland 1989, Crufts BOB 1990). Regrettably, she was unable to produce puppies and pass on her many virtues. Whilst unable to keep many hounds, Mr and Mrs Campbell have been lucky enough to own and/or breed 10

Ch Rittyrig Wallis.

hounds who have won CCs or Reserve CCs and many others that gained entry to The Kennel Club Stud Book.

Doreen has awarded CCs in Basset Hounds since 1987, and was Secretary of The Basset Hound Club of Scotland from 1979 for 15 years.

Rossfell

Rosemary and Ron Parker started in Bassets in the mid-1970s. They bred the occasional litter, mainly to pick a puppy for show. Their first litter (Ch Jeffrone Red Admiral ex Drawdell Kalamity

Kate) produced 11 puppies, most of which were shown and won extremely well. This litter included Ch Rossfell Long John Silver. A year later they mated their other lovely bitch, Drawdell Weeping Willow, to Ch Harecroft Magnus of Balleroy, producing a super litter of dark tri-colours, including the extrovert male Ch Rossfell Crazy Horse, who loved the show ring and won many BIS awards.

Ron and Rosemary have not shown much lately, as starting a new business has accounted for a large proportion of their time, but they hope that they will soon be back on the show circuit.

Ron is a championship show judge of Basset Hounds.

Ch Rossfell Long John Silver.

Siouxline

Mrs Sue Ergis obtained her first Basset in 1973 from Wendy Thomas (Coastal). She bred her first champion, Ch Siouxline Matthew (Ch Langpool Scrumpy ex Siouxline Kelly), in 1979. Matthew won well in the 1980s and continued in his veteran years. At the age of eight he was the first Basset in the United Kingdom to qualify for the Pedigree Chum Veteran Stakes.

Matthew's litter sister, Siouxline Miriam, when mated to Verwood Varne, produced Sue's second champion, The Senator of Siouxline, who gained his first CC at six-and-a-half months. Senator, when mated to Verwood Mercedes at Siouxline (Verwood Diamond Cutter ex Ch Zondas I'm A Muddy Girl of Verwood), produced Siouxline Angelica (one CC). Angelica, mated to Bascor Royal Nugget, produced the multiple winners Siouxline Reuben (Junior Warrant and one CC) and Siouxline Rudolph. Reuben sired four champions: Ch Barrenger Demon King, Ch Taormina January Gem, Swedish Ch Verwood Glitz and Ch Suzanna of Siouxline, who was Top Basset Hound Bitch in 1989. Her first litter, to Ch/Dutch Ch Brandydale Equerry for Barratini, produced Siouxline Corinna (two CCs, five Reserve CCs). Her second litter, to Barratini Ambassador to Siouxline (Ch White Gold of Andyne ex Brandydale Evita) in 1992 produced Ch Siouxline Doyle of Dereheath and Ch Siouxline Daniella (see overleaf), Top Puppy in breed 1993 (see overleaf). Siouxline Corrina, mated to Ambassador in 1994, produced Siouxline Grant who, like his great-great-grandfather, gained his first CC at six-and-a-half months. Siouxline Gideon (Grant's brother) was a slow maturer but has won several championship show firsts and sired four championship show winning puppies in 1996 when mated to Daniella. Siouxline Lizetta and Leonara have yet to make their debut.

Sue awards CCs in Bassets both here and overseas and judges all hounds at open show level. She holds the posts of Secretary of the Basset Hound Club and Vice-President of Poole Canine Society.

Switherland

Jo and Phil Freer became interested in Bassets in 1971 when they had a pet Basset. In 1979 they started to show with Cwmdale Kanine, purchased from Jean Elliot-Jones. Their first litter in 1983 was from Bascor Royal Nugget ex Sarah of Switherland, and this produced Switherland Ellie. In 1986 they purchased the brother and sister Karipat Wildair of Switherland and Karipat Penelope of Switherland (Bascor Royal Nugget ex Karipat Shooting Star), and later Karipat Sweetbriyne (Karipat Olympic Banner ex Ch Karipat Spring Mist).

The success of the Switherlands was built on these three hounds. Wildair and Sweetbriyne both became champions. Karipat Penelope of Switherlands, mated to Karipat Olympic Banner, produced their first home-bred champion, Ch Switherland Wild Rose. This bitch, mated to Ch Karipat Lawrence, produced Ch Switherland Wild Orchid. Wild Orchid and Sweetbriyne were both mated to Bassbarr on Parade, and these two matings produced Ch Switherland Desert Orchid from Wild Orchid and three champions from Sweetbriyne: Ch Switherland Sage, Ch Switherland Strudel and Ch Switherland Surprise. Switherland Ruby, sister of Switherland Rose, when mated to Fredwell Fidelio produced Ch Switherland Camilla, who was mated to Ch Bassbarr O'Sullivan to produce Switherland Georgia, winner of two CCs. Ch Karipat Wildair of Switherland was mated to Ch Karipat Sweetbriyne to produce Switherland By Design, who was in turn mated to Sw/Norw Ch Switherland Sandpiper to produce Switherland Designer Jeans and Ch Switherland Desert. Orchid, mated to Switherland Designer Jeans, produced the two top winning youngsters Ch Switherland Blue Jeans (BIS Scottish Kennel Club 1996) and Ch Switherland Betabuy Design (Pet Plan Junior of the Year 1996 and Reserve BIS at Midland Counties Championship Show 1996 at just 20 months). This brother and sister combination gave the Switherlands their fourth generation of home-bred champions.

Ch Siouxline Daniella. Photo: Michael M Trafford

Tanneron

Mrs Felicity Luxmoore-Ball campaigned her first Basset Hound to his title in 1976. This was Ch Beacontree Teazel (Langpool Friar Tuck U The Beacontree ex Beacontree Chervil), bred by Mrs Barbara Golding. Mrs Luxmoore-Ball paired Teazel with Tanneron Jinty to produce her first home-bred champion, Tanneron Staffa.

Felicity's son, Nigel, still shows hounds under the Tanneron affix and awards CCs in Basset Hounds.

Ch Switherland Blue Jeans and
Ch Switherland Betabuy Design. Photo: Carol Ann Johnson

Verwood

Veronica Ross had her first Basset, Sungarth Quizzical (Sungarth Dashing ex Sykemoor Amorous), in 1961. He sired a litter, and Rosscap Orthras was retained as a foundation bitch. In 1965 a litter was born from Rowynan Janvrins Desty, and Verwood Chinook was kept from this litter, gaining many championship show firsts before being mated to It Ch Dreymin Dusky Knight, a Lyn-Mar Acres Dauntless son, strengthening the American strain. Lines introduced over the years have included Am Ch Long View Acres Bonza, Am Ch Lyn-Mar Acres Endman, Hess Sampson and recently Ch Morkebergs It's Now or Never at Balmacara. In the 1980s Am Ch Tal-E-Ho's Upstart II was imported and went on to gain her British title. Duskie Knight and Chinook produced Veronica's first British champion, Verwood Mirus, and also a bitch, Verwood Macra.

Ch Zondas I'm A Muddy Girl of Verwood, bred in Sweden by Mr and Mrs Samuelsson and imported by Veronica, was mated to Ch Kuntree Rhodes at Belvere and produced Veronica's second home-bred champion, Verwood Raphia. Fresh Lettuce of Verwood, by Verwood Royal Swede, bred by Mrs Austin, was campaigned to her championship, as was Kentley Marmalade of Verwood, sired by Verwood Hyper Hyper and bred by Mrs Humphrey. Thirteen Bassets have been exported and made champions in EEC countries, Canada, Scandinavia and Australia.

Veronica is a championship show judge in Basset Hounds and judged Crufts in 1992. She also judges PBGVs at championship level. Some of her Verwood hounds have been used for advertising purposes.

Viness Vinell

Lavinia Ness bred her first litter in 1980, mating her foundation bitch Tanneron Eriskay of Vinell (one CC) to Ch Beacontree Gelarista Gold Blend to produce four puppies, three of which were shown. These were Ch Vinell Antimony, who won BOB at Crufts 1982 when only 15 months, her sister Ch Vinell Adorable, owned by Mrs Luxmore Ball, and brother Vinell Auric, who gained his stud book number. When mated to Ch Brackenacre The Viking, Antimony produced Ch Vinell Digeri-Doo, Ch Vinell Dapper Dandy and Ch Vinell Double Diamond (owned by Heather

Redford). Her second litter, to Lodway Micky Finn, produced the well-known Ch Vinell Hooray Henry (10 CCs and 10 Reserve CCs), who took pride of place on the front page of the *Sunday Express* after Crufts.

Ch Digeri Doo became the foundation of the Viness Vinell kennel as it is today. Mated to Ch Lodway Lancer of Islwyn, she produced Ch Viness Vinell Vice Versa, and her second litter, to her long-time love Ch Henry, produced Ch Viness Vinell Whoops a Daisy. Both these girls, aged nine and ten, are still happily hunting. Vice Versa and Daisy have

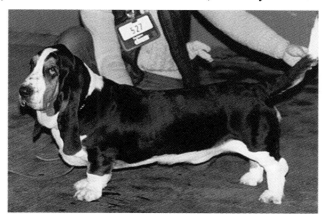

Ch Vinell Dapper Dandy.

both made excellent contributions to the Viness Vinell stock. Vice Versa, mated to Verwood Hyper-Hyper, produced two puppies: Ch Viness Vinell Just William, BOB at Crufts 1995, and Viness Vinell Bizzy Lizzy, owned by Lauren Armstrong. Daisy, mated to the import Ch Bassbarr Fred Astair, produced Ch Viness Vinell Yum Yum of Lelaurin, owned by Jan and Peter Laurie. Yum Yum returned home to be mated to her half-brother Viness Vinell Zoic, and another champion emerged: Ch Viness Vinell Ko Ko. Her litter sister, Viness Vinell Pitti Sing, owned by J Harvey, has two CCs and two Reserve CCs, and brother Viness Vinell Pooh Bah, owned by Lauren Armstrong, has won his stud book number and proved himself as a sire.

Vinny awards CCs in Basset Hounds and has judged in Germany, Sweden and Ireland.

Wellboy

Liz Hogarth obtained Saxonsprings Patience, bred by Jean Blythe, and Saxonsprings Leona. Shortly afterwards, Kortebin Belfalas was added to the kennel. When mated to Verwood King of The Castle, she produced Wellboy Bertie (two Reserve CCs). Her second mating, to Verwood Royal Swede, produced Wellboy Will-I-Am who was sold to Carole and Sam Laverty and became an Irish champion and sire to several Irish champions. Wellboy Val-N-Teena was mated to Ch Lodway Lancer of Islwyn, producing Ch Wellboy Luck Lady.

Witchacre

Jack and Agnes Ryan became interested in showing Bassets in 1972 when they took two puppies to a club championship show in Scotland and won firsts with them. They later purchased Brackenacre Jingle Bell (Ch Brackenacre Fino de Paris ex Ch Brackenacre Daisy Bell) as a show and brood bitch. She became a champion and, when mated to Bezel Action Man, produced a litter which included Witchacre Magpie of Brackenacre and Pendlewitch of Brackenacre, both obtained by Mr and Mrs Nixon, and Witchacre Jim Lad, who won one CC and three Reserve CCs.

Pendlewitch and Magpie won several Reserve CCs and a CC between them. Pendlewitch produced two champions: Brackenacre The Witch and Brackenacre The Challenger. Magpie produced the great champion Brackenacre The Viking. Another Brackenacre was added to the kennel: Brackenacre Hue and Cry, winner of one CC and several Reserve CCs.

A bitch purchased from a different line was Trevaylor Tambourine who, mated to Ch Trevaylor Thomas John, produced Ch Witchacre Tom Tom, a very extrovert lemon-and-white who won many

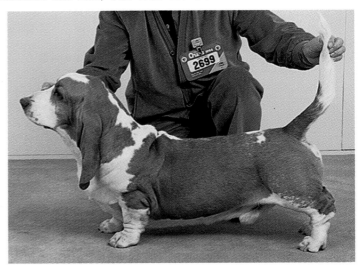

Ch Witchacre Stroller, BOB Crufts 1995.

awards in the 1980s. Jack and Agnes took a home-bred bitch, granddaughter to The Viking, and mated her to Ch Gladsomes Harvest Gold to produce the outstanding winner, Ch Witchacre Stroller. Stroller was Top Dog Basset 1990, Top Basset 1991, BIS at the Hound Championship Show and the Scottish Hound Show in 1991, Reserve BIS at Manchester Championship Show 1992, and won innumerable other top awards, including BOB Crufts 1995. He was a superb showman who never faltered in the ring.

Jack believes in giving his Bassets plenty of exercise, which probably stems from his early days as a professional roller skater. Both Jack and Agnes award CCs in Basset Hounds.

Basset Hounds Worldwide

Europe
Denmark
There are some extremely good Bassets in Denmark that combine American and European bloodlines.

Pioneers of the breed were Mrs Ries and her daughter, Esja, who is still involved. Kresten and Birte Scheel have also been involved in the breed for many years. Kresten's parents bred Bassets, and Birte obtained her first one in 1971. During 1982-1987, four Bassets were imported from the American kennel Tal-E-Ho. Two were American champions and three gained their Danish championship. Am/Dk Ch Tal-E-Ho Tiffany was the dam of Am/Dk Ch Scheels First Edition, who was Top Basset Hound in the 1980s and sired 50 champions. Two sons were retained from First Edition: Dk/Am Ch Scheels Riveredge Rubber Duck and Dk/Am/Nu Du Ch Scheels Excalibur, No 1 Hound in Denmark in 1995 and 1996. The Danish Basset Hound Club is an active, go-ahead organisation, and its current Secretary is Bent Rasmussen.

Finland
The Finnish Basset Hound Club was formed in 1972, and 25 years on it is still going strong; it is not a very large club but has dedicated followers. Mrs Marita Massingberd (Billhill) had her first Basset, Bazzets Nightman, from Rose-Marie Hartwig in Sweden, and he went on to become a Finnish champion. Marita imported from Great Britain several Bassets who became champions. In 1971 she purchased Maycombe Plocates from Mildred Seiffert and Int/Nu/Fin Ch Sykemoor

Fin Ch Sykemoor Redbone.

Rufus, Fin Ch Sykemoor Betsy and Int/Nu Du/Fin Ch Sykemoor Redbone from Mr George Johnston. From Norway came Fin/Nu Su Ch/W 80 Baseknap Yankie Hill, bred by Mrs Elizabeth Knap of Norway. Basset Artésien-Normands are also popular in Finland and several have been imported from France. They are used mainly for hunting.

France

It is generally accepted that the Artois-Normand Hound is the ancestor of the Basset Hound. It is the influence of the Bloodhound on the breed in England that has caused the Basset Hound to develop into the hound seen today. Mr John Miller of the Club de Basset Hound in France wrote to me with the following observations:

The first basset scenthound club (for both smooth- and rough-coated), organised under the auspices of the Société Centrale, saw the light of day in 1896, and the first breed standards appeared two years later. The first independent basset club, the Club du Griffon Vendéen, was started by Paul Dézamy in 1906, and the Club du Basset d'Artois, forerunner of the present Club du Basset Artésien-Normand, was founded in 1910.

I feel that the divergence between British and French breeding of smooth-coated bassets came right at the start, the British Breed Standard making explicit reference to the Bloodhound while the French Standard described the breed type of the Artois hound. By definition, the latter is heavy-headed, thick-skinned and flat-eared, having nothing of the type appreciated in Great Britain at the

Fr Ch Brackenacre Kathleen one of Jaques Médard-Ringuet's foundation bitches.

outset. However, through the efforts of Léon Verrier, a Norman-type basset gradually gained a following in France, becoming the standard in the breed in the 1920s (hence the name, Artésien-Normand).

Jean Rothéa wrote a report on the Walhampton Pack after looking at it in 1932, prior to its dispersal sale. His commentary, reflecting his own prejudices, dwells on the heaviness, the large variety of colours, the abundance of skin (*too much flew*) and on the poor fronts in the pack. One can infer that by this time the French were more interested in an aristocratic, thin-skinned, lighter hound. It seems that one of the Walhampton hounds, Walhampton Melrose, was still imported into France at that time to be used as an outcross.

Obviously, the written ideal isn't always easy to achieve in the kennel. The pictures we have from one of the most important French kennels in the late 1930s show a pretty mixed kettle as far as type is concerned, and one of the most successful hounds in the show ring did not look much like our present interpretation of the Standard. World War II didn't help, either; in France as in Great Britain the Basset Hound had to be rebuilt from scratch afterwards. As I look at the changes that have taken place over the last 30 years, resulting largely from better feeding, better care and more intelligent breeding, I think all our breeds are very modern.

In the last 20 years there has been an increased interest in a heavier type of hound, and Carla Gerber's breeding has had a great deal of influence. The founding President (equivalent to Chairman in Great Britain) of the Club du Basset Hound, Paul Liot, retired in 1983, and Jacques Médard-Ringuet became President at the next Annual General Meeting. It is through his efforts that the breed has achieved its present quality. After the Basset Fauve de Bretagne, which has more than 900 pups registered each year, the Basset Hound, with more than 600 registrations, is the most popular scenthound in France.

The Basset Hound is now different from any of the French basset scenthound breeds. In France, as elsewhere in Europe, Basset Hounds should follow the British (Kennel Club) Breed Standard. Two of the most influential kennels in France today are Josette Aubert's Rally de Sequigny and Nicole Poiret's Clos Simon.

Ireland

Mr and Mrs Bridgham of the Ballymaconnel affix were instrumental in establishing the Basset Hound in Ireland.They purchased Sungarth Placid as their foundation bitch. Placid was mated to Ch/Am Ch Crochmaid Bold Turpin of Blackheath, and she produced Ballymaconnel Araminta and Ballymaconnel Arabella. Arabella became an Irish champion and produced Ir Ch Ballymaconnel Forester, who came to England and, in the capable hands of Mildred Seiffert, became a British champion. Forester also sired some promising stock; for example, Ch Stormfield Hugo was his son.

As the breed became more popular, more people became interested in forming a Basset Hound Club. The Basset Hound Club of Northern Ireland Branch of the BHC was formed in 1965. In 1964, Belfast gave the Basset full classification with CCs for the first time. In 1973, the branch became a club in its own right, and it has a membership between 30–40.

The Basset Hound Club of Ireland, affiliated to the Irish Kennel Club, has a membership of 145. Mrs Betty Mitchell of the Montpelier Bassets was actively involved with the club for many years and bred some very good winners. Peggy and Colin Martin of Wicklow also have bred some good Bassets. Gill and Roddy McDowell (Knockfinn) have bred several champions. Knockfinn King Charlie came to England to live with Mrs Mildred Seiffert, who campaigned him to his British title.

Gypsy Bridgham with Ir Ch Ballymaconnel Charmeuse.

Phil McGarry Arthur is Secretary of the Basset Hound Club of Northern Ireland and, with his wife, owns the Faburn affix. Their first show Basset was Coastal Walnut of Aberthin (Montague of Aberthin ex Coastal Agnes), bred by Wendy Thomas. Although not shown very often, she won a CC and had two litters with some winning progeny. Another Basset bitch was obtained: Kenstaff Alethea (Uproar of Aberthin ex Helen of Boseley). Her grandmother was Coastal Winifred of Aberthin, litter sister to Walnut. Alethea became an Irish champion, also winning one CC, one Reserve CC and BIS at the Basset Hound Club of Ireland in 1981 and 1982. Alethea was mated to

Ch/Ir Ch Faburn Gypsy. Photo: Joyce Crawford-Manton

Ir Ch Lyndthorpe Dauntless (two CCs and five Reserve CCs) and a tri-colour bitch was retained: Ir Ch Faburn Chanel. Chanel was mated to Ch Lodway Lancer of Islwyn, to produce Ir Ch Faburn Damlia and Faburn Dahlia. Damlia was mated to Ch Bashur Zorba The Greek, and a tri-colour bitch, Faburn Folly, was kept. Folly won numerous green stars before being mated to Ch Bassbarr O'Sullivan and, from a litter of seven, producing Ch/Ir Ch Faburn Gypsy, BIS at the Basset Hound Club of Ireland Championship Show in 1996, Ir Ch Faburn Gemima of Larkhund, Ir Ch Faburn Geranime and Ir Ch Faburn General. These four hounds have shared the Green Star and Reserve Green Star positions in 1995 and 1996 at the Basset Hound Club of Ireland Championship Show. The remaining three pups in the litter are championship show winners. A repeat mating of Folly and O'Sullivan produced three pups. Faburn Harlequin and Faburn Honey are, at 10 months, winning well at championship shows under the Irish Kennel Club Rules.

Sam and Carole Laverty (Lisnoe) purchased Wellboy Will-I-am (Verwood King of the Castle ex Kortebin Belfalas of Wellboy). Will-I-am gained his Irish crown, winning 33 Green Stars, and was Top Winning Basset Hound in Ireland 1989, with two Reserve CCs, at Belfast in 1988 and Basset Hound Club in 1990. He was used on Danny Boland's Knockfinn Perdita (Ir Ch Knockfinn King Charlie ex Kingfuze Leonie of Knockfinn) for her first litter. Sam and Carole chose Bishoplands Alexis to campaign and the litter started the Bishoplands affix.

Ir Ch Bishopsland Alexis. Photo: R Smith

Alexis gained her Irish championship at 15 months and went on to win many more awards, including 57 green stars, one CC and BOB at Belfast 1991. A repeat mating produced Bishoplands Brahms at Lisnoe, who also became an Irish champion. A third mating produced Bishoplands Diva at Lisnoe, BIS at the Basset Hound Club of Ireland Show in 1992 aged eight months and BIS again the following year. She became an Irish champion and won 26 green stars. Diva, mated to Ch Karipat Lawrence (Ch Karipat Wildair of Switherland ex Karipat Lizzie) after Sam and Carole had purchased him, produced three live puppies that were retained, two of them becoming Lisnoe Lohengrin and Lisnoe Brunhilde, who were made up to Irish champions in 1996. Brunhilde won the bitch CC in 1996 and Lohengrin was the top winning Basset in Ireland in the same year.

Netherlands

The van Hollandheim kennel of Carla Gerber has been one of the leading kennels in Europe for many years. Carla's first import, Wingjays Pardon, was from Jeanne Rowett-Johns. In 1972, Beacontree Calender joined the kennel, and a year later Beacontree Ebonite joined his kennel mate. The two Beacontrees were mated and produced Carla's first champion, Don Quichotte van Hollandheim. Calender was mated again, this time to Akerwood Boots, producing Nl Ch

Multi-Ch Lonesome Lover v Hollandheim.

Phoebe van Hollandheim, a red-and-white bitch. When mated to Longfellow Anthony Adam (Akerwood lines) Phoebe produced the legendary Nl Ch Lonesome Lover van Hollandheim. Lover produced good Basset type: beautiful heads, deep lip and good bone. To improve movement, Ch Tal-E-Ho Top Gun was imported from the United States. Six bitches were kept from him and, paired with Lover, produced the combination of type and movement so desired. This combination is in almost every pedigree in Holland. The Lover/Top Gun pairing produced Nl/German/Swiss/Lux Ch Forester van Hollandheim out of Madison van Hollandheim, and also Nl/Dk/Swiss/German/Lux Ch Haya v Hollandheim. Forester and Haya produced Vogue van Hollandheim, JW96, JAW and W96/Europasieger97 – according to Carla, the best bitch she has ever bred.

Sweden

The first Basset to be imported into Sweden was the in-whelp bitch Grims Charlotte, in 1958. Shortly afterwards a male, Barnspark Rambler, joined her. These were purchased by Ulla and Erik Pettersson of the Astor kennel. Bassets bred in the Astor kennels were sent to Norway, Denmark and Finland and were the first Bassets in these countries. During the ensuing years, 20 Bassets have been obtained from the United Kingdom, including hounds from the kennels Fredwell, Appeline and Brackenacre. The Petterssons are proud to have owned 60 champions, among them NuDu Ch Fredwell Fluke,

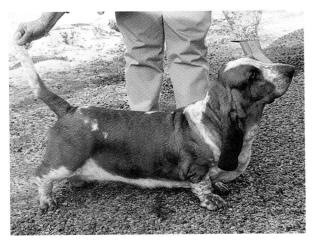

Su Ch Islwyn Simply Red for Langpool.

NuDu Ch Astors Posy, NuDu Ch Red Baron of Ide, NuDu Ch Astor Bella, Su/Nu Ch Astors Charlotta, Su/Nu Ch Astors Kimoko, Su Ch Astors Olivia and NuDu Ch Brackenacre Crystal Clear. This is just a small selection from the Astor kennel.

Several other breeders in Sweden are breeding quality hounds, including Dr Elizabeth Andrews (Langpool) and Rose-Marie Hartwig (Bazzets), who has been involved with the breed for over 25 years.

Switzerland

The Basset and Bloodhound Club of Switzerland (BBCS) was founded in 1970. Breeding regulations, based on those of the Swiss Kennel Club (SKC), were brought into force by the BBCS. Then as now, there were breeding selections every six months. Among those present at a breeding selection are a conformation judge, the BBCS Breeding Controller, one or more members of the Breeding Commission, possibly one or more trainee judges, and of course the dog to be examined and its owner. The examination takes 30–40 minutes. Over the years, the breeding regulations have become increasingly restrictive. In 1997, partly because of pressure from an influential parliamentary lobby which alleges that it is cruel to breed certain breeds (including Basset Hounds) for exaggerated, unsound features, the AGM decided to make it compulsory to X-Ray for elbow and hip dysplasia, as well as to have the eyes examined for glaucoma. It also voted for obligatory identification by tattooing or microchip.

Int/Swiss/Lux/VDH/BHF/Dk Ch Bellecombe Eugenie.

At present, only three regular breeders remain, making it clear that it is not easy to breed Bassets in Switzerland.

Prominent Swiss Basset kennels include:

Of Kind Kernel – Maja Altorfer: The Bassets of this kennel are based on Balleroy, the American line Sanchu, and the German line Longfellow. Two champions have been bred: Ch Nugget of Kind Kernel and US Ch Daphne of Kind Kernel. Maja also had three dogs and two bitches that were BBCS Show winners in 1984–1985 and 1994–1996.

Big Bone – Françoise Schick: Françoise Schick started to breed in 1981. By 1997 she had bred 36 litters, including ten champions – three Swiss, two French, two Portuguese, one Italian, and the two International (Fédération Cynologique Internationale) winners Big Bone Busybee Barbara and Big Bone Ginger-Katharina. Five of her Bassets obtained working certificates.

Bellecombe – Grace Servaise: Grace Servaise acquired Maycombe Danseuse, her first Basset, from Mildred Seiffert in 1978. Ten years later she imported from the United States the bitch Am Ch Lochopt Fantastic. 'Fan', when mated to Kevin van Hollandheim, produced three dark tri-colour bitches and a mottled tri-colour dog. The dog went to Italy to become It Ch Bellecombe Edward Elgar, owned by Francesco Trantarossi, and was used extensively, exerting considerable influence on the breed in Italy. One of his daughters was Bellecombe Eugenie (Jenny), the only Swiss Basset to have achieved six championships: International (FCI), Swiss, German (VDH and BHF), Luxembourg and Danish. Jenny produced five puppies in May 1997.

Elkington – Corinna Roch: Corinna Roch was one of the pioneer Basset Hound breeders. Her foundation bitches were Langpool Blue Ribbon and Tanneron Camilla. Corinna bred Ch Elkington Felicity, the only Swiss Basset hound ever to have been made up as a British champion. She was campaigned in England by the Luxmoor-Balls. In addition to three home-bred champions, Corinna made up Tanneron Camilla and Fauntleroy v d Klejne Hoeve as Swiss champions.

North America

The history of the Basset Hound in America is very interesting. I would have to devote many chapters to it to do it justice. Within the context of the book it is only possible to give an outline. Most of the information was kindly provided by Mr R Frederiksen, who is well known in British Basset Hound circles. For those wishing to undertake an in-depth study of the breed in North America, I would recommend the works of Mercedes Braun, Margaret Walton and, if it can be found, the early volume by Carl Smith.

Although the American Kennel Club (AKC) first accepted Basset Hounds for registration in 1885, it is known that some low-set hounds had been sent to George Washington in 1785 by the Marquis de Lafayette.

The first recorded importations of Bassets were in 1883, when the English breeder George Krehl of London sent a hound, namely Nemours (Jupiter ex Vivien), to Mrs Chamberlain in New York State, and a couple more by Jupiter to Lord Aylesford, an Englishman residing in Texas, whom a fellow baronet, Lord Lonsdale, described as a 'cattle baron and a whisky drinker' – excellent credentials! Nemours was the first Basset Hound to be exhibited in the United States when he was entered at the Westminster Kennel Club show in 1884.

The breed slowly established itself and attracted a small group of fanciers whose interest was not only in exhibiting, but also in hunting and field trialling. Gerald Livingstone founded his pack, the Kilsyth, on Long Island in 1921 – the first known organised Basset Hound pack in America. His interest rubbed off on Erastus Tefft, a New York stockbroker who, with imports from the Walhampton, formed his Staridge pack. Other prominent fanciers in this period were Consuelo

Dalby Hall Vanguard, 1925.

Ford (Bijou of Banbury) and Lewis Thompson (Stanco), but perhaps the doyen of the pioneers was Carl Smith of Xenia, Ohio who, with his brother George, inherited a love of hounds and hunting from his father. Their Smiths kennel was large. They imported many hounds from England and France and also, by a circuitous route, obtained 'Russian' Bassets Old Deck and Dolly M. Early imports in 1930 included Walhampton Passion, Walhampton Andrew, Walhampton Aaron, Walhampton Nicety and Amir of Reynalton.

Mr Tefft is reputed to have paid £1000 for Lavenham Pippin. Dalby Hall Bassets also imported Drifter, Dormouse and Diligence (1924). Most of the French stock (technically not Basset Hounds, but Bassets d'Artois or Bassets Normands) were shipped to America by Henri Baillet of Rouen, whose hounds were descended from those of Leon Verrier, author of the classic *Les Bassets Francais*. Baillet's Trompette, Corvette and Veilleuse, imported in 1925, and several others helped to form the nucleus of the American Basset Hound.

Carl Smith's kennel records were sent to his friend in England, George Johnston. These make fascinating reading and reveal how, during the Depression era and Wall Street Crash, the Smiths acquired whole packs from their bankrupt owners. A disagreement between the American Kennel Club and French Kennel Club meant early imports were registered with the United Kennel Club, and it was not until after the formation of the Basset Hound Club of America in 1935 that the American Kennel Club accepted the registration of French hounds.

The litter brothers Smiths Red Pathfinder and Am Ch Smiths Red Powder figure in the ancestry of the majority of American Bassets. Their dam was Walhampton Passion.

These early breeders had, at great effort and no small expense, laid a solid foundation for the breed's progress in America. They were eventually joined by others who had little need to import stock from Europe and who placed a different emphasis on various breed points, which eventually resulted in a type of Basset somewhat different from the English hounds. After the formation of the Basset Hound Club of America, the flow of European imports slowed down and the breed in America gradually became heavier-bodied and deeper-chested. At least, this was the preferred type for the show ring. The Basset Hound Club of America also organised field trials, and this aspect is still important and very popular in the United States. Photographs of American show champions and their field trialling counterparts show a difference in type, the latter being considerably lighter in construction. However, it was possible for a hound successfully to combine looks and ability: Kazoo's Moses The Great (1964) was the first dual champion.

Leslie Kelly of New Alexandria, Pennsylvania, had stock from Carl Smith and, being an accomplished stockman, he quickly produced many champions carrying his Belbay affix, such as Xtra Handsome and Winning Look. Many of Kelly's hounds were red-blanket, and he tried to perpetuate this colouring in his stock. Other prominent breeder exhibitors in this period were Mrs Travis Look, a Director of the Basset Hound Club of America and author of the booklet *Pet Basset Hound* (1960), Nancy Evans and Mercedes Braun. Affixes which figured prominently in the 1940s–1960s and can be noted in European stock were Seifenjagenheim, Long View Acres, Musiclands, Orangepark, Tallyrand, Cloverleaf and Santana-Mandeville. The appearance on American television of the Basset Hounds Mr Morgan and Cleo put the breed in the public eye and consequently Bassets became very popular as pets. Many of the pet-buying public caught the bug and became enthusiasts: some in the show ring, others field trialling, and many others were attracted to obedience training.

There is not enough space here to list every major American breeder or affix. Some have had great influence on the development of the breed, not only in North America but also, in recent years, in Great Britain and Continental Europe. I have stated that the American breeders ceased importing stock in numbers, but some still took in hounds. Among these were Mr and Mrs Basset (Notrenom), who imported Rossingham Barrister from Angela Hodson, and Alfred Bissell, who in 1960 added Sykemoor Charmer, a daughter of Hercule de L'Ombrée to his pack in Delaware.

M Pierre Leparoux sent de L'Ombrée Artésiens-Normands to Mr Thompson in Massachusetts, Mr and Mrs Meyer of the Orangepack kennels purchased Sykemoor Fencer and Farthing, and Foyewyn Flirtie of Maycombe, a Ch Wingjays Ptolemy daughter, went from Mrs Mildred Seiffert to Mrs Walton's Lyn-Mar Acres kennel.

In 1968, the well-known Scottish breeders Jim and Rosemary McKnight emigrated to Canada, taking several of their Chantinghall Bassets with them. Their Can/Am Ch Chantinghall Airs'N'Graces was Top Canadian Hound in 1975 and 1976, and Can/Am Ch Chantinghall Dominic, who combined British and North American bloodlines, became an influential sire.

The Basset Hound Club of Canada was formed in 1960 and the first Basset Hound entry into the Canadian Kennel Club stud book was Bess of Banbury, born 1942, bed by Consuela Ford of the United States and owned by Charles Perrault of Montreal.

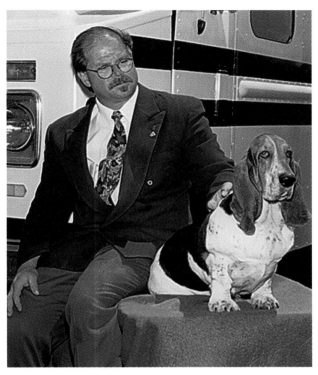

Am Ch Lyn-Mar Acres Hit The Road. Photo: Perry Phillips

Mrs Babson had her celebrated hounds (she also had Bloodhounds and Otterhounds) in Illinois, and to her goes the honour of breeding the first British/American champion – Bold Turpin of Blackheath, who gained his title in 1962. A dark tri-colour dog, he was owned by Mrs McArthur-Onslow and her daughter, Mrs Kewley (Crochmaid), in Dumfrieshire. Bold Turpin's export to England had been preceded by that of Lyn-Mar Acres Dauntless, who was purchased in 1958 by the Basset Hound Club for $250, from Mrs Peg Walton of New Jersey. Mrs Walton had her first Basset in 1943 and, with her husband, founded the Lyn-Mar Acre kennel. Since that time many Lyn-Mar Acres hounds have attained championship status: Topbrass, His Lordship, Clown, M'Lord Batuff, Endman, Extra Man, Scalawag and de March. The influence of this source of carefully-bred hounds has had a great impact on North American Basset Hound breeding. The opportunity to use Lyn-Mar Acres bloodlines has been available to breeders all over the globe, as Mrs Walton has exported to Great Britain, Scandinavia and Australia.

As my readers will note, the AKC standard for Basset Hounds differs from that approved by The Kennel Club. The Kennel Club standard was revised and re-written in 1986, the AKC version is unchanged since 1964.

Ambrican is the kennel affix of Randolph and Penny Frederiksen. Ambrican is a show-oriented kennel that had its beginnings in three different countries before it eventually came together in America. Penny Frederiksen began her career in Bassets following her mother's (Mrs Audrey Charman's) lead in England. She acquired her foundation bitch in 1970 and later took her hounds with her to Canada. Penny's original kennel affix was Charford. In America, Randy Frederiksen was successfully showing under the Coran affix; he began breeding and showing in 1972. The current kennel name of Ambrican came from a combination of the countries involved –

America, Britain and Canada – and was first used in 1982. Mrs Bert Salyers also was invited to become a named partner in Ambrican Basset Hounds.

Since its beginning the kennel has completed 30 titles on 20 hounds. Including the previous affixes, the kennel has completed 47 bench champions, 10 obedience titles and 4 tracking titles. The obedience and tracking titles were acquired through the patient work of Mike Salyers, Nancy Chapman and Kay and Craig Green.

When the Ambrican kennel moved to England in April 1990 for 12 months, they brought a few Bassets with them. Ch Strathalbyn Lugano joined them later, remaining in England when they returned to America. Lugano sired several litters here and became Top Basset Stud Dog 1992.

Am Ch Bon View Old Fashion Olga LV. Photo: Ashbey Photography

Len and Marge Skolnick, of Slippery Hills, Maryland bred their first Basset litter in 1961. The rest of their show stock was bred from the Santana Mandeville kennel. Over the years the Skolnicks bred more than 30 show champions and 30 field trial champions. Am Ch Slippery Hill Hudson still holds the record for BIS wins – 29 times BIS.

Bon View Bassets are owned by Amy and Keith Jones, who started in 1960 as a family hobby. Amy did the showing and was successful in junior handling. Their Bassets were related to Ch Abbot Run Valley Brassy, one of the major prepotent sires of the time. When Amy went to university, showing Bassets ceased. In 1984, Amy was in Texas and looking for a Basset again. She obtained a Bevlee hound, and a dog puppy obtained later became Ch Bevlee Baxter Birney. At about the same time a bitch puppy, Moonbeans Abigail Adams, was purchased from Linda Bean. In 1988 this pair had a litter that contained two hound-group-winning females: Am Ch Bon Views Old Fashion Mariah and Ch Bon Views Maggie Magoo. As Amy had to move around a lot with her job, Jane Baetz from Old Fashion Bassets became co-owner of the two young bitches and took over campaigning them. Amy later had two puppies from Jane, both sired by Ch New Old Fashion van Hollandheim from Carlo Gerber's kennel in Holland. Amy, who is at present in England with her Bassets, intends to use Mr and Mrs Freer's Ch Switherland Blue Jeans as a stud for one of her bitches and return to America with a couple more puppies.

Australia

Bassets were imported from Great Britain in 1957 by Dr and Mrs H Spira and Mrs J McInolty. Grims Vanquish and Grims Caroline were the first, soon followed by other imports. Sykemoor Dauphin and Ch Kierhill Donald had a good influence on the breed.

The Basset Hound Club of New South Wales is the oldest Basset Hound Club in Australia. It was founded in 1960 and its first championship show was held in 1961.

As the Basset progressed and improved it became a force to be reckoned with in the show ring.

In the mid-1970s Ch Lacaza Jericho, bred by Mrs Liz Soain and owned by Carol Woolcock, won 19 championship all-breed BISs. More imports arrived from Great Britain, the United States and New Zealand. Affixes such as Langpool, Barnspark, Verwood, Kortebin, Brackenacre, Balleroy and Meddgoed can be seen in the pedigrees of today's winning hounds.

Bassets are now in most Australian States. In New South Wales, Mrs Janet Beckman (Wahabi) has bred Bassets for many years and enjoyed a great deal of success, producing many Australian champions. Her latest success is the import Aust Ch Burnvale Quintessential of Wahabi, whom she campaigned to his championship.

Jean and David Jackson (Abattu), who live just outside Perth, have a small kennel of quality Bassets. They concentrate on soundness with good movement and good temperament. I was most impressed with free-moving, bi-colour bitch Aust Ch Abattu Misty Morning when I gave her BOB at the Ladies Kennel Club of Western Australia Show, September 1994.

Keith and Anne McGinn (Ammidan) of Queensland have imported Bassets from Great Britain and the USA, from kennels including Langpool, Verwood and Lyn-Mar Acres. These successful breeders win well with their hounds.

Aust Ch Wahabi Wentworth.
Photo: Michael M Trafford

The Basset Hound Club of South Australia was formed on 20 April 1970, and its first championship show was held on 23 October 1973. In 1959, Mrs Ruth Rogers introduced Bassets into this State by purchasing Carillon Forrester (Ch Grims Vanquish (import) ex Carillon Corky), bred by Mrs McInolty and Dr and Mrs H Spira of New South Wales. Thirty-eight years later, the breed is still flourishing in the hands of a small band of dedicated breeders.

Ron and Raylen Brock (Goldchamp) have bred Bassets for 23 years. Deschamp Miss Jennifer is their foundation bitch. They have bred many champions, among them Aust Ch Goldchamp Deal a Joker and Aust Ch Goldchamp Autumn Mist, who both won BIS and Group awards.

Mrs Chris Lawrence (Beauchasseur) has a small kennel of very good Bassets, recognised by fellow breeders for their quality. Chris handles Bassets and has helped many to their title. She has titled winning stock in South Australia, Western Australia, New South Wales and Tasmania.

Mr and Mrs G Faux (Wellingtess) reside in Victoria and have bred Bassets for 25 years. Several quality hounds have been sold or leased to fellow exhibitors and many champions bred. Pride of place must be Aust Ch Wellingtess Frazer, multiple BIS all breeds, BOB Melbourne and Sydney Royals and so on. He has produced nine Australian champions from six litters.

Aust Ch Hushanda Lyndon Johnson.
Photo: Sally Margot Everard Stasytis

The Basset Hounds Club of Victoria held its Silver Anniversary in 1993, and Mrs Grace Venturo (Hushanda) is a founder member. The Hushanda Bassets have probably had the greatest impact on Australian Bassets. Grace has bred over 100 Australian champions and her stud dogs have sired many more. Aust Ch Hushanda Ezaruffyn has sired no less than 45 Australian champions. I was particularly impressed with Aust Ch Hushanda Lyndon Johnson when I awarded him BOB at Adelaide at the Canine Fanciers Kennel Club in South Australia in September 1994.

Africa

South Africa

The Greystones kennel was founded in the mid-1960s, in what was then Salisbury, Rhodesia (now Harare, Zimbabwe) by Mrs Hermione Whitfield, who was shortly joined by Sheila Tarr. The original stock was from South Africa, with lines going back to Sykemoor Landmark and Deschamps Tess of Lynacre.

The first imports from the United Kingdom were made in 1959 by Jean Newby-Frazer. These included Sykemoor Westward. In 1974, a red-and-white dog called Fredwell Marsala (Badger of Cwmdale ex Fredwell Maiden), bred by Mrs Joan Wells-Meacham was imported, together with Wingjays Peter Rabbit (Ch Wingjays Ptolemy ex Crepe Suzette of Wingjays). Both hounds easily won their titles. On the bitch side, Brackenacre Hells Bells (Ch Fredwell Varon Fawkes ex Ch Brackenacre Daisy Belle) had been imported from the Nixons in 1972. In 1976, the litter sisters Brackenacre Laughter and Brackenacre Lily the Pink (Ch Brackenacre James Bond ex Brackenacre Bell of Freedom) joined the kennel. In 1975, Mrs Whitfield moved to South Africa with the bitches, leaving Mrs Tarr in Rhodesia with the dogs – long range breeding. Laughter won well in 1978, gaining BOB under Jeanne Rowett Johns in a strong entry. These bitches, bred to the Wingjays, produced some quality hounds. More imports came from Great Britain: Wingjays Alligator and Wingjays Chongololo. The standard of Bassets was improving. In 1989, Blaby Jolly Conqueror (Balleroy Jazzman at Andyne ex Blaby Camilla) arrived from Great Britain and lived up to his name, becoming Dog of the Year 1990 and three times Hound of the Year, with many other top awards. To complement his bloodline, Andyne Lady in Red has been imported from Mrs Andy Dyne and Switherland New Yorker from Mr and Mrs Phil Freer. These, with Ch Fredwell Faldo, comprise the current show team.

SA Ch Blaby Jolly Conqueror at Greystones.

Basset Hound Breed Standards

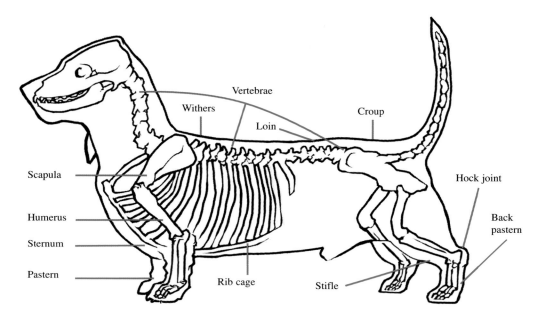

Fig 1: The structure of the Basset Hound.

The Kennel Club Breed Standard 1994 – Basset Hound

Reproduced by kind permission of The Kennel Club

General Appearance Short-legged hound of considerable substance, well balanced, full of quality. A certain amount of loose skin desirable.

Characteristics Tenacious hound of ancient lineage which hunts by scent, possessing a pack instinct, a deep melodious voice and capable of great endurance in the field.

Temperament Placid, never aggressive or timid. Affectionate.

Head and Skull Domed with some stop and occipital bone prominent; of medium width at brow and tapering slightly to muzzle; general appearance of foreface lean not snipy. Top of muzzle nearly parallel with line from stop to occiput and not much longer than head from stop to occiput. There may be a moderate amount of wrinkle at brow and beside eyes. In any event skin of head loose enough as to wrinkle noticeably when drawn forward or when head is lowered. Flews of upper lip overlap lower substantially. Nose entirely black except in light coloured hounds when it may be brown or liver. Large and well opened nostrils may protrude a little beyond lips.

Eyes Lozenge-shaped neither prominent nor too deep set, dark but may shade to mid-brown in light coloured hounds. Expression calm and serious. Red of lower lid appears, though not excessively. Light or yellow eye highly undesirable.

Ears Set on low, just below line of eye. Long; reaching well beyond end of muzzle of correct length, but not excessively so. Narrow throughout their length and curling well inwards; very supple, fine and velvety in texture.

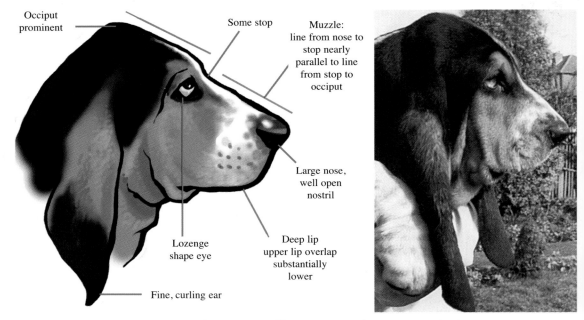

Occiput prominent

Some stop

Muzzle:
line from nose to
stop nearly
parallel to line
from stop to
occiput

Large nose,
well open
nostril

Lozenge
shape eye

Deep lip
upper lip overlap
substantially
lower

Fine, curling ear

Su/Fin Ch Brackenacre Crystal Clear demonstrates the correct Basset head:
excellent planes, depth of lip and fine, curling ear.

Mouth Jaws strong, with a perfect, regular and complete scissor bite, ie upper teeth closely overlapping lower teeth and set square to the jaws.

Neck Muscular, well arched and fairly long with pronounced but not exaggerated dewlap.

Forequarters Shoulder blades well laid back; shoulders not heavy. Forelegs short, powerful and with great bone; elbows turning neither in nor out but fitting neatly against side. Upper forearm inclined slightly inwards, but not to such an extent as to prevent free action or to result in legs touching each other when standing or in action; forechest fitting neatly into crook when viewed from front. Knuckling-over highly undesirable. Wrinkles of skin on lower legs.

Body Long and deep throughout length, breast bone prominent but chest neither narrow nor unduly deep; ribs well rounded and sprung, without flange *[projecting edge of rib]*, carried well back. Back rather broad; level; withers and quarters of approximately same height, though loins may arch slightly. Back from withers to inset of quarters not unduly long.

Hindquarters Full of muscle and standing out well, giving an almost spherical effect when viewed from rear. Stifles well bent. Hocks well let down and slightly bent under but turn neither in nor out and just under body when standing naturally. Wrinkles of skin may appear between hock and foot, and at rear of joint a slight pouch resulting from looseness of skin.

Feet Massive, well knuckled up and padded. Forefeet may point straight ahead or be turned slightly outwards but in every case hound always stands perfectly true, weight being borne equally by toes with pads together so that feet would leave the imprint of a large hound and no unpadded areas in contact with ground.

Tail (Stern) Well set on, rather long, strong at base, tapering, with moderate amount of coarse hair underneath. When moving, stern carried well up and curving gently, sabre fashion, never curling or gay.

Gait/Movement Most important. Smooth free action with forelegs reaching well forward and hindlegs showing powerful thrust, hound moving true both front and rear. Hocks and stifles never stiff in movement, nor must any toes be dragged.

Coat Smooth, short and close without being too fine. Whole outline clean and free from feathering. Long-haired, soft coat with feather highly undesirable.

Colour Generally black, white and tan (tri-colour); lemon and white (bi-colour); but any recognised hound colour acceptable.

Size Height 33–38cm (13–15in) at withers.

Faults Any departure from the foregoing points should be considered a fault and the seriousness with which the fault should be regarded should be in exact proportion to its degree.

Note Male animals should have two apparently normal testicles fully descended into the scrotum.

Thoughts on the Breed Standard

The Kennel Club Breed Standard seeks to describe the ideal animal in relation to the function of the breed concerned. It is used as a guide by breeders in their efforts to produce that elusive *perfect* Basset and by judges when assessing and comparing the hounds in classes at shows.

The Basset has been developed for a specific purpose: to hunt small game with a pack. Even if most current Bassets get little or no opportunity to indulge in such activities, their original task will have influenced the standard against which they are to be judged. Bassets should be physically and mentally capable of doing the job, should the need arise.

What follows is my personal analysis of the Breed Standard with observations and comments.

General Appearance

I feel that all dogs, given the opportunity, should be capable of actually working at the job they were originally bred for. The Basset is a true hound, whose quarry is the hare. The legs should not be so short that movement and free action are impeded when the hound is hunting over rough or ploughed land. Clearance is essential, and there should be some daylight under the hound.

Sometimes a Basset who conforms correctly to the Breed Standard is considered to be plain because it lacks emphasis of certain points and is therefore under-rated. Breed standards warn about *undue exaggeration,* but it does creep into a breed, beyond the requirements of the Standard. This can be visible in head properties, the over-abundance of loose skin, and size.

Consider the weight of some champions in the past:

* Ch Grims Whirlwind (1954) – 26kg (56lb)
* Ch Fredwell Varon Vandal (1960) – 26kg (56lb)
* Ch Sykemoor Emma (1962) – 23kg (49lb)
* Ch Maycombe Vaisya (1965) – 25.5kg (55lb)
* Ch Brackenacre Annabella (1966) – 25.5kg (55lb)

Some modern champions must weigh 38–42kg (80lb–90lb). Given that the welfare and feeding has improved for our hounds, care must be taken to ensure that their weight does not increase even more excessively. Moderation must always be a key word.

The standard states *a certain amount of loose skin desirable.* Again, the loose skin will help a hunting hound as it hunts through dense thickets or undergrowth; thorns, jagged twigs and so on will not easily pierce or tear the skin that rolls. One only has to experiment with a pin and a balloon to see it is easy to pierce a fully-inflated, taut balloon, but not so easy when the balloon is semi-deflated. The loose skin is one of the great characteristics of the Basset – but again, watch this does not become exaggerated.

Considerable substance is another inexact phrase that is open to abuse. It does not mean that the hound has to be enormous. Sometimes *fat* can be confused with *substance*, but fat can only make a hound obese. The weight of any Basset should be determined by the size of the bones in the skeleton and of the body organs, but depends most of all on the muscles; between a third and a half of the body weight is muscle.

A Basset's shape is decided mainly by the underlying skeleton, but the size of the muscles in the different parts of the body will also influence its silhouette. The function of the skeleton is to support the body and to protect it, especially the delicate brain and spinal cord, and to provide a system of levers on which the muscles can act to make the Basset move.

Finally, a Basset of *quality* must have balance and personality, plus that extra charisma and ring presence.

Characteristics

Tenacious hound of ancient lineage which hunts by scent. The Basset that is strong in breed characteristics will be observed as the very embodiment of the breed's heart and character. It is not just balance or sound action, but a living example of the distinguishing features that make a Basset one of a special breed.

The ancestors of the Basset were the great hounds of France. Although the Basset is a dwarf relation, the pack and hunting instinct, the deep, melodious voice, the colours, the sensitivity and the endurance still remain.

Many people think their Bassets deliberately stubborn or disobedient. This is not the case; it is the tenacious streak in the character, coupled with great endurance, rising to the fore. Once a Basset's mind is motivated to a certain action it does not hear or see anything else – whether it is chasing a cat, chewing a hole in the fence, or digging up the newly-planted herbaceous border! But remember that the Basset is also tenacious in its love for its owner. It will ignore all human frailties and be a devoted companion for life.

Temperament

Placid, never aggressive or timid. Affectionate. This is a good description of the Basset; they are rarely aggressive and, if anything, are more inclined to be the opposite. A Basset can be most sensitive, especially when young. Even the French breeders, many of whom hunt their hounds, recognise this fact and find that the smooth-coated breeds – Basset Artésien Normand, Basset Hound and Bleu-de-Gascogne – do not come easily 'under the whip' (*sous le fouet* in French). Nor do many of their large ancestor breeds. A Basset puppy can be ruined very easily by rough handling in the first few months of its life. The Basset is extremely affectionate. Unfortunately, at times it loves to sit on a lap to watch television. The legs of the recipient of this honour usually go numb after 10 minutes, and the offending Basset is removed to the floor, much to its disgust.

Head and Skull

In the original Breed Standard, the description of the Basset's head was *most perfect when it closest resembles the head of a Bloodhound.* I think this was stated because, at that time (the 1800s) most people were familiar with Bloodhounds but not Bassets. However, because so much of the Basset's charm derives from the head, it is essential that it is of the correct structure. The skull should be domed, the occiput clearly visible, and a heavy, coarse, rounded skull is a bad fault. The skull should be of medium width at the brow, tapering slightly to the muzzle. The foreface *lean but not snipy* indicates a wedge-shaped appearance from the nose to the rear of the skull when viewed from the front. The cheeks should be flat, with no signs of muscling. The lines from the nose to the stop and the stop to occiput should be nearly parallel. The muzzle from nose to stop can be slightly longer than stop to occiput. The occiput should be prominent. Unfortunately, these

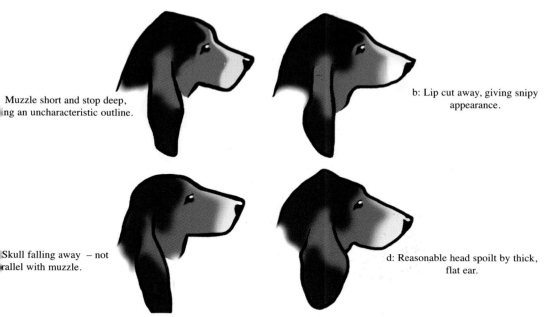

Muzzle short and stop deep, ...ing an uncharacteristic outline.

b: Lip cut away, giving snipy appearance.

Skull falling away – not ...rallel with muzzle.

d: Reasonable head spoilt by thick, flat ear.

Fig 2: Head faults. Compare these with the picture of Brackenacre Crystal Clear and accompanying diagram on page 68.

nearly-parallel lines of the head are rare at present; one tends to see Bassets in which the top of the muzzle is straight from nose to stop, but the cranium or sagittal crest falls away from behind the brow to the occiput. It is a point worth watching, or this could gradually become the type of head that is bred for, thus losing one of the most important aspects of the contours of the head.

The true Basset head type depends to a considerable degree on the stop. The stop is capable of misinterpretation. A Basset should have a *moderate* amount of stop; neither a right angle where the muzzle joins the skull, like a pointer, nor straight enough to give an almost Borzoi look.

The Basset's muzzle is made up of part of the nose and the upper and lower jaws. The Basset's acute sense of smell is a well-known feature, and some scientists have estimated it to be a million times keener than our own. While the 'smell-receiving' region of the human nose contains some 20 million sensitive cells, a Basset's may contain 300 million. Bassets can enhance this sense of smell by sniffing, so that they sample as large a volume of inspired air as possible. For scenting, the nostrils are flared, so air is strongly drawn in and passed over the smell-sensitive layers. Bassets, with their large, open nostrils, are well adapted to take full advantage of the sniff.

Nose

The nose is black on tri-colours, but may be brown or liver to blend in with a lemon-and-white coat. The nose is large and may protrude slightly beyond the lips. When a Basset Hound pup is born, the nose will be pink. The black pigment will permeate the nose within a few weeks. Sometimes, a pink spot will remain, but usually this will fill in by the time the Basset is adult. If the pink spot, usually by the nostril, remains, the Basset has a *butterfly nose*, which is a fault.

Head Furnishings

Having dealt with the bone structure and nose, I will now describe the head furnishings, although the Standard is explicit. The skin on the head should always be loose. A Basset, when standing normally and facing straight ahead, may have a wrinkle of skin from the brow down past the side of the eye to the flews, and one or two wrinkles on the brow. When the Basset's head is lowered, the loose skin is more noticeable and falls in distinct wrinkles over the brow and beside the eyes. The flews of the upper lip overlap the lower considerably, but again not to excess. I think Bassets with over-long muzzles and very deep flews (pendulous upper lips) look ugly and unbalanced in the head. There should be plenty of depth to the flews under the nose to give an almost square appearance; shallow flews give the muzzle an incorrect wedge shape when viewed in profile. The flews continue back over the jaws, gradually getting deeper until they blend with the loose skin under the neck to form the dewlap.

Eyes

The *lozenge shape* mentioned in the Standard describes the shape of the eyelids, the corners of the eyelids being two points of the lozenge, the upward sweep of the upper eyelid being the third point

Kortinas Adonis demonstrates the correct, lozenge-shaped eye.

and the centre of the lower eyelid, drooping as it does, being the fourth. At one time the Standard said *diamond shape*. I have noticed recently the appearance of Bassets in the show ring with incorrectly set eyes. Their eyes are set on the side of the skull and drawn back in a slant-eyed way, because of lack of frontal bone.

The upper and lower eyelids serve to cover and protect the delicate front of the eye against damage. The blinking action clears the front of the eye of debris and spreads tears over the entire eye surface. A third eyelid of nictitating (blinking) membrane is located in the inner corner of each eye and can be drawn across the eye when occasion demands. This consists of hairless gristle and has the same function as the main eyelid. Sometimes this membrane ruptures, and what looks like a small pink pea appears in the corner of the eye. To remove this ruptured membrane involves surgery by a veterinary surgeon, which in most cases is very successful.

The colour of a Basset's eye is determined by a structure called the *iris*. It is formed from blood containing a layer of the eye's sphere and is made of muscular tissue. The colour is determined in a similar way to that of the coat.

The eyes shade from deep brown in the tri-colours to mid-brown in the lighter-coloured hounds. The Basset's expression should always be rather sad, calm and serious, belying the joy they have in living. The red of the lower lid (normally referred to by Basset breeders as the *haw*) appears, though not excessively. Very pale or light eyes are discouraged as a fault, as they alter the expression.

Ears

The Standard is very clear regarding the ears. They are set far back on the head, below the level of the eye, never above. They should be very fine and thin, soft and velvety to the touch, and curling inwards, corkscrew fashion, ending in a point rather than rounded. The ears are long and should extend beyond the end of the muzzle, but not excessively. A thick, flat, cabbage-leaf-like ear is very ugly and a fault. The ears are rather like a picture frame to the face, enhancing the soft, sad expression that is so endearing.

Mouth

Fig 3 (overleaf) shows the correct jaw structure for a Basset. The upper set of incisors should overlap the lower set in a correct scissor bite (3a). An adult Basset should have 42 teeth (figs 3b–d): 6 incisors above and below (12), 4 canines and 4 premolars top and bottom on each side (16) and 10 molars. Basset exports to Europe must have the correct number of teeth, as judges there are most particular regarding this aspect.

Occasionally, an overshot puppy appears in a litter (fig 4b overleaf). This could be a throwback to their ancestors, as many early hounds of the *Le Couteulx* strain had this type of mouth. The original Breed Standard did not condemn the overshot or undershot jaw. Undershot (fig 4c) is when the lower incisors overlap the upper. Until the revision of the Breed Standard, the level or edge to edge mouth (fig 4d) was permitted.

For its size, the Basset has relatively small teeth, which can be twisted quite easily when it chews bones – or the kennel door!

Neck

Muscular and well arched aptly describes the neck contours from the point behind the occipital bone down to the shoulder blades. This arch not only makes the hound look elegant and attractive but also serves a functional purpose. One of the most powerful muscles, the *brachicephalicus,* is attached to the head and shoulder blade. Other muscles extend from shoulder blades to the neck vertebrae. Since the shoulder blade muscles are attached to the neck, an arched neck is structurally stronger to withstand the pull from the shoulder blade muscles.

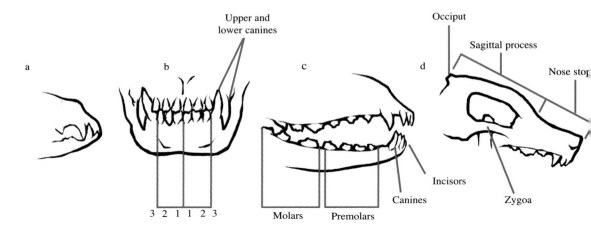

Fig 3: The scissor bite – structure.
a: Upper incisors fit over lower incisors. b: View from the front. c: View from the side. d: In relation to the skull.

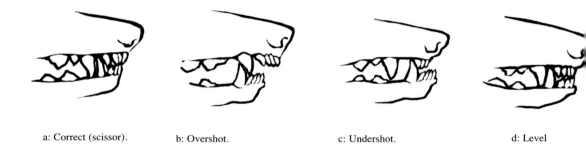

a: Correct (scissor).   b: Overshot.   c: Undershot.   d: Level

Fig 4: Various bites.

The neck should be fairly long; Bassets with long necks normally have well laid back shoulders. A lengthy, well arched neck adds elegance, while a short neck makes a Basset look stuffy and unbalanced. The loose skin under the neck forms into two pouches: the dewlap. This is one of the Basset's characteristics, and little or no dewlap would be a fault.

Forequarters

The most vulnerable and also the hardest working part of the Basset is the front assembly, as it has the most functions to perform. It supports the major part of the weight of the Basset, leaving the hindquarters comparatively free to deliver maximum drive, although I do not imply that the front does not supply power and forward thrust. As the Basset is propelled forward, it is the front assembly that checks the fall and receives the impact of hitting the ground. It also maintains a comparatively level centre of gravity, thus reducing the fatigue that is suffered in moving. The front assembly also assists the hindquarters in propelling the Basset forward. During the rear portion of each step, it adds additional thrust.

The anchor of the forequarters is the *scapula*. The scapula and its angulation, more than any other individual part, determines what kind of movement the Basset has. Good shoulders come as

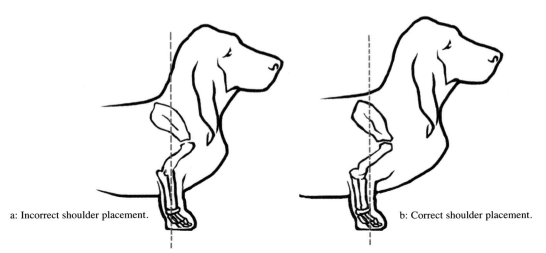

a: Incorrect shoulder placement.

b: Correct shoulder placement.

Fig 5: Shoulder placement.

a result of the scapula sloping well to the rear as well as being inclined towards the centre line of the Basset's body, so that they fit closely to the rib cage and can move smoothly over the ribs, held in position with long, smooth muscles. The length of the scapula and humerus varies depending on the total leg length. In the Basset these are approximately equal. The scapula which lies back at a 45° angle, in conjunction with the humerus relatively equal in length, will give the required power and stride – the smooth, free action, with foreleg reaching well forward, that is required in the Basset.

Even if the bone structure is correct and the scapula and humerus at the correct angle, fronts can still go wrong in a Basset through

- incorrect feeding – overfeeding and getting a young puppy very fat and heavy.
- overfeeding or underfeeding certain vitamins and minerals.
- over-exercising a puppy.
- allowing puppies to jump down onto hard surfaces or go up and down steps or stairs.

Fig 6 overleaf shows the correct Basset front and various ways in which it can be incorrect. Breeding from good-fronted Bassets with generations of sound-fronted hounds behind them eliminates much of the risk. Even so, close attention to the rearing points is needed for best results.

The Basset is not built for speed, but for stamina and endurance when hunting, so good strong bone is essential. The elbows should fit neatly against the side. Common causes for 'out at elbows' are loaded shoulders and incorrect shoulder placement.

The front legs support the heaviest part of the Basset, and the deepest point of the chest will be immediately between the front legs. The upper forearms incline slightly inwards, and the forechest fits neatly into the crook (Fig 6a–b). There should be neither excess crook, causing the legs to touch in front, nor so slight a crook that the chest is not supported. Knuckling over (Fig 6f) is a bad fault. There should be wrinkles of skin on the leg. The pastern joints should be flexible. A short pastern functions at a superior mechanical advantage and imparts better endurance.

Body

The body of a Basset is long and oblong in shape; under no circumstance should it be short or cobby. Even so, it should be balanced. Enhancing the length is the sternum or breastbone, which should be easy to see at all times, protruding in front of the forelegs; some hounds have a mass of loose skin on their chests, disguising the absence of a prominent sternum. This usually goes with an upright shoulder – definitely a fault.

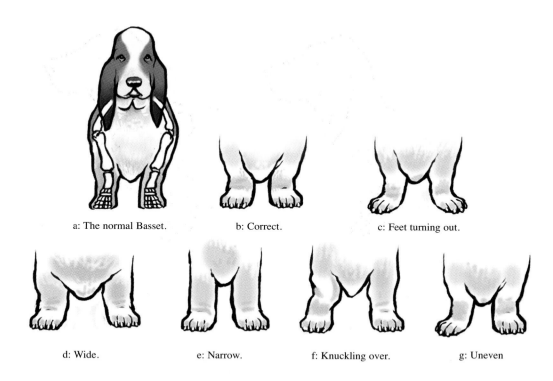

a: The normal Basset.   b: Correct.   c: Feet turning out.

d: Wide.   e: Narrow.   f: Knuckling over.   g: Uneven

Fig 6: Basset fronts.

The length of the body is derived mostly from the rib cage, which is well rounded and free from any flangeing (protruding ribs). The rib cage should be smooth when felt, especially underneath the hound; there should be no indentations or lumps. The rib cage is very important, as it protects the lungs, heart and diaphragm. A well rounded rib cage allows for plenty of expansion of the lungs.

There are thirteen pairs of ribs (see fig 1 on page 67), nine of which are *sternal* (attached by cartilage to the sternum). Three are *asternal* (attached by cartilage to the ninth rib). The last is *floating* (attached to the vertebrae only, with the shaft projecting outwards). The liver, stomach and kidneys receive some protection from the last four or five ribs. The Basset's rib cage is not unduly deep.

The back is rather broad and level, with the withers and quarters approximately the same height. The back should be strong, hard and muscular, well capable of withstanding the pressure of a judge examining it. The loin, which is the part of the back above the flank, should be relatively short, perhaps just over a handspan. There are no ribs below the loin; the *slight arch* mentioned in the Standard is referring to well-toned muscle under the skin. When running, a Basset can flex this part of the back. The back from withers to inset of quarters is not unduly long.

Fundamental to the structure of the Basset is the spine, made up of *vertebrae*. This is what decides the animal's size, balance, proportions and, to some extent, the function it is able to perform. Most of the Basset's body is linked directly or indirectly to it. The spine is immensely strong and flexible. Nearly all dogs have the same number of vertebrae in each segment of the body: seven in the neck, thirteen in the rib cage, seven in the loin, three in the pelvis and an irregular number in the tail. In all dogs the scapula muscles are attached to the same vertebra. The longer the rib cage, the further back the scapula is attached, and the further it is laid back.

Hindquarters

Standing behind a Basset, you should be able to see that the upper and lower thighs are very muscular, standing out to make them appear almost spherical. I liked the old standard which stated *round as an apple*. A well bent stifle has a marked angle at the stifle or knee joint. A Basset with well bent stifles has longer rear reach and greater flexibility. The angle of the pelvis must also be noted at this point: a 30° pelvis slope permits a more efficient delivery of power to the hind movement than any other angular arrangement. It is very important that the hindquarters – the propelling power of the Basset – should have the correct angulation, strength and sturdiness. Again, when viewed from behind, with stifles and feet pointing forward, the hocks should be parallel. Loose skin may appear between the hock and foot, and at the rear of the joint there should be a pouch of loose skin.

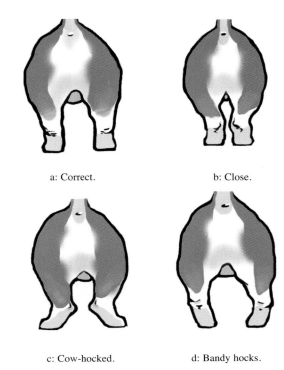

a: Correct.　　　　　　b: Close.

c: Cow-hocked.　　　　　d: Bandy hocks.

Fig 7: Hindquarters.

Feet

These must be massive, well knuckled-up and padded. Deeply cushioned pads help to absorb the shock of impact. Thin or splay feet, with toes spreading, lack compactness and strength. The massiveness of the foot is a continuation of the heavy bone of the leg. Since the front feet of a Basset carry more weight than the rear, the front feet are larger. The forefeet may point straight ahead or be turned slightly outwards but, in all cases, the weight must be borne equally on all the toes with the pads together.

The feet should leave an imprint of a large hound, with no unpadded area in contact with the ground. Good feet are bred, although they can be helped by correct nutrition – by feeding to help bones, such as the digits in the toes and the metacarpus, to develop. Keeping the nails well trimmed and exercising your hound correctly also help. The front and hind feet of a Basset are similarly constructed, with only slight anatomical differences in shape and size, the hind feet being somewhat narrower and longer.

In a heavy breed like the Basset, the surface of the runs in kennels may contribute towards feet problems. It has been proved that smooth concrete does not help a Basset to attain good feet; a rougher or sandy surface is much better.

Tail (stern)

The stern should be strong and thick at the base indicating the heavy bone continuing from the vertebrae. When the hound is moving the stern is held up in a gentle curve, sabre fashion. There should be no kink in the stern and it should never curl over the back.

Because the first bone of the stern articulates with the last one in the sacrum of the spine, the angle at which the stern is held depends very much on the angle of the sacrum to the rest of the vertebrae column. To my mind, the stern curving gently upwards and out from the body balances an elegant, arched neck. The hair on the underside of the stern is normally coarser and slightly longer than on the top. The tip of the stern is always white, with the hair normally ending in a slight whorl. In some countries the underside and tip of the stern is trimmed, but in Great Britain the stern is not tampered with or trimmed at all.

Gait/Movement

The Breed Standard is explicit on this point: the Basset must have a smooth, free action, the forelegs reaching well forward. This free, smooth action is dependent on drive from behind, in conjunction with excellent forequarter conformation. A good reach of neck and correctly angulated shoulders give the ideal length of movement to the front legs. The hindquarters are the driving force. As the Basset moves away, the legs should maintain the vertical alignment of the hips, stifles, hocks and feet, and should move forward with a coordinated driving action, reaching well forward and back in a long, low stride. The pads of the feet should show as the Basset moves away, but there should be no wasteful throwing up of the hocks or hackney action (high stepping) in front. The current fetish for fast movement, and the assumption that such action is correct, is incorrect. Strong, forceful, steady movement is what is looked for in a hound.

Coat

Smooth, short and close, without feathering. At one time it is thought that, either by misalliance or intention, a Clumber Spaniel was crossed with a Basset, and occasionally a Basset puppy with a soft-textured, long coat like a Clumber appears in a litter. These long-coated puppies usually have very heavy bone, reminiscent of a Clumber. This type of coat is a fault, and highly undesirable. Bassets kept in outdoor kennels with minimum heating will grow denser coats.

The skin of the Basset is supple and loose, with great elasticity.

Colour

The usual colours are black-white-and-tan (tri-colour) and lemon-and-white (bi-colour), but any recognised hound colour is acceptable. One of the most pleasing aspects of the Basset is the glorious range of colours and markings, from the traditionally marked tri-colour (white collar, black back, shading to chestnut brown on the shoulders, thighs and tops of legs) to the pale lemon-and-white, with all the shades and markings in between. The range of colours is a clear indication of the Basset Hound's ancestry and descent from the large, smooth-coated French hounds, the rare black-and-tan being indicative of the Bloodhound outcross.

Soundness and Type

Two words not mentioned in the Breed Standard, but which the standard is describing, are *soundness* and *type*.

Soundness represents conformation, construction, movement, temperament and health. If the function of a Basset is understood, the requirements of soundness become much more easily identifiable. What is wanted is a happy, poised Basset, eager and responsive to its owner, whose every part is complete and functioning correctly: a hound capable of working all day over all kinds of terrain.

Type must be inter-related with soundness to breed a Basset that can perform a specific function, and the correct balance between type and soundness must be maintained. There are many hunting breeds, but type differentiates between them. I feel that the head plays a great part in the keynote of type. Every breed has a head that is individual to that breed – some may look similar but are not identical. Type is best described as the sum of the points that make a Basset look like its own breed and no other: the ideal for which breeders should aim. It is subject to slight variation according to how people interpret it.

So far, I have commented on the current Kennel Club Breed Standard for Basset Hounds. For comparison, I shall now include the Basset Hound Breed Standard of 1879, the Fédération Cynologique Internationale (FCI) Standard for the Basset Artésien Normand and the current American Breed Standard.

The Basset Hound Standard 1879

Points of the Basset Hound

Head, skull, eyes, muzzle and flews	15	(14)
Ears	15	(10)
Neck, dewlap, chest and shoulders	10	(18)
Forelegs and feet	15	(18)
Back, loins and hindquarters	10	(18)
Stern	5	(5)
Coat and skin	10	(5)
Colour and markings	15	(5)
'Basset character' and symmetry	5	(7)
	100	100

1   *Head* The head of the Basset hound is most perfect when it closest resembles a Bloodhound's. It is long and narrow, with heavy flews, occiput prominent, *la bosse de la chasse* and forehead wrinkled to the eyes, which should be kind and show the haw. The general appearance of the head must present high breeding and reposeful dignity, the teeth are small, and the upper jaw sometimes protrudes. This is not a fault, and is called *bec de lièvre*.

2   *Ears* Very long, and when drawn forward folding well over the nose – so long that in hunting they will often actually tread on them. They are set on low, and hang loose in folds like draperies the ends inwards curling, in texture thin and velvety.

3   *Neck* Powerful, with heavy dewlaps. Elbows must not turn out. The chest is deep, full and framed like a man-of-war. Body long and low.

4   *Fore-legs* Short, about 4in, and close-fitting to the chest till the crooked knee, from where the wrinkled ankle ends in a massive paw, each toe standing out distinctly.

5   *Stifles* Bent, and the quarters full of muscle, which stands out so that, when one looks at the dog from behind, it gives him a round, barrel-like effect. This, with their peculiar waddling gate, goes a long way towards Basset character – a quality easily recognised by the judge, and as desirable as terrier character in a terrier.

6   *Stern* Coarse, underneath, and carried hound fashion.

7   *Coat* Short, smooth and fine, and it has a gloss on it like that of a race horse. To get this appearance they should be hound-gloved, never brushed. Skin loose and elastic.

8   *Colour* Black, white and tan. The head, shoulders and quarters a rich tan, and black patches on the back. They are also sometimes hare-pied.

The scale of points was not approved by some of the earlier breeders, especially those who hunted their hounds. In 1898, Captain Godfrey Heseltine, Master of Hounds Walhampton, drew up his own scale of points for distribution amongst his puppy walkers. These points are in brackets alongside the official standard.

Basset Artésien Normand Breed Standard

Reproduced by kind permission of the Fédération Cynologique Internationale (FCI)

Origin: France

Date of publication of the valid original Standard: 22 October 1992

Utilization

Small game hunting dog used for hunting with the gun. Hunts as well by himself as in a pack, with giving tongue. His short legs allow him to penetrate the most dense vegetation, there where the big dog cannot go, and to flush out the hidden game. His favourite is hunting the rabbit, but he can just as well hunt the hare as the deer. He tracks and flushes with great determination driving the game not fast, but with perseverance and giving voice.

FCI Classification

Group 6: Scent hounds and leash hounds.

Section 1.3: Small sized hounds

Brief Historical Summary

The controlled breeding of the short-haired French Basset began in the year 1870. From Bassets having an apparently common origin, Count Le Couteulx of Canteleu has fixed a utilitarian type with straight front legs called *d'Artois*, whereas Mr Louis Lane has developed a more spectacular type, with crooked front legs, called *Normand*. Only in 1924 the name *Artésien-Normand Basset (Basset Artésien Normand)* was finally adopted for the breed and the club. Mr Léon Verrier, who took over as chairman of the club in 1927, at the age of 77, has wanted to strengthen the Norman character of the breed and in the book of standards of hunting dogs of 1930, where the two breeds, Basset d'Artois and Basset Artésien-Normand figure, we find the following reference to this breed: The committee of the Société de Vénerie (Game Society) decides and notes that the Basset Artésien-Normand should not be but one stage of transition towards a *Norman* type, without any trace of Artois.

General Appearance of the Dog

Long dog in relation to its size, well balanced, compact, recalling in his head the nobility of the big Norman hound.

Important Proportions

Height at withers	: length of body	=	about 5 : 8
Depth of chest	: height at withers	=	about 2 : 3
Width of skull	: length of head	=	about 1 : 2
Length of muzzle	: length of skull	=	about 10 : 10

Behaviour/Temperament

Gifted with an excellent nose and a melodious voice. Perseveres but not too fast on the line, he permits his master to fully enjoy the hunting work.

Temperament: Outgoing and of very affectionate nature.

Head

Skull: Dome shaped, medium width; occipital bone apparent. On the whole the head must have a dry look.

Stop: Marked without exaggeration.

Facial region

Nose: Black and large, slightly protruding over the lips; nostrils well open.

Lips: Upper lip covering considerably the lower lip, without, however, being too pendulous nor too tight lipped.

Muzzle: Approximately the same length as that of the skull and slightly aquiline.

Cheeks: Formed by one or two folds of skin.

Teeth: Scissor bite, ie upper incisors covering the lower ones in close contact are squarely set in relation to the jaws.

Eye: Oval shaped, large, dark (in harmony with the coat), expression calm and serious, the haw (conjunctival lining) of the lower lid may sometimes show without excess.

Ears: Set as low as possible, never above the line of the eye, narrow at the base, well curled inwards corkscrew fashion, supple, fine, very long, reaching at least the length of the muzzle and preferably ending in a point.

Neck: Rather long, with some dewlap but without exaggeration.

Body

Back: Wide and well supported.

Loin: Slightly tucked up.

Rump: Hips a little oblique, giving a slight slant to the rump.

Chest: Of ovalized section, long, sternum well prolonged backward and prominent in front, with developed brisket. Full flanks. The brisket sternal line is distinctly below the elbows.

Ribs: Long, carried well back.

Tail (stern): Quite long, thick at base and thinning down progressively. At rest the tip of the tail must just touch the ground. Carried sabre fashion but never falling on the back; its extremity must not be like a plume. On that subject it is absolutely forbidden to modify the look of the stern of show dogs.

Forequarters

Seen on the whole, forelegs are short and well-boned; they are half-crooked or a little less than half-crooked, provided there is a sufficient principle of crook visible. Some folds of skin, without excess, on the pasterns, must be considered as a quality.

Shoulders: Muscular, oblique.

Elbows: Close to the body.

Feet: Oval shaped, a little elongated, toes rather close and placed firmly on the ground giving maximum support.

Hindquarters

On the whole and seen from the back, a vertical line going from the point of the thigh (buttock) goes through the middle of the leg, the hock, the metatarsal and the foot.

Thighs: Fleshy and muscular.

Hocks: Strong, quite low, relatively bent, which places the hind foot slightly under the dog when he is at rest. A small pouch of skin at the point of the hock (calcaneum) is not a fault.

Metatarsals: Short and strong.

Gait/Movement: Even, quite effortless and steady movement.

Skin: Supple and fine.

Coat

Hair: Close, short and smooth without being too fine.

Colour: Fawn with black blanket and white (tri-colour) or fawn and white (bi-colour). In the tri-coloured dog, the head should be largely covered with tan hair and show a circle of darker hairs on each temple. The black blanket or the black patches should be composed of solid black hairs or black hair with 'grizzle' (realising thus the former characteristic of 'hare-pied' or 'badger-pied').

Size and Weight

Height at the withers: Males and females, 30–36cm with tolerance of ±1cm on the recommended limits for the exceptional subjects.

Weight: 15–20kg.

Faults

Any departure from the foregoing points must be considered a fault which should be penalized in proportion to its seriousness and importance.

Head:	Flat skull
	Wide forehead
	Medial furrow too pronounced
	Ears flat, too round, thick, high set and broad at base
	Eye light, round and protruding, showing too much haw
Neck:	Short
Body:	Topline
	Stern too long, deviated or coarse
	Xiphoid process (cartilaginous process of the rear end of the sternum) either too short or absent.
	Ribs flat or deformed
Forequarters:	Shoulder straight, short, insufficiently muscled
	Pasterns touching each other, knuckling over
	Out at elbows
	Exaggerated crook with feet turning out excessively
	Flat feet
	Splay feet
Hindquarters:	Thighs flat
	Hocks close, too wide apart

Coat: Soft, distinctly long or fringed

Colour: Black shading on the head

Behaviour: Timid subjects

Eliminating Faults

* Lack of type.
* Height at withers other than that of the standard.
* Undershot or overshot mouth.
* Eye very light.
* Rear end of sternum too short with absence of xiphoid process.
* Ribs very much deformed.
* Forelegs completely straight.
* Legs too weak.
* Too much dark shading on the head.
* Too much black-mottled giving the white a bluish tint.
* Timid or aggressive subject.
* Serious anatomical anomaly.
* Hereditary identifiable and disabling defect.

Note: Males should have two apparently normal testicles fully descended into the scrotum.

American Basset Hound Breed Standard

Reproduced by kind permission of the American Kennel Club

General Appearance – The Basset Hound possesses in marked degree those characteristics which equip it admirably to follow a trail over and through difficult terrain. It is a short-legged dog, heavier in bone, size considered, than any other breed of dog, and while its movement is deliberate, it is in no sense clumsy. In temperament it is mild, never sharp or timid. It is capable of great endurance in the field and is extreme in its devotion.

Head – The head is large and well proportioned. Its length from occiput to muzzle is greater than the width at the brow. In over-all appearance the head is of medium width. The **skull** is well domed, showing a pronounced occipital protuberance. A broad flat skull is a fault. The length from nose to stop is approximately the length from stop to occiput. The sides are flat and free from cheek bumps. Viewed in profile the toplines of the muzzle skull are straight and lie in parallel planes, with a moderately defined stop. The skin over the whole of the head is loose, falling in distinct wrinkles over the brow when the head is lowered. A dry head and tight skin are faults. The **muzzle** is deep, heavy and free from snipiness. The **nose** is darkly pigmented, preferably black, with large wide-open nostrils. A deep liver-coloured nose conforming to the colouring of the head is permissible but not desirable. The **teeth** are large, sound and regular, meeting in either a scissors or an even bite. A bite either overshot or undershot is a serious fault. The **lips** are darkly pigmented and are pendulous, falling squarely in front and, toward the back, in loose hanging flews. The **dewlap** is very pronounced. The **neck** is powerful, of good length, and well arched. The **eyes** are soft, sad, and slightly sunken, showing a prominent haw, and in color are brown, dark brown preferred. A somewhat lighter-colored eye conforming to the general colouring of the dog is acceptable but not desirable. Very light or protruding eyes are faults. The **ears** are extremely long, low set, and when drawn forward fold well over the end of the nose. They are velvety in texture, hanging in loose folds with the ends curling slightly inwards. They are set far back on the head at the base of the skull and, in repose, appear to be set on the neck. A high set or flat ear is a serious fault.

Forequarters – The **chest** is deep and full with prominent sternum showing clearly in front of the legs. The **shoulders** and elbows are set close against the sides of the chest. The distance from the deepest point of the chest to the ground, while it must be adequate to allow free movement when working in the field, is not to be more than one-third the total height at the withers of an adult Basset. The shoulders are well laid back and powerful. Steepness in the shoulder, fiddle fronts and elbows that are out, are serious faults. The **forelegs** are short, powerful, heavy in bone, with wrinkled skin. Knuckling over of the front legs is a disqualification. The **paw** is massive, very heavy with tough heavy pads, well rounded and with both feet inclined equally a trifle outward, balancing the width of the shoulders. Feet down at the pastern are a serious fault. The **toes** are neither pinched together nor splayed with the weight of the forepart of the body borne evenly on each. The dewclaws may be removed.

Body – The rib structure is long, smooth and extends well back. The ribs are well sprung, allowing adequate room for heart and lungs. Flatsidedness and flanged ribs are faults. The topline is straight, level and free from any tendency to sag or roach, which are faults.

Hindquarters – The hindquarters are very full and well rounded, and are approximately equal to the shoulders in width. They must not appear slack or light in relation to the over-all depth of the body. The dog stands firmly on its hind legs showing a well let down stifle with no tendency towards a crouching stance. Viewed from behind, the hind legs are parallel, with the hocks turning neither in nor out. Cowhocks or bowed legs are serious faults. The hind feet point straight ahead. Steep, poorly angulated hindquarters are a serious fault. The dewclaws, if any, may be removed.

Tail – The tail is not to be docked, and is set in continuation of the spine with but slight curvature and carried gaily in hound fashion. The hair on the underside of the tail is coarse.

Size – The height should not exceed 14in. Height over 15in at the highest point of the shoulder blade is a disqualification.

Gait – The Basset moves in a smooth, powerful, and effortless manner. Being a scenting dog with short legs, it holds its nose low to the ground. Its gait is absolutely true with perfect coordination between the front and hind legs, and it moves in a straight line with hind feet following in line with the front feet, the hocks well bent with no stiffness of action. The front legs do not paddle, weave or overlap, and the elbows must lie close to the body. Going away, the hind legs are parallel.

Coat – The coat is hard, smooth and short, with sufficient density to be of use in all weather. The skin is loose and elastic. A distinctly long coat is a disqualification.

Color – Any recognised hound color is acceptable and the distribution of color and markings is of no importance.

Disqualifications
- Height of more than 15in at the highest point of the shoulder blades.
- Knuckled over front legs.
- Distinctly long coat.

Choosing a Basset Hound

Buying a Basset puppy, in fact any puppy, is a commitment and a responsibility. It should also be a family decision. It will be no good if your partner is house proud and cannot abide hoovering needle-like short hairs from the carpet two or three times a week or clearing up the odd mistakes a puppy tends to make in the middle of the carpet, or has an impeccable garden and does not want the occasional plant (or border) uprooted and taken indoors as a trophy. The children must also be sensible and taught that a puppy is not a toy; it needs respect, gentleness and periods of rest. All these things must be considered and, when the family is in agreement that all members will cooperate fully in bringing up a new addition, then serious consideration can be given to obtaining the puppy. But before this, you must also ask yourself whether you really want a Basset Hound.

Do You Really Want a Basset Hound?

Anyone who wants to be owned by a Basset Hound will need the following:

* A great sense of humour.
* A placid and forgiving nature.
* Stamina – if not equal to that of a Basset, then as near as possible.
* Preferably unlimited resources.

It is hoped that your Basset puppy will be part of the family for the next 10–12 years. A fully-grown male Basset can weigh up to 35kg (75lb) and a female around 30kg (65lb); easily the size of a Labrador or Boxer. A boisterous Basset – yes, they can be boisterous when playing – does not realise its own strength and, if it runs into a child's legs, it can easily knock the child over without realising it has done anything wrong.

Caught red-pawed! Photo: B Muttock

The Basset has a character with a multitude of facets: faithful, loving, stubborn, endearing, exasperating, to name but a few. It may fail to hear you calling when it is on the scent of a rabbit in the countryside or rolling in some malodorous manure delivered for the flower bed, and it may also suffer functional deafness and turn into a lump of immovable jelly when you try to remove it from the best armchair in front of the fire on a cold winter's night. Finally, with a twitch of the eyebrows and a body-trembling sigh, it slides seal-like onto the floor, leaving you feeling rather bad about repossessing the seat. But its loyalty to its owner will never fail.

A Basset could teach Fagin a trick or two in the art of stealing. That soft, lumbering, soulful-eyed creature can be as quick as greased lightning, with a tongue like a giant anteater's, when food is left unguarded on the table. It loves a good romp in the country, but preferably when the weather is nice. It doesn't really like getting wet so, when the rain is pouring down, it will quite happily do a quick U-turn in the garden, lying down on the settee for the rest of the day.

Once trained, the Basset will love travelling in the car. It regards the car as an extension of its home and, provided that there is a blanket to stretch out on and a bottle of fresh water to drink at various stops, it will accompany its owner contentedly for hundreds of miles and be a very pleasant travelling companion.

Bassets love company, as Ch Bracenacre Navan and Ch Brackenacre Mary Anne can tell you.

The Basset has a very determined streak in its nature (the tenacity of the hound) and should not be allowed to get the upper hand. If a Basset is required to act in a certain way for good manners' sake (for instance, *not* to take the ice cream out of a child's hand and devour the treat in a second) it must be trained from a very early age, with firmness and kindness.

Always remember that the Basset is a hound and will, if not on a lead in open countryside, take off on the scent of hare, rabbit or deer, and no amount of shouting will bring it back. This is the basic hunting instinct coming to the fore.

Bassets are pack animals, and for generations were hunted, kennelled, fed and watered as a pack. They are therefore very gregarious, enjoying the company of humans or other animals. Because of this background and love of companionship, it is cruel to leave a solitary Basset for long periods. If left alone for several hours, Bassets become bored. They then turn to digging at carpets, chewing furniture and so on to relieve their boredom, and the ensuing destruction would make a demolition gang feel inadequate. They can be stubborn, obstinate and sometimes awkward, but never stupid.

The charm of the Basset lies in its versatility: an armchair clown with a tremendous love for its family, a dedicated hunting machine in the field, and, in the show ring, a film star attracting a multitude of admirers.

Where Should You Buy Your Basset Hound?

If you have decided that you really do want a Basset, the next question is, where to obtain a nice puppy, either as a companion or as a companion and show dog. Dogs are advertised in several places: the local newspaper, the *Exchange and Mart* advertising paper, and the local veterinary surgery normally has a board advertising pets for sale. The Telephone Directory Yellow Pages also may have local breeders advertising. However, two weeklies deal exclusively with dogs, giving reports on shows, breed notes and articles of canine interest. These papers, *Dog World* and *Our Dogs*, are available at newsagents, although they usually have to be ordered. The Kennel Club (see **Useful Addresses**) will also give information, and all pedigree breeds have breed clubs. You will find the address of the Secretary of the Basset Hound Club in **Useful Addresses**. The Secretary will no doubt ask many questions regarding the family to establish their suitability as Basset owners. This is in no way meant to be impertinent – it is merely a way of finding the correct breed for the correct home.

At this stage, most people would prefer to own a puppy that can be trained into the ways of the family. However, if the carpet soiling, garden digging, and possible chewing of such objects as chair legs and children's toys needs to be obviated, thought should be given to obtaining an older hound who, through no fault of its own, has been placed in the hands of Basset Hound Rescue. There are many reasons why this happens. Among the most frequent are marriage break-up, a new baby arriving, family bereavement and emigration. The adult hound will probably be fully house-trained and inoculated and, more than likely, lead- and car-trained, and will be very happy and more than content to settle into a new home. If a Basset has to be rehomed from a kennel, more time will have to be taken to house train it. The Basset Hound Rescue coordinator at the time of writing is Mrs Pat Green (see **Useful Addresses**). Again, she will probably ask many questions to establish your suitability. The organisation will expect a remuneration to help the work of the Basset Hound Rescue to continue.

Which Pup?

Two points on which you should be quite clear are whether you want a male or female and whether the dog is to be primarily a companion or a potential show dog, with the possibility of breeding in the future. If a potential show dog is required, go to a breeder with a good reputation who has sold puppies that have won well in the show ring, and be prepared to wait for a suitable puppy if one is not immediately available. *Potential* is the operative word, as even the most promising puppies may not turn out to be show winners.

Basset colours: lemon-and-white and tri-colour.

The majority of reputable breeders are striving to breed the perfect Basset. Given the law of averages, not all the puppies bred will be top quality show specimens; one may have a lighter coloured eye than desired, another may have ears that are slightly thicker than preferred, yet another may have a mouth that is not 100%. None of these faults will stop the puppy from growing into a fine healthy animal and living a long life, and it would still make a splendid companion.

If a puppy is obtained from a well-bred litter, no doubt the buyer would be able to see the dam, and possibly grandparents, great-grandparents and other relations. Unless the breeder owns the sire (and quite often the bitch will have been taken to a stud), the sire cannot be seen by the prospective buyer, but the reputation, quality, temperament and condition of the hounds you see should be a good enough guide.

Without previous experience, it can be very hard for a novice buyer to pick a puppy. To be confronted with eight to ten puppies running all over the place can make the decision difficult. I feel the best way is for the breeder to ascertain from buyers whether they want a male or female puppy. The next consideration is the colour: tri-colour or lemon-and-white. The final consideration is whether show potential is required or whether the puppy is to be simply a pet. This will narrow the choice until there may be just three puppies suitable for viewing, making it a much easier task for the buyer to choose a suitable pup.

If possible, I prefer the prospective owner to see the puppies for the first time when they are six weeks old; at this stage they will be showing all the Basset characteristics: virtually adult Bassets in miniature. It is sometimes very difficult to convince a prospective buyer that, for the first two weeks, Basset puppies never resemble adult Bassets; in fact they could be any short-haired breed. By six weeks the puppies should be alert, playful and inquisitive.

Choosing a Potential Show Puppy

It is almost impossible to choose a puppy and say with conviction that it will be a show winner. Rest assured, many breeders with years of experience have picked out promising puppies for themselves to show, only to find that, at six to ten months, the pup starts to turn a foot, or perhaps the jaw becomes undershot or overshot, or the hind movement is not true. These and so many other minor faults can appear, so that in the end the youngster is sold on as a pet. There is no golden rule for picking a potential champion from a litter, but I list the points to look for in a puppy.

First and foremost, take advice from the breeder, who has raised and watched the litter grow and will probably know every detail about each one.

Look for a puppy with a bright, clean, shining coat. This should be short, like velvet. Avoid a puppy with a fluffy coat, hairs between its toes and curls like a cocker spaniel on its leathers, as this could develop into a long and incorrect coat. Sometimes puppies may have a little scurf, through being raised under infra red heating, but this will soon go when the puppy is in a home environment.

The ear canals should be clean, and the ears fine textured and set on low. They should feel like a piece of silk, and will easily crumple in your hand. Avoid the heavy, thick ears, as these usually develop into thick, flat, incorrect adult ears.

The mouth should have a correct scissor bite, the upper teeth closing slightly over the lower.

The feet of a good Basset puppy must be large and well knuckled, with the nails trimmed short.

The puppy should have heavy bone in its legs, and a thick base to its tail (which should not be too long), indicating good bone.

The prosternum (breast bone) should project well forward of the pup's shoulders, forming a keel, like on a boat.

The eyes have adequate haw and a sorrowful expression. Eye colouring should be dark in a tri-colour, but can be lighter in a lemon-and-white.

The rib cage will be smooth and round, carried well back. The Basset is a long dog, but the length comes from a good length of rib cage, not a long loin.

A good bend of stifle should be apparent, almost exaggerated, as this tends to straighten as the pup grows older.

Overall, the pup should have fine supple skin. When you pick up the puppy, the skin will hang about the head in wrinkles and folds, and it will come away easily from the body when lifted by the hand.

Although the puppy will appear very ungainly at eight weeks, it should be coordinated enough to move correctly, both fore and aft, with the shoulders well laid back.

The topline must be reasonably strong, with no dips, roaching or weakness. Overall, the puppy should look balanced from every angle.

A dark, shiny nose with large, open nostrils, as befits a hunting animal, is preferred but, in lemon-and-white puppies, the nose will probably be brown, or it can even be patched, gradually turning brown at a later stage.

A pot-belly on a puppy is usually indicative of worm infestation.

The puppies will probably run to the owner at the sound of his (or her) voice, associating him with food,

A long-haired bitch: lovely, but incorrect.

grooming and play. I am a little wary of allowing prospective owners to pick up and fondle the puppies, as at this age the pups will not have been inoculated against any diseases and could easily pick up an illness from contact on clothing or shoes. Do not be tempted by the little shy pup that runs and hides in the corner, especially if you have children. A shy puppy needs a lot of tender loving care to bring it out of its shell, and a household with boisterous children would be most frightening. If you have children, you would do better to choose the most outgoing, daring puppy, or the bully of the litter – it will join in the games and be unafraid.

Are You a Suitable Basset Owner?

Another reason why I prefer the new owners to view the puppies at six weeks is because it gives me a chance to talk to them about the breed, and thereby assess their suitability, and also to see their reactions to a couple of adult

This pretty eight-week-old shows excellent front and wrinkling.

A Basset Hound with its long-haired 'cousin',
a Petit Basset Griffon Vendéen. Photo: Kim Dent

Bassets. I show them the largest Basset I own so that they can see the size a Basset can attain when adult. I allow them to play with a young, active Basset, so that they know what the puppy could be like in a few months' time. It may turn out that they eventually decide to obtain a smaller breed, and far better this than a puppy needing to be rehomed in six months' time because 'they hadn't realised it would grow so large'.

These are the four main questions I ask a prospective buyer:

• Is someone at home all day?
• Do you have an enclosed garden to which the pup can have direct access?
• Have you any very young children? (I always think a mother with a very young baby must have her hands full without taking on a puppy.)
• Have you had a Basset before?

If the answer to the last question is 'yes', I always breath a sigh of relief; here is someone who has lived with one Basset, is well aware of the breed's requirements, and still wishes to own another.

It is unfair for a puppy to be sold into a home where everyone is out at business all day, unless special arrangements are made for a neighbour or relative to take in the pup while the owners are away. A Basset needs companionship, especially in puppyhood, because this is the formative time of its life. The training needs to begin from the moment it enters the new home. It is pointless to try to train the pup to do something between 7.00–7.30 am and then leave, expecting it to remember what it was told 10 hours earlier when you return in the evening. During the ensuing time, your pup will probably have howled, barked and whined, driving the neighbours to distraction, and possibly chewed half way through a chair leg, simply because it is bored and lonely.

Preparing for the New Arrival

It is at this time that advice is given to buyers about preparing their homes for the forthcoming puppy.

It is advisable to build a small pen in the corner of the room where the puppy will sleep, or it could be worth investing in a folding puppy pen or crate, available from pet shops, at dog shows or direct from the manufacturers, whose advertisements appear in the weekly dog papers. Put plenty of newspapers on the floor in the puppy pen. For the first few weeks, a strong cardboard box with a U-shaped cut-out in the front to let the puppy get in and out easily can be used as a bed. A Basset puppy will chew its bed, and a cardboard box can be replaced easily. Never leave a Basset in a wicker basket. I made this mistake with my first puppy and, within a few weeks, the basket was chewed to pieces. By then it was not very safe for a puppy, with spiky pieces of bamboo sticking up from a wooden base.

The pen, furnished with the bed, a warm blanket or vet bed and a few toys, will be your puppy's own place. This is where the pup will sleep; a secure and comfortable place, away from small children, however good their intentions. It can also be the first step to introducing it to a wire cage, invaluable for carrying the pup in the car or for using in an hotel bedroom if the youngster has to be left alone while the owners go for a meal.

I also tell new owners that the puppy must not be allowed to jump down steps or stairs or from furniture. Make sure the pup cannot run upstairs when you are not looking: a baby-gate is ideal to put across the foot of the stairs. I also show owners how to pick up and put down a young Basset. Always put one hand between the back legs and the other under its chest, so that, when the pup is lifted, its back and body are supported. When placing the puppy on the floor, put its back feet down first, then its front. This prevents its shoulders from being jarred.

If there is another dog already in the family, introduce them gently, preferably out in the garden. Do not let the puppy jump up and scratch at the older dog; conversely, do not allow the older dog to crowd the pup. Be sensible and, with plenty of supervision, they will become firm friends within a few days.

Have the food bowls ready for the pup, preferably stainless steel dishes for its meals; it could easily chew up a plastic dish, and stainless steel is easy to clean. A heavier porcelain dog bowl should be provided for the pup's water; again, this can be cleaned easily.

Safety in the House

Beware of hanging or trailing electrical wires from a household appliance such as a refrigerator, deep-freeze, microwave, electric fire, television or telephone. There is nothing a puppy enjoys more than chewing on electrical wires; it doesn't realise it could be electrocuted.

Do not leave small plastic toys around, or small rubber balls; the pup could swallow these, which would cause an obstruction in its stomach. Rubbish should be placed in a dustbin with a clip-on lid. Plastic bin liners can be ripped open in seconds by sharp puppy teeth.

Bottles of bleach and other chemicals should be stored in cupboards or on shelves above Basset level.

Safety in the Garden

Ensure there are no plants with poisonous berries.

All gates must have good, strong hinges and bolts on them. Ensure also that the fencing is strong, with no holes that the puppy can squeeze through. Bassets are notorious escapologists, and will soon find a weak point.

It is a good idea to provide a paved area for the puppy's toilet. An outside tap with hose to wash the toilet area is also useful.

If you have a fish pond or swimming pool, ensure that it is well covered and that the puppy cannot get under the covering. I have known of Basset puppies who disappeared, only to be found hours later, tragically drowned in a covered swimming pool. Water butts should always be kept covered.

A garden shed can be like an Aladdin's cave to a puppy, but the pup could easily pick up slug pellets or damage itself on lawn mower blades. Ensure that a good bolt is fitted and that the door is kept shut when the shed is not in use. Do not allow the puppy into a garage, where it may tread in oil or lick at antifreeze, which could poison it.

Collecting Your Puppy

When the new owners arrive to collect the puppy at eight weeks, all the paperwork should be available from the breeder. This should include:

- Pedigree
- Registration certificate
- Feeding instructions
- Name and address of the Basset Hound Club Secretary
- A note of when the puppy was wormed and when it should be wormed again
- Insurance certificate

Huckleberry demonstrates that Bassets enjoy fun with their humans.

A quick peep over the fence.

I always feel it safer to insure the puppy for the first month as this is when it is most vulnerable. The insurance company will contact the owner during the ensuing four weeks to see if they wish to continue with insurance. I think anyone with only one or two dogs would be foolish not to insure, as the cost of veterinary fees can be astronomical. Health care cover is available with Kennel Club registration. The new owner must register the transfer of ownership with The Kennel Club within 10 days of purchase to qualify for this cover.

It is sensible to bring along another person to carry the puppy, armed with a blanket to wrap around it and paper towels in case it is travel sick. If the new owner is alone, he or she will need a carrying cage to put the puppy in, with plenty of newspapers laid inside it. It would be incredibly foolish for only one person to arrive to take a puppy home, expecting it to sit on the back seat for the whole journey. The puppy would be between the front seats causing a nuisance within minutes.

The puppy will have been with the rest of the litter up until the time of departure, with lots of siblings to play with and cuddle up to for warmth, and plenty of competition for food. The pup is now out in the big, wide world and slightly frightened of new sights and smells, with no brothers or sisters to play with and with strange people wanting to pick it up. My advice is to let the puppy investigate its new home in peace and quiet. If you have children, make sure they do not get over-excited and start screaming and laughing loudly over the puppy.

For comfort and safety during car travel, it is best to place the Basset in a cage.

After an hour or so, offer a drink of slightly warmed milk, and later, when the new surroundings have been thoroughly explored, offer a meal from the breeder's feeding guide. The puppy may or may not eat this first meal, depending on how excited or tired it is. If it is excited, play with it for a while and keep talking, constantly using the chosen name, thus allowing the pup to get to know your voice and smell. Get down to the same level as the pup to play; it must be very intimidating for a puppy in a strange environment to have a person towering over it. When the puppy is tired, put it to bed, which should contain a blanket or a piece of Vetbed and plenty of furry toys to cuddle. Make sure there are newspapers around the bed inside the playpen. When the pup wakes from its first sleep, take it outside to where you hope, in time, it will know it should relieve itself.

The first night with a new puppy is usually traumatic. Put a well-wrapped hot-water-bottle in its bed and have a ticking clock nearby, to remind it of its mother's heartbeat. Obviously, the puppy will be lonely during the first night away from its litter mates, and no doubt it will whine and howl its distress. Do not be tempted to go to the pup and remove it to the bedroom, as it will be an even harder task the following night to keep it in the allotted place. The pup will eventually go to sleep, but may take three or four nights to learn that, once it is put into bed at night and the light is turned out, it must sleep or play until the next morning. With plenty of newspapers in the pen it can get out of its bed and relieve itself, and this can easily be cleared up the next morning. This will be the pup's first training session: to learn that it must be quiet at night when separated from its owner.

A Basset puppy aged eight weeks cannot control its bowels and bladder all night, but no doubt the puppy will already have been partially trained to use newspapers when with the rest of the litter. Puppies usually wish to relieve themselves as soon as they awake from sleep, and quite often after eating a meal or drinking thickened milk. The normal behaviour is for the pup to run about a bit sniffing before turning around two or three times prior to squatting down to relieve itself. When the owner recognises the signs, the pup should be picked up and taken outside. In the early stages of toilet training, when the puppy is out of the puppy pen, put newspaper by the door through which it will go to the garden; the pup will no doubt relieve itself on this paper. The next step is to leave the door open; the pup will soon learn that it has to go outside. A dog is not a naturally dirty creature. I make no apologies for quoting in part the article written by Kay White regarding puppy toilet training, by kind permission of The Kennel Club:

Toilet Training

It is important to remember that a puppy will make mistakes during the time you are teaching it acceptable toilet habits. Some of the mistakes will be the fault of the humans, who are not paying enough attention to the puppy at the critical time. House training is much easier in summer, when garden doors can stand open and the pup will sometimes eliminate in the right place without needing to attract the attention of a human. Summer house training is much less arduous but it is important to remember that, come the autumn, mistakes may be made indoors just because the pup is not used to doors being closed. House training isn't easy, it is not quick, it is time consuming and needs tolerance and patience – but in the end 99.75% of pups do reach the stage of absolutely reliable perfection in house manners.

I cannot emphasise too much that house training largely depends on the owner, and relatively little on the dog. The crucial factor, especially in the early days, is the owner being present at the vital time. Young puppies cannot wait very long to urinate; neither can some adults, and elderly dogs may also have a very short waiting ability. Dogs do not soil their beds, except in acute illness or in very old age, or when recovering from anaesthetic, but most dogs will compromise by using the carpet if they are prevented from getting to the place where you have taught them to go. Usually the soiling will be as close to the door as they can get, but for some dogs, anywhere will do!

Dog Door

An equally important lesson for the new owner is that punishment does not help the house training cause. Absolutely not at all. House training is a habit in the dog, not a moral resolution. Think the idea through, relate the concept of punishment for inappropriate elimination to the human situation. Unless you really know that a human adult or baby, or a dog, adult or puppy is deliberately eliminating in the wrong place as revenge or provocation, what is the use of punishment? Punishing a puppy for defecating or urinating indoors just sets back your whole house-training programme.

Do you want to make your puppy afraid to pass faeces even if the need is very urgent? Even if there is acute pain? Even if there is diarrhoea overnight through a gastric upset? Of course you will not punish the pup, that would be brutish. You may do a bit of under-breath grumbling as you clear up the mess just to show the pup his behaviour is not desirable, but nothing more violent than that. Your resolution will undoubtedly be to keep a closer watch on the pup, to get home sooner, or to get up earlier.

Housetraining mistakes will rarely occur when you are actually with the pup. If you are aware that your absences are likely to be in flexible time, then it helps a great deal to have a dog-flap fixed into your kitchen door, so that the puppy can get outside when it needs to do so. Our dog door gives on to a small enclosed paved yard, so that the dogs are not actually achieving the freedom of the garden via this exit. The small yard is used exclusively for overnight elimination as it is easily cleaned down. If you do arrange for a dog door please do not make this an excuse for leaving puppy or adult dog alone for lengthy periods, because aside from elimination purposes, your dog may still be incited to bark to excess, or to embark on mischief and destruction if it is lonely and frustrated.

Dogs do not use inappropriate defecation and urination behaviour in the way cats do, to express or protest at a change in the household. If your dog defecates indoors, you can be sure it is a case of 'gotta-go'.

Gold standard house training may take a variable time to teach, so it is useless to allocate two weeks' summer holiday to acquiring a puppy and teaching it all it needs to know before you return to work. Six months is more like the time scale which must be allowed before your pup will be acceptable socially in friends' homes, in a hotel or in the office.

Overnight

Getting a puppy to be clean overnight depends very much on the length of the owner's nights and the amount of local disturbance, as well as where the puppy sleeps. If the pup is in your bedroom then you will be able to respond when it wakes and needs to urinate. If the puppy is left in the kitchen, then the pup will realise its needs at first light, or when the world around it starts to stir. Milk or newspapers being delivered, other animals around being put out in the gardens and fields, up gets the pup, all inquisitive and eager and whoosh goes the urination impulse. Can you beat the paper boy seven days a week?

Cleaning Up

There are many cleaning up systems on the market now; your veterinary surgeon will almost certainly be selling one or more sets. New owners would do well to invest in one of these chemical cleaning systems to protect your household furnishings. The important thing to remember is not to use anything containing ammonia; otherwise you will be compounding the smell of urine and the puppy will be likely to use the same spot again, because the smell of the familiar is all-important to a puppy. Do not be too ready to clear up deposits in the garden, as the pup may well be drawn to the same area there, once the smell wafts into his nose.

Urine deposited on concrete or paving will dry up in the summer sun and smell terrible! The remedy is to hose down the area with large quantities of cold water, before you attempt any disinfection. Disinfectant is useless on a soiled surface, so always wash well with water and detergent first. Stains of all kinds on carpet or upholstery respond wonderfully well to Vanish, which can be bought as a stick of soap or a liquid spray.

Solid Accidents

Most of what I have written about inappropriate urination also applies to passing faeces in the house, unless, and this is a big unless, the need to pass excessive quantities of loose faeces is owner-induced, as it all too easily can be. Sudden changes in type or quantity of food, and over-feeding of unsuitable titbits; or that overwhelming desire we have not to waste anything, so we give last night's curry to the dog – this is the cause of many of the explosive loose motions which cause so much trouble. This is not true diarrhoea, as it will stop once the offending substance has been got rid of.

Other food should be withheld for up to 24 hours to allow the digestive system to clear, but always make sure that the puppy has access to clean water, perhaps frequently given in small amounts if the puppy is drinking cold water greedily. We just had a load of horse manure delivered; excellent for the roses, not so good for puppies and adults, all too eager to eat the excreta of other animals. This will produce another owner-induced diarrhoea, and if the pup cannot get outside when it needs to, the owner will be punished by having an unpleasant clean-up job. Never, never, ever, no matter what your grandmother or the odd-job man says, descend to the ugly and undignified action of 'rubbing' the pup's nose in it. What does it give you but a puppy with a smelly face, and possibly a simmering dislike of being handled or even approaching its owner?

Anger makes us do things which can have far reaching consequences, especially when training a young animal. We must try to be reasonable in our expectations of cleanliness in a young animal; remember, the human race is far slower in learning and we tend to be much more tolerant of children's failures.

Socialisation

Basset puppies from 8–12 weeks should be socialised with people. Kept in an enclosed environment, away from people and other animals, they may tend to become withdrawn. At this age the puppy can be very sensitive and impressionable so, although it must be socialised, make sure it feels safe and protected and is allowed enough time each day to rest and be quiet. It has been noted that failure to allow a puppy sufficient rest away from constant stimulation of human attention can be one of the causes of a nervous temperament. Most hounds, puppies, juniors or adults, like 'quiet periods', and allowances must be made to provide such opportunities.

Bassets thoroughly enjoy the company of children, but make sure that young puppies have enough time to themselves to rest.

'Let sleeping dogs lie!'

Veterinary Examination

When a puppy is obtained it is advisable for the new owner to make an appointment with the veterinary practice that, hopefully, will be looking after the pup for the rest of its life. As soon as possible, arrange for the puppy to be seen by the veterinary surgeon for an examination. Most breeders will encourage new owners to do this, as they do not want to be told six months later there was something wrong with the pup when it was obtained. Veterinary examination within 48 hours will no doubt leave both the breeder and new owner pleased that the puppy is in good health. Some vets will give an eight- or nine-week-old week puppy its first vaccination against distemper, canine parvovirus, canine leptospirosis and infectious canine hepatitis, and this will normally be mixed in one dose and injected into loose skin at the back of the puppy's neck. This will be repeated at twelve weeks. Ten days after the second vaccination, it should be safe to take the puppy to puppy training classes and for further socialisation.

Although the puppy of eight to twelve weeks, which has not had the second vaccination, must not socialise with other dogs, there is nothing to stop the new owner taking it out for short drives in the car. Perhaps a friend who likes dogs but does not own one would enjoy playing with the new puppy in her home and garden; the change of environment and company for the pup is very bene-

Train your Basset to walk on your left-hand side.

ficial. Drive the puppy in the car to a safe lay-by on a fairly busy road and sit with the window down, so that the pup can watch and listen to the traffic. Smooth the pup with your hand and speak to it calmly, letting it get accustomed to the noise of traffic.

Training for Separation

There are times when the puppy must be left for a period on its own; for example, at night, or when the owner has to go shopping. Much time is spent training the puppy what to do when the owner is there, but it must be trained also to be left alone for certain periods. It is best to start this training when the owner is in the vicinity. Play with the puppy and, when it seems to be getting sleepy, put the pup in bed with a favourite toy and leave it for approximately 15 minutes. If it barks and whines ignore it. After a period, the pup will be quiet. This is when the new owner should return

and give praise. In time the pup will realise its owner will only return when it is quiet and not when it is making a noise.

With a Basset, this training may take several weeks or even months, as the breed hates being alone. A radio left on at this time may give the pup comfort, and so may an old pair of socks or a garment that retains the owner's smell that the pup can cuddle into. With practice and patience, the puppy will learn that the separation will be short-lived and is a small price to pay for the hours that will be spent with its master.

Whinneywoods Queen Bea demonstrating show stance.

To train a Basset to sit, press gently but firmly on the hindquarters repeating the command 'Sit!'

Collar and Lead Training

As soon as the puppy has adjusted to its new home, perhaps after four or five days, put a collar on it, making sure that it is soft leather. A cat collar is very good as it has a piece of elastic inserted in it so, if it does get caught on anything, it will stretch and the puppy can wriggle out of it. The puppy will probably scratch at it frequently, but continue to put it on each day. After a week, the pup should be accustomed to it, and the next step is to place a lead on the collar and allow the pup to trail it behind for a few minutes. It might be a good idea to put

it on just before a meal, then put the meal down across the room; the pup will then walk across the room to eat with the collar and lead on, all the time getting accustomed to the feel of the collar and lead. The next step is to encourage the pup to walk beside the owner. It will probably object strenuously to being led. Do not let the pup get frightened; speak calmly, with a special titbit in your hand (perhaps a sweet biscuit or a piece of liver). Hold the lead and the titbit in the left hand, allowing the pup to smell the titbit. Encourage the pup to follow it. The pup will not realise it is being led – it just reaches out to try to eat a piece of liver. The process is rather like dangling a carrot in front of a donkey. Plenty of praise is important.

To train to stay down, from Sit position, press the Basset gently on the shoulders with the command 'Down!'

Training sessions should be kept relatively short, to maintain the pup's interest as far as possible. The exercise can be repeated a couple of times a day and, if carried out regularly, the pup will quickly become accustomed to the lead. Always keep the pup on the left hand side so that, when you are walking in the direction of on-coming traffic, you will be between your hound puppy and the road. Additionally, if your pup is a potential show dog, it will have to be kept on the left when in the ring so that the judge can see it at all times. If you have an older dog who already walks steadily on the lead it is much easier, as the pup will trot along quite happily with the older dog, not knowing it is on a lead.

Train the puppy to a collar and lead during

For extra control, use a Halti, but with a collar and lead.

the first four to six weeks it is with you. This should take place in the garden so that, when your pup has been fully vaccinated and can be taken outside for short walks, it will be steady on the lead. First walks should never exceed 100m.

Be extremely careful of the fit of the collar when taking the pup out near traffic. Should a pup or even an adult Basset be frightened by something or someone, it will endeavour to get away. In many cases it could probably jerk out of an ordinary collar. I do not advocate a choke chain on a puppy, but prefer a nylon collar that can be adjusted with two buckles. This is inter-linked with a small circle of chain, with a ring onto which the lead can be clipped. If adjusted correctly with buckles, the collar will fit nicely around the pup's neck but, should the puppy pull or try to get away, the collar will tighten, keeping the pup safe on the end of the lead. Also keep the lead at a reasonable length, so that the pup cannot run off the pavement into the gutter or road. I have known of two dogs who were killed while still on the lead because the lead was too long, allowing them to jump out into the road. Another puppy slipped out of his collar, ran into the road and was killed by a car. Very traumatic occurrences for the owners but, with the correct collars and lengths of lead, all three accidents could have been prevented.

A fully mature Basset is a very strong animal. A male who decides to pull can easily assert his authority, even when on a choke chain. I always use a *Halti*: a halter head collar training aid. It is slipped over the head very much like a halter on a horse, and a lead is clipped under the jaw. Used in conjunction with a collar and lead, this enables you to keep the strongest Basset under control.

Training on a Table

It is easier for the owner if a puppy can get used to standing on a table from a very early age. Make it an enjoyable time for the pup; give its coat a good brush, and then rub it over with a square of chamois leather or velvet to get a good shine. Check for any evidence of fleas or any inflamed skin under the front or back legs. Inspect the ears, but do not poke the ear canal of a puppy. If it should have excess wax, put a little Benzyl Benzoate into the ear canal, massage lightly, and then, using cotton wool balls, clear away any visible excess wax. If the pup is obviously in distress, constantly scratching at the ear and holding its head on one side, seek veterinary advice, as it may have a grass seed or some other foreign object in its ear.

Check the nails to see if they need to be clipped. It is easy to clip a pup's nails; just cut off the amount of nail that is in front of the nerve. This is usually just the sharp point.

Examine the teeth, and clean them if necessary. Special dog toothpastes and brushes are available from pet shops and veterinary practices. If this is done regularly it could help dental care in later life.

If the pup is a show prospect, start training it to stand in show pose. If the pup has been bought as a potential show dog, the new owner will probably have been to dog shows and noted how Bassets are shown to accentuate their various good points. Training a Basset to stand can take several weeks, even months. Usually, it will sit down as soon as the front legs are placed correctly; by the time the back legs are placed, the pup will have its front legs stretched out in front of it with its head on them. A most graphic description heard from an exasperated breeder recently when trying to stand his most recent young hopeful was: 'It's like trying to stand a melting ice cream.' But with patience, kindness and firmness, it will eventually click, and the pup will stand in show pose for the delighted owner. Whenever the 'show stance' lesson begins, repeatedly say 'Stand!' to the pup. This is essential for a show dog, as it enables a judge to assess the hound properly.

'No!'

The final lesson I feel a Basset must learn when still a very young puppy is the meaning of 'No'. It can be very funny to see an eight-week-old puppy hanging on to the hem of a skirt, the shoelaces or a trouser leg but, unless it is admonished at this stage, it will wonder why it cannot play the same game when it is a young adult and probably weighing 20–25kg (40–50lb). The pup must be made to realise that certain actions are not allowed. As soon as it attempts to chew at shoelaces or whatever, push it away and say 'No', and the pup's name – for example, 'No, Rover!' Point a finger at the pup when saying 'No' to emphasise the point. It will probably come back several times, but keep repeating the exercise. Finally, if it will not stop, roll up a newspaper loosely and, when it starts again on the shoelaces, give it a light smack. This will make a loud noise, but will startle the pup rather than hurt it. Keep repeating this. When your pup retires to the corner with the sorrowful look only a Basset has, do not run and pick the pup up – give it a couple of minutes to let the lesson sink in, and then instigate a game with a favourite toy. This lesson will probably have to be repeated several times but, eventually, the pup will learn that 'No' means it must stop what it is doing. When it stops being naughty, give it plenty of praise.

Slow Maturing

Always remember that the Basset Hound is a very slow maturing breed, both physically and mentally. Most Basset Hound breeders agree that the terrific growth rate of a Basset, the massive bone and elasticity of muscles and ligaments and the weight compared to body length make the Basset very ungainly. Up to the age of six months, the Basset should never be allowed to jump down steps or stairs, or off the furniture. The pup should not be taken for long walks; just allow it to play in the garden.

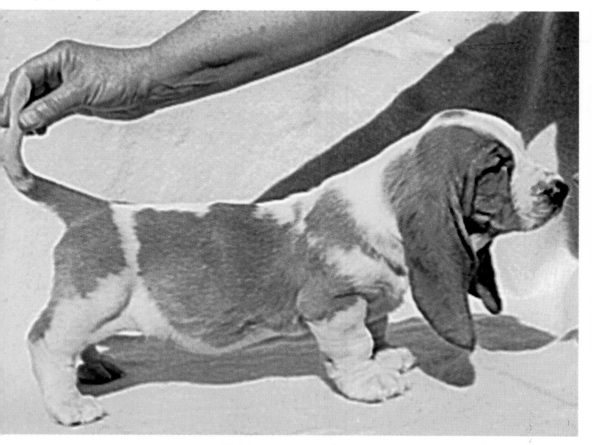

Training a puppy to stand.

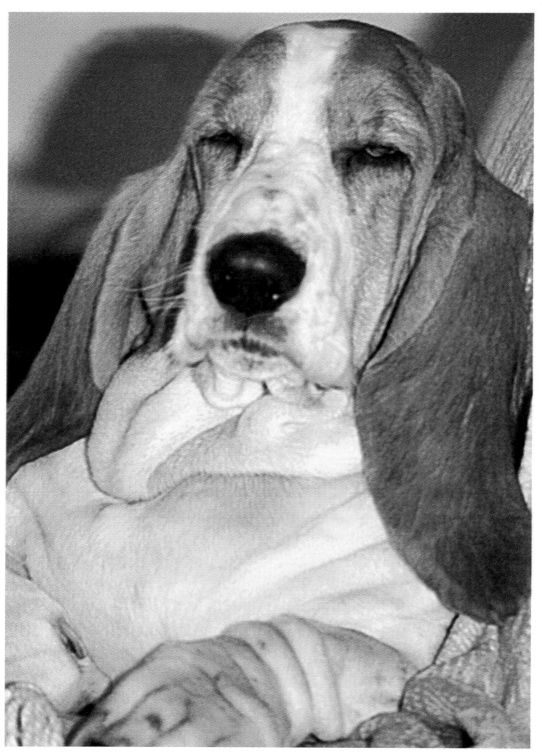

'I'm not really asleep!'

Puppy Training Classes

After the final vaccination, the youngster can be taken to puppy training classes. These are very good places in which to let your puppy socialise with other breeds and to start lead training in earnest. Most cities and towns have local dog societies that run events like dog shows and training classes. You can find out the name and address of the Secretary of your nearest dog club by writing to The Kennel Club (see **Useful Addresses**).

I would not attempt more advanced training than for the basic good manners required in a Basset puppy until it is more than 12 months of age. A puppy would be unlikely to be mentally or physically adjusted to cope with the training necessary for obedience or agility, for example, at less than 12 months.

Mother with five-day-old puppy.

Health and General Care

Basset Hounds have a great deal in common, but each one is an individual, with its own personality, its own particular likes and dislikes and its own unique behavioural quirks. As a result, its precise care and needs are likely to differ from those of other Bassets. Only through practical experience will you become sensitive to your Basset's requirements and adapt to how it should be looked after.

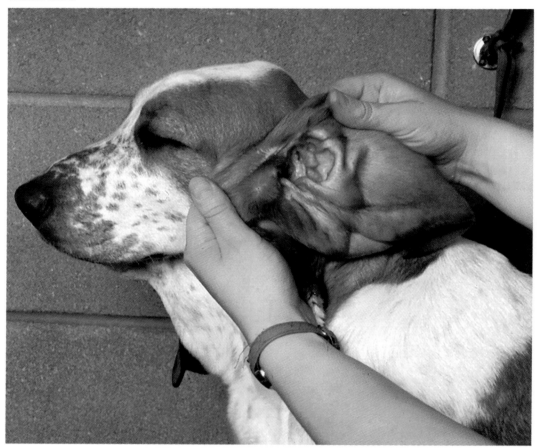

A Basset having its ears examined at the vet's. Photo: Frank Naylor

Insurance

Veterinary expenses can mount up alarmingly if a Basset has to have treatment. It makes sense to take out an insurance policy to help pay the veterinary bills.

Check around the various canine insurance companies. It is better to insure with a company dealing and specialising in animal insurance. All schemes exclude preventive vaccination and most companies have age limits beyond which they will no longer insure. However, there are insurance companies that will insure the Basset for life, provided that it is enrolled when young.

Third party insurance is a social necessity in case your Basset trips up or injures someone quite unintentionally by jumping up and knocking them over.

Nutrition

The nutritional requirements of an adult Basset – or, indeed, any other dog – are many and varied. Preparing a healthy diet is a complex science, and the major pet food manufacturers employ skilled scientists to work out these dietary requirements. It is well known that food is transformed into the living animal: its muscles, nerves, blood-cells, bone, skin, teeth, hair, and so on. Contained in the various foods are vitamins, minerals, carbohydrates, fats and proteins.

Vitamins

Vitamin	Source	Function
E	Wheat germ oil, evening primrose	Reproduction
A	Fish oils, liver, vegetables	Vision and maintenance of skin
D	Cod liver oil, eggs, animal products	Calcium balance and bone growth
K	Green vegetables, and liver	Blood clotting

Water soluble B group vitamins include:

B1 (Thiamin)	Dairy products and cereal	
B2 (Riboflavin)	Milk, animal tissues	
B12	Liver, meat, dairy products	
B6 (Pyridoxine)	Meat, fish, eggs, cereal	
Folic acid	Offal	
Pentothenic acid	Cereals, animal products	
Biotin	Offal, egg yoke	
Choline	Plant and animal materials	

Minerals

Mineral	Source	Function
Calcium	Bones, cheese, milk, white bread	Bone, nerve and muscle formation
Phosphorous	Bones, meat, milk	Bone formation, energy utilisation
Potassium	Green vegetables, bones, cereals	Nerve function, water balance
Iron	Eggs, liver, green vegetables	Part of haemoglobin (oxygen transport)
Copper	Bone, meat	Part of haemoglobin
Zinc	Cereals, meat	Digestion, tissue maintenance
Manganese	Cereal, nuts, tea	Fat metabolism, several enzyme functions
Iodine	Dairy produce, fish	Part of the Thyroid hormone
Cobalt	Milk, organ meat	Part of Vitamin B12
Selenion	Fish, cereal	Associated with Vitamin E function

Carbohydrates

These provide energy, and may be converted into the body fat. They also affect the digestive system.

Fats

Concentrated sources of body fuel. They help in the absorption of certain vitamins and provide the essential fatty acids required for some important body functions.

Proteins

Broken down, proteins provide the body with amino acids. Proteins are vital for repair and growth. They are used by the body to make hormones, and can be turned into fuel and energy.

A seven-week-old broken tri-colour female. Puppies need a special diet to maintain their rapid growth.

Selecting a Prepared Food

As you can see, the provision of all these various components in the correct proportions can be a veritable minefield. For instance, if too much calcium is given, this can result in bone deformities; if too little, rickets can ensue. If too much vitamin D is given, malformation of the bone may result; if too little, night blindness and skin lesions can follow. It is far better to leave it to the experts.

There are four types of prepared food: complete dry food to which water is added, complete dry food nuggets, moist food and semi-moist food. Always read the labels carefully so that you know what ingredients are in the prepared food. Choose whichever is most convenient and most palatable to the Basset. Most quality pet foods are similar in nutritional content.

A premature puppy born by caesarean. It is vital to weigh puppies regularly to make sure they're growing steadily.

When you give your Basset the prepared food, whether it is dry or moist, do not be tempted to slip in extra vitamins or minerals. Prepared food has all the nutrients required, correctly balanced.

Always have fresh water available. Water is one of the elementary nutritional essentials. It flushes the system and helps to regulate the Basset's temperature. Denied water, the Basset will dehydrate and become seriously ill.

Your Basset's dietary requirements will vary throughout its life. Puppies need a special diet to maintain their rapid growth, and a mature, active hound requires more food than an old, sedate one. Beware of obesity: if calorie intake exceeds requirements, the result is an accumulation of fat and body weight gain. Several problems are associated with obesity, including, arthritis, breathing difficulties, diabetes mellites, reproductive problems and shortening of life.

Regular Weighing

To assess weight gain, weigh the pup each week. When the pup is very young, normal kitchen scales can be used but, as it grows older and heavier, the easiest way is to stand on scales yourself, remount the scales holding the puppy, and subtract your own weight, leaving the weight of the pup.

Preventive Care

The owner must make decisions about the Basset's health. Some illnesses and accidents are unavoidable, but preventive health care throughout its life is extremely important. A Basset that is full of life and enjoying food and walks is easy to care for but, when it is depressed, does not wish to eat, and is reluctant to go out, it cannot tell you how it feels. At such times experience, common sense and the veterinary surgeon's scientific knowledge must be relied on.

An adult male broken tri-colour.

Preventive care begins from the moment a Basset puppy enters its new home. Ensure that nothing toxic or harmful can be chewed or licked. The area where the pup's bed is situated must be draught-free and warm. The diet the puppy's breeder has devised for it must be adhered to, and all food dishes and water bowls must be kept scrupulously clean. Always ensure that plenty of clean, fresh water is available.

It is advisable to find out about the local veterinary practices, and then decide on one and register the puppy. The day after the Basset puppy has been brought home, take it to the veterinary surgeon for a health check, and ask when it should have its first vaccination. Prevention is better than cure, so it is essential to have Basset puppies vaccinated against the dreadful diseases mentioned below. Booster doses are given at 12-monthly intervals to maintain immunity.

Two three-month-old puppies, one lemon-and-white and one tri-colour.

Spot the odd one out! Bassets love close contact – and so do Miniature Wire-haired Dachshunds.

Immunisation Against Specific Diseases

Probably the puppy will be vaccinated between 8–12 weeks by means of an injection under the loose skin at the back of its neck. Normally, the Basset pup will not take much notice, being more interested in looking around the surgery. The vaccination will be against distemper (hardpad), leptospirosis, canine hepatitis and parvovirus.

Distemper (Hardpad) This virus infection can be deadly, and there can also be secondary bacterial occurrence. The puppy will be listless, off its food and coughing, and its eyes could be inflamed. It could also be vomiting and have diarrhoea. This infection is nearly always accompanied by a high temperature. The virus is also likely to attack the nervous system and subsequently, should recovery take place, the puppy could have nervous signs, such as twitching, fits, and paralysis. The pads of its feet could thicken, which is why at one time it was thought to be another disease, known as *hardpad*.

Leptospirosis This is a bacterial disease carried by rats. Dogs can be infected from rat urine on the ground or in water bowls. The Basset, by its very nature – nose into everything, sniffing, hunting – could easily pick up this disease from ditches, old farm buildings or river banks, in fact anywhere that rats like to live. The symptoms are constant drinking, high temperature, coated tongue, vomiting and frequent urination, and there can also be abdominal pain and possibly an ulcerated mouth. Jaundice can accompany this disease. The bacteria, *Leptospira*, can be excreted in the urine for many weeks after apparent recovery; this can infect other dogs and humans. The disease is called Weils Disease when contracted by humans.

Canine Infectious Hepatitis Puppies are most susceptible to this, although adults are sometimes affected. The first signs are raised temperature, pale gums, vomiting, diarrhoea and stomach pain. Jaundice also may occur, as the disease affects the liver. A patient recovering from this may show blue colouring over the eyes, but in most cases this will disappear.

Parvovirus This disease first appeared in 1980, and many puppies and older dogs died while a vaccine was being sought to counteract this virus. I lost three puppies in one litter, and they had never been off the premises. This virus can be transmitted by direct or indirect contact. The signs in the puppy are lack of appetite, depression, severe vomiting, profuse diarrhoea (often blood-stained) and dehydration. The patient will either die or recover within five days.

Kennel Cough This disease, like the common cold in humans, is transmitted most easily where there are many dogs under the same roof (for instance, in boarding or breeding kennels, or at dog shows). For this reason, it is wise to have a preventive vaccine if the Basset is to be shown. Although no one single organism is responsible for kennel cough, a vaccine against the bacterium *Bordatella bronchiseptica* has been developed. It is given intra-nasally (dripped into the nostrils). Although an adult Basset with kennel cough may also have tonsillitis, it will probably remain fairly cheerful and retain its appetite, but in a very old dog or a puppy there could be complications like secondary pneumonia, which can cause death.

Rabies This most deadly viral disease, associated with dogs and certain other animals, can be transmitted to humans, not only through a bite, but also through saliva from an infected animal

Enjoying a tug o' war with a Plaque Attacker Dental Floss from Nylabone. Photo: Frank Naylor

entering an open wound, for instance a cut on the hand. At present the United Kingdom is rabies free, and animals entering the country have to undergo six months' quarantine in a licensed kennel. In Europe, dogs are protected from rabies by vaccination, but this is not permitted in the United Kingdom except for dogs being exported or arriving in quarantine.

Grooming and Checking

A Basset Hound is easy to groom. Put aside 10 minutes a day to comb out dead undercoat, using a comb with round-ended teeth, and then give a good brushing, at the same time checking for any problems. Check the ear leathers for any sign of swelling or cuts, ensuring that the ear canal is free from bad odour. Inspect the eyes, making sure that they are clear and bright and that there is no discharge or clouding over the cornea. Make sure that your hound's nails are trimmed to a reasonable length and that there is no inflammation in the nail bed. See that its teeth are clean and free from tartar and that the gums are pink and healthy with no inflammation. Check the skin and coat, looking for evidence of excessive scratching, in case your hound has picked up a flea or a tick, and also feel for warts or lumps under the skin.

Specific Checks for Females Look for signs of swelling of the vulva and loss of a small amount of blood; these are indications that she is in season. For the three months after her season, if she has not been mated, monitor her for a false pregnancy. Check for the presence of milk by gently squeezing the teats. If she builds up excessive milk, beware of mastitis. In this case, the mammary glands will become enlarged, hard and very inflamed, and veterinary treatment must be sought at once. Also ensure that she does not have a putrid discharge from the vulva, as this may indicate an open pyometra. Monitor her drinking in these three months. If she has excessive thirst and seems off colour, seek veterinary advice; it could be an enclosed pyometra building up. Pyometra occurs when the uterus becomes filled with an accumulation of fluid that could contain bacteria. It is potentially life-threatening, and the vet will probably perform an ovarian hysterectomy (spay her).

Specific Checks for Males With a male, check his testicles to ensure they remain the same size. If one testicle starts to enlarge, seek veterinary advice; he may have developed testicular cancer.

Controlling the Oestrous Cycle

If a Basset bitch is to be shown, she should not be spayed unless the vet considers it necessary for her health. The Kennel Club must be informed by the owner, and a letter from the vet stating the reason for the operation must be forwarded to them. The Kennel Club, in genuine cases, will issue a certificate for exhibitors to carry and show to judges, if required. The notification of the operation and permission to show will be published in *The Kennel Gazette*. Spaying removes the risk of pyometra and false pregnancy.

The Basset bitch can have her season controlled by modern chemical methods. She can have her season suppressed by a course of tablets or an injection from the vet. This can stop her season but, should a litter be wanted at a later date, she can be mated when she comes into season in her normal six-to-nine-month cycle.

Hereditary problems

Eye Defects

Testing for eye defects such as Progressive Retinal Atrophy (PRA), primary glaucoma and hereditary cataract is advised. Basset eyes can be tested and checked at 12 months by a specialist on the British Veterinary Association/Kennel Club/International Sheep Dog Society Panel for these defects. The specialist checks the whole eye and comments on any problem that may be present. This information will be given to The Kennel Club and will appear on the dog's registration.

Primary Glaucoma This term relates to a large group of ocular disorders. The most common is an abnormal rise in the internal fluid, causing pressure on the eye and resulting in damage to the retina and optic nerve, affecting the sight. It can be extremely painful and requires immediate veterinary treatment.

PRA This is an irreversible blindness in dogs as a result of retinal degeneration, and occurs because of the presence of certain recessive genes. I have never seen or heard of a Basset with PRA, but we must not be complacent.

Hereditary Cataract Cataract is the clouding of the lens of the eye, and it can be hereditary. Again, I have never heard of hereditary cataract in Basset Hounds. Non-hereditary cataracts are sometimes seen in elderly Bassets.

Entropion This is a condition in which the eyelids turn in, so that the eyelashes are resting on the corneal surface, causing irritation and discomfort. Treatment will depend on the severity of the condition and the distress of the animal, but surgical correction of the deformity may be the only answer – your vet will advise you. Again, if it is a show dog, The Kennel Club has to be informed.

Ectropion This condition, commonly called 'red eye', is the turning out of the lower lid, with the exposure of the inner conjunctiva. Again, depending on the severity and your vet's advice, surgical correction may be the answer. If so, The Kennel Club has to be informed if the patient is a show dog.

Hip Dysplasia (HD)

In this condition the head of the femur or main thigh bone is abnormal and does not fit properly into the hip socket. The first symptoms of HD are a reluctance to rise from the sitting position and an unsteady gait, first noticed when the pup is four to six months old. There are varying degrees of dysplasia. Some are slight, and the dogs may live their lifespan without surgery; the more severe cases may respond to orthopaedic surgery. In all cases, the diagnosis and treatment must rest entirely in the hands of your vet.

Umbilical Hernia

An umbilical hernia is a part of an abdominal organ or a pad of fat protruding through an incompletely-closed umbilical ring. A small umbilical hernia may disappear as the pup grows. If it is large, a relatively simple operation can be performed by the vet to correct it. Should this operation occur, The Kennel Club must be informed, as the Basset will no longer be eligible to enter at Kennel Club licensed shows. Umbilical hernia can be hereditary.

Parasites

External Parasites

Fleas These parasites breed, and can live part of their life cycles, away from the dog's body. Eggs are laid in carpets or the Basset's bedding and develop through larvae stage into a flea within three weeks. With central heating, the house can be kept warm all the year round, so the flea can be a constant problem.

A Basset can be affected with fleas at any age. Repeated scratching and biting will indicate the unwelcome visitors, in some cases the Basset is so irritated that it will break the skin, endeavouring to rid itself of the problem. A most reliable way to check for fleas is to run a flea comb through its coat; the fleas tend to gather around the base of the stern. If fleas are detected there are a variety of products on the market, both to bath and spray the Basset with. Be sure to treat the bedding and any area where the flea eggs and larvae could be.

Lice There are two species of lice:

* *Linognathus setosus* suck the fluid through the skin and usually remain anchored to one place.
* *Trichodectes canis* move around more and bite intermittently.

Lice lay eggs that stick to the hair, and these egg cases are known as *nits*. Lice and nits are easily eradicated by means of special medicated shampoos, available from the veterinary practice.

Ticks Ticks can be picked up in areas where sheep and deer are abundant. The tick transfers itself to the Basset and anchors onto its host's skin by means of its mouth part. It then sucks its host's blood and, when fully distended, drops off. To remove a tick, cover it with petroleum jelly. This will block its breathing pore and make it drop off. Surgical spirit dabbed on has the same effect. Never try to remove a tick by pulling with tweezers, as this will make it break, leaving the mouth part in the skin, which can then result in a localised infection.

Cheyletiella (Mange) Mites These cannot be seen by the human eye, but live on the surface of their host, feeding on tissue fluid. They lay eggs similar to lice. The presence of these mites should be suspected if the Basset is constantly scratching and appears to have scurf or dandruff. Stand the Basset on a sheet of black polyurethene, comb some of the 'dandruff' onto the plastic and then, with a magnifying glass, watch to see if the dandruff moves. If it does, remember that the common name for this mite is 'walking dandruff' and request the appropriate medicated shampoo from your vet. Like fleas, cheyletiella mites can live away from the host, so all carpets and bedding should be thoroughly cleaned. They can also transfer to humans, causing immense localised irritation.

Harvest Mites The so-called 'harvest mite' is not really a mite, but a parasitic larva that burrows under the skin, producing an inflamed spot. Sometimes during the summer the Basset may pick up it up between the toes. The Basset will then bite and lick its feet constantly. Treatment is available from the veterinary surgery for this problem..

Scabies Sarcoptic mange (scabies) can cause very irritating skin lesions on legs, face and ears. The mite burrows into the surface layer of the skin and lays eggs, which keep hatching. Skin scrapings will identify the particular mite to the vet, who will advise on the appropriate medication, which is usually a course of medicated baths.

Demodectic Mange A much more serious type than Sarcoptic, because the parasite buries itself deep into the skin and usually takes a powerful bacterium called *Staphylococcus* with it. It is the bacterium that causes the characteristic lesions, especially around the eyes, nose and feet, with the characteristic odour. It may not be so itchy as scabies, but this mite can be transferred from bitch to puppies. Long and protracted veterinary treatment is necessary to eradicate this type of mange.

Internal parasites

Roundworms The many types of roundworm include heartworms, hookworms, ascarids, whipworms, and lungworms. Most common in the United Kingdom is *Toxocara canis*. These worms are creamy-coloured and can grow up to 15cm (6in) long, looking like pieces of string.

Most newborn puppies have *Toxocara canis* growing in their intestines, despite the dam having a worming programme prior to mating. The puppies gain the infection before birth, as the larvae can move across the placental barrier. By the age of three weeks a puppy can have egg-laying worms in its intestine. The adult worm can produce thousands of eggs a day, which pass through the pup and out in its faeces. These eggs remain alive for up to three years. Many adult dogs have dormant worms in their tissue and, in a pregnant bitch, these worms become active again. At approximately the sixth week they migrate into the young foetus. A puppy should be wormed at three weeks, then every two weeks until it is about twelve weeks of age, and then every three months until adult. Adult Bassets should be wormed twice yearly.

Unfortunately, *Toxocara canis* can infect humans. Eggs picked up on the hand and transferred to the mouth can hatch in the intestine. Serious effects are rare, in fact in the United Kingdom only two persons in a million have been recorded as having Toxocara-induced illness. Cleanliness and basic hygiene must be adhered to by children and adults, especially when handling anything that has been in contact with the ground. When exercising a Basset, always have a plastic bag to clean up where he has defecated.

Tapeworms These worms are different in shape and length from *Toxocara canis*. A tapeworm *(Dipylidium caninum)* consists of segments and can grow more than a metre long. They are white and flat and look like a long piece of narrow ribbon. Flea larvae eat tapeworm eggs, the larva develops in a flea, and the flea hops onto a dog who, in an effort to remove the flea, may swallow it; thus the immature tapeworms are put back into the intestine. Unless the Basset is heavily infected with tapeworm it may seem perfectly healthy. The first signs may be segments wriggling on the hair near the anus. There are special medications on the market, or from the veterinary surgery, to deal with these parasites.

Other Health Problems

It may be thought that, because of its shape, loose skin, long ear leathers and long back, the Basset could be subject to a multitude of health problems. Nothing is further from the truth. Provided that its vaccinations and boosters are kept up to date and it is groomed, fed on a good diet, has adequate exercise, a good place to sleep undisturbed, and plenty of companionship, the Basset should remain a remarkably healthy hound. However, various problems can occur in its lifetime. Since there are many books on the market specialising in canine medicine, I will not try to deal with everything that could happen, but will list a few of the more common problems.

Bloat

The first symptom is that the Basset's stomach rapidly enlarges and the skin becomes as tight as a drum. The Basset is in great pain and distress, trying to be sick but only able to bring up frothy saliva. If torsion (twisting of the stomach) has taken place, it will block both the entrance from the throat and exit to the small intestine. The stomach is full of fermenting food and gas. When this happens, it is a **veterinary emergency**. Take the Basset to the surgery immediately, having first informed the vet so that he or she is ready either to operate or to release the gas by means of a tube. I must stress that the quicker the Basset is seen by a vet, the higher its chance of survival: this condition can be fatal in a very short time.

No definite cause of bloat has been established, but suggestions have included exercise after feeding, excess drinking of water after a meal, and dried food. However, no-one has yet pinpointed the real reason for this distressing problem. Many Basset breeders give their hounds two small meals a day instead of one large meal, hoping to prevent this syndrome. Also, charcoal granules can be obtained to sprinkle over the food; these help to absorb gas.

Cervical Spondylo-myelopathy (Wobbler Syndrome)

In simple terms, the spinal cord is compressed by the vertebrae in the cervical region. The signs, in an affected animal, are usually related to the hindlegs. The puppy has difficulty in getting up and turning, and has a characteristically wobbly and swaying gait. This problem can sometimes be corrected by surgery. The cause is thought to be related to breed conformation coupled with incorrect feeding during the early formative months: over-eating or excess of calcium could be contributory factors.

Cleaning up the beach. Outdoor exercise is beneficial to all adult Bassets, but keep an eye on what they pick up!
Photo: C Millard

Un-united Anconeal Process

This is usually characterised by lameness in the front leg at around the age of five months. An X-ray will show that a small piece of bone in the elbow joint, the anconeal process, has not fused correctly to the ulna. The vet will operate to remove this piece of bone, which will relieve the pain.

Bladder Stones

Calculi are stones in the bladder that can irritate and cause cystitis. The indications will be blood in the urine and frequent urination. These stones must be removed surgically to relieve the pain.

Juvenile Pyoderma

This usually affects a puppy around the age of three to five weeks. Characteristically, the ear leathers appear to swell and the ear canals are moist. If it is not treated with medication, the muzzle will swell and an abscess appear. It is caused by a *Staphylococcus* bacterium, but will respond to antibiotics if caught in the early stages.

Haematoma

Sometimes through constant shaking of the head or a knock, a Basset will rupture blood vessels in

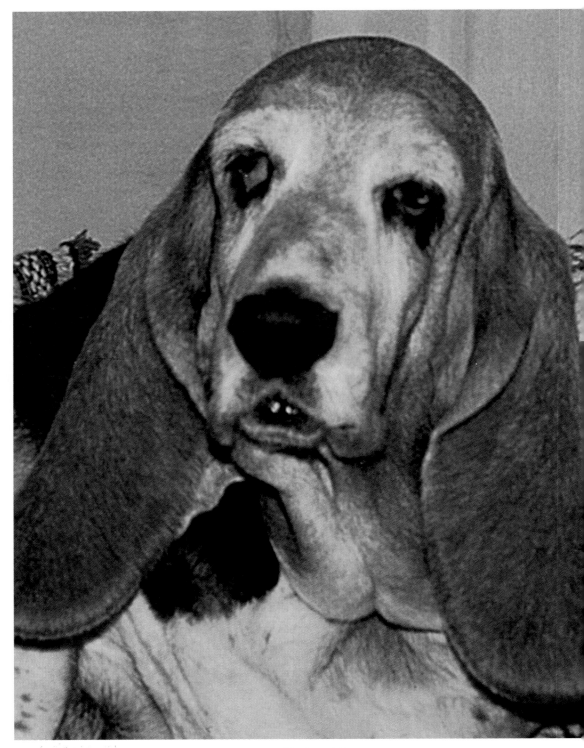

Brackenacre Zinnia aged 13 years.

an ear leather. This will cause a blood-filled swelling. If this swelling is left untreated, the blood clot will be replaced by scar tissue and pull the ear leather out of shape. The vet can operate under anaesthetic to cut the swelling and drain the blood, bringing the ear leather back to its normal shape.

Wasp/Bee Sting

Very rapid soft swelling can be dangerous if it is in the mouth. Check for a sting (a bee will leave its sting behind). Remove the sting and bathe the area with bicarbonate of soda solution. If there is no sting, assume it was a wasp, and bathe the area with vinegar. A bee sting is acidic, a wasp alkaline. If your Basset is in great discomfort or the swelling is in the mouth, seek veterinary attention, and your Basset will probably be given an antihistamine injection.

The Basset in Old Age

I have always maintained that, the older the Basset is, the more character it develops. After a number of years with a family it will interpret every action and comprehend many spoken words.

After years of devotion, it is only fair to endeavour to make your Basset's autumn years comfortable and happy. If it has been a kennel dog for most of its life, perhaps a place indoors could be arranged. However, I know that some kennel Bassets are happier in their kennel with their own particular companions. If this is the case, ensure that the kennel is warm in the winter and cool in the summer, with ample shade for your old friend to relax in. Perhaps provide a soft mattress for the Basset to lie on.

An elderly Basset can be compared to an elderly person. Both slow down as old age approaches. The hair around the Basset's muzzle will turn grey, its hearing becomes less acute and its eyesight a little dimmer. It does not enjoy chasing after balls any more, and its heart may not be so strong. Females should not be allowed to have puppies; in fact, it is against Kennel Club regulations to mate a bitch over eight years of age. If a few teeth have been lost over the years, give it softer food to eat. Ensure that the teeth are kept free of tartar as much as possible. Maintain a healthy diet for the older Basset; several specially compiled 'all in one' foods for the elderly dog are now on the market.

Elderly Bassets become creatures of habit and do not like their routine to be disturbed. They like their meals to be on time, their favourite armchair to be vacant, a thick rug in front of a fire when it is cold, and a cool place when it is hot.

Any unexpected lumps must be viewed with suspicion, particularly in the mammary glands of bitches. These are the most common tumours, and early diagnosis is vital to ensure successful treatment. Arthritis is another ailment that can make the old Basset's life a misery and, as many people know, it is painful. Medication from the vet can help relieve the pain. Unfortunately, as senility creeps in, so may incontinence.

Eventually, when quality of life is very poor, euthanasia is the last great service that can be performed. For my Bassets, the vet is always called to the house for the final injection. Over the years, all of my Bassets have visited the veterinary surgery, and most have disliked the experience. I find that the last act of kindness I can extend to an old and trusted friend is to allow them the comfort of their favourite armchair at the end.

Many people worry about the disposal of the body. Discuss this with the vet, as many practices are in touch with dog crematoriums and will even contact them to arrange for the cremation.

The Beginning of Dog Shows

The earliest recorded exhibition of dogs was held in the bar of a public house in London. The show was named *A Fancy dog show* and was organised by a well-known character, Charles Ainstrop. The first specialist show, for Pugs, took place on 30 May 1850, and the first organised dog show for a variety of breeds was held at Newcastle-Upon-Tyne on 28–29 June 1859.

In 1860, the Birmingham Dog Show Society held their first exhibition at Cheapside, Birmingham. This was the first general dog show ever held. Dog shows were now becoming more popular: Leeds, Birmingham and Manchester were holding shows, and more were being held in London.

Until 1873, no dogs were registered and many bad practices were creeping in. For instance, mongrels were shown in classes for the breeds they most closely resembled, and high prices were being asked for them.

It was therefore decided to form The Kennel Club in April 1873. Rules and regulations were drawn up and Mr Shirley, MP, of Ettington, organiser of several excellent shows at the Crystal Palace, was elected Chairman.

The Kennel Club Stud Book was finally issued in 1874, after much research had been completed by Mr Frank C S Pearce to complete the entries and pedigrees. This stud book was an immediate success, and has continued to be issued annually.

The Purpose of Showing

The purpose of showing a Basset, apart from to satisfy the natural competitive streak in most people, is to allow a judge knowledgeable in the breed to compare and assess hounds in various classes, according to their age and previous wins, in order to pick the best. That Basset, in the judge's opinion, most closely adheres to the Breed Standard. The top five Bassets in each class are placed in order of merit, First to Very Highly Commended, and finally The Kennel Club Challenge

BORDER UNION AGRICULTURAL SOCIETY

Canine Section

KENNEL CLUB AWARD CARD FOR

BEST OF BREED

19 June 1993

Breed ___*Basset Hounds*___ Sex __Bitch__

Name of Exhibit __Brackenacre My April Fool__

Signed __R. J. Price__

Judge

The Big Card that everyone covets: Best Of Breed (BOB).

Certificate (CC) for Best of Sex from the class winners is awarded. Bassets who win three coveted CCs under three different judges, subject to Kennel Club approval, are endorsed as *champions*. Breeding from champions gives a much higher chance of breeding quality offspring, thus perpetuating top-class Basset Hounds.

Attending shows enables a novice exhibitor to look at his or her Basset in a really critical way, acknowledging its faults and virtues and, from this experience, to know what type of Basset must be obtained or bred for success in the show ring.

The Art of Showing

The art of showing is presenting a Basset as close to the Breed Standard as possible, in the peak of condition, trained to stand and move with its handler to show off its good points and enable the judge to assess and compare it with all the other exhibits in the class.

Showing and judging outside: the Hound Show, 1994. Judge: Miss Wendy Thomas.

Showing can become an obsessive pastime, albeit a very expensive one. It breaks down all social barriers, and leads exhibitors to travel many hundreds of miles every year. Lifelong friends can be made through exhibiting. An exhibitor must have the temperament to take the bad times with the good. No one Basset can win every time; conversely, a well-constructed Basset will not lose all the time. However, it can be very frustrating to a novice owner to see the same breeders winning time and time again with different Bassets. If the novice owner was to step back and view these breeders and their Bassets with an objective eye, he or she would see that these breeders are producing Bassets of a similar stamp and showing only top-quality hounds in the peak of condition. Such breeders are also expert at exhibiting hounds to advantage.

Types of Show

All the under mentioned must be Kennel Club approved and licensed. Dogs competing should not have been exposed to the risk of any contagious or infectious disease during the period of 21 days prior to the show. All dogs exhibited must be over six months old.

Except in exemption shows, all dogs exhibited must be registered with The Kennel Club.

At matches, exemption shows and limited shows, no dog who has an award towards being a champion is eligible to exhibit.

Match

A match is a form of competition in which the dogs are judged in pairs, one against the other, in an elimination process. All exhibitors at matches should be members of the canine society running the match. The entries are made at the time of the match.

Exemption Show

An exemption show is licensed for the purpose of raising money on behalf of charities. Classes for pedigree dogs are confined to four, but in addition there can be several fun classes; for example, *Dog with Most Appealing Eyes*, or *Dog The Judge Would Most Like To Take Home*. These shows are usually held in the summer in conjunction with fêtes.

Limit Show

The entry is limited to members of the show society. A schedule will be issued with an entry form, and entries close several weeks before the show. There could be two or three judges, according to the number of classes. Usually there are a few breed classes, and then some variety classes.

Open Show

These shows are open to all exhibitors and, depending on the number of classes, they may be benched. Sometimes open shows cover two days. More judges and breed classes are usually scheduled for an open show than for the other types. An entry form and schedule will be available from the club holding the show, with entries closing several weeks prior to the first day.

Championship Show

These shows are open to all, unless the organising society impose restrictions. The Kennel Club, for instance, controls entry to Crufts. The only difference between open shows and championship shows is that Kennel Club Challenge Certificates (CCs) are on offer at championship shows. Most championship shows have approximately 12 classes for each breed, divided into 6 for each sex. A breed specialist will probably judge the breed. Championship shows can last two, three or four days. The cost of an entry at a championship show is much higher than at an open show because of high overhead costs. At time of going to press, the average cost of first entry to a championship show where CCs are on offer is approximately £16, with a second costing a further £2.

Breed Club Show

These are confined to the breed represented by the club holding the show and can be at limited, open or championship show level.

Definition of Classes

Qualifying Wins

In estimating the number of awards, all wins up to and including the seventh day before the date of closing of entries shall be counted when entering for any class.

Wins in variety classes do not count for entry in breed classes, but when entering for variety classes, wins in both breed and variety classes must be counted. A first prize does not include a special prize of whatever value.

In the following definitions, *C/O* applies to championship and open only and *L* applies to limited shows only. Where there is no qualification, the definition applies to all types of show.

Showing and judging inside: Crufts 1997. The judge is Mrs Jean Elliott-Jones.

Classes

Minor Puppy For dogs of six and not exceeding nine calendar months of age on the first day of the show.

Puppy For dogs of six and not exceeding twelve calendar months of age on the first day of the show.

Junior For dogs of six and not exceeding eighteen calendar months of age on the first day of the show.

Beginners *C/O:* For owner, handler or exhibit who has not won a first prize at a championship or open show. *L:* For owner, handler or exhibit who has not won a first prize at any show.

Maiden *C/O:* For dogs that have not won a CC or first prize at an open or championship show (minor puppy, special minor puppy, puppy and special puppy classes excepted, whether restricted or not). *L:* For dogs that have not won a first prize at any show (minor puppy, special minor puppy, puppy and special puppy classes excepted whether restricted or not).

Novice *C/O:* For dogs that have not won a CC or three or more first prizes at open or championship shows (minor puppy, special minor puppy, puppy and special puppy classes excepted, whether restricted or not). *L:* For dogs that have not won three or more first prizes at any show (minor puppy, special minor puppy, puppy and special puppy classes excepted, whether restricted or not).

Tyro *C/O:* For dogs that have not won a CC or five or more first prizes at open or championship shows (minor puppy, special minor puppy, puppy and special puppy classes excepted, whether restricted or not. *L:* For dogs that have not won five or more first prizes at any show (minor puppy, special minor puppy, puppy and special puppy classes excepted, whether restricted or not).

Debutant *C/O:* For dogs that have not won a CC or a first prize at a championship show (minor puppy, special minor puppy, puppy and special puppy classes excepted, whether restricted or not). *L:* For dogs that have not won a first prize at an open or championship show (minor puppy, special minor puppy, puppy and special puppy classes excepted, whether restricted or not).

Undergraduate *C/O:* For dogs that have not won a CC or three or more first prizes at championship shows (minor puppy, special minor puppy, puppy and special puppy classes excepted, whether restricted or not). *L:* For dogs that have not won three or more first prizes at open or championship shows (minor puppy, special minor puppy, puppy and special puppy classes excepted, whether restricted or not).

Graduate *C/O:* For dogs that have not won a CC or four or more first prizes at championship shows in graduate, post graduate, minor limit, mid limit, limit and open classes, whether restricted or not. *L:* For dogs that have not won four or more first prizes at open or championship shows in graduate, post graduate, minor limit, mid limit, limit and open classes, whether restricted or not.

Post Graduate *C/O:* For dogs that have not won a CC or five or more first prizes at championship shows in post graduate, minor limit, mid limit, limit, and open classes, whether restricted or not. *L:* For dogs that have not won five or more first prizes at championship and open shows in post graduate, minor limit, mid limit, limit and open classes, whether restricted or not.

Minor Limit *C/O:* For dogs that have not won two CCs or three or more first prizes in all at championship shows in mid limit, limit and open classes, confined to the breed, whether restricted or not, at shows where CCs were offered for the breed. *L:* For dogs that have not won three or more first prizes in all at open and championship shows in minor limit, mid limit, limit and open classes, confined to the breed, whether restricted or not.

Mid Limit *C/O:* For dogs that have not won three CCs or five or more first prizes in all at championship shows in mid limit, limit and open classes, confined to the breed, whether restricted or not, at shows where CCs were offered for the breed. *L:* For dogs that have not won five or more first prizes in all at open or championship shows in mid limit and open classes, confined to the breed, whether restricted or not.

Limit *C/O:* For dogs that have not won three CCs under three different judges or seven or more first prizes in all at championship shows in limit and open classes, confined to the breed, whether restricted or not, at shows where CCs were on offer for the breed. *L:* For dogs that have not won seven or more first prizes in all at open and championship shows in limit and open classes, confined to the breed, whether restricted or not.

Open For all dogs of the breeds for which the class is provided that are eligible for entry at the show.

Veteran For dogs of not less than seven years of age on the first day of the show.

Champion For dogs that have been confirmed as champion, show champion or field trial champion. Champion classes may not be scheduled for individual breeds or varieties of breeds.

Rare Breeds Confined to those breeds not granted CCs in the current year, with the exception of breeds whose registration is confined to the Imported Register.

Field Trial For dogs that have won prizes, Diplomas of Merit or Certificates of Merit in actual competition at a field trial held under Kennel Club or Irish Kennel Club field trial regulations.

Working Trial For dogs that have won prizes in competition at a Bloodhound working trial and Kennel Club licensed working trials held under Kennel Club regulations.

Stud Dog For stud dogs and at least two progeny, of which only the progeny have to be entered and exhibited in a breed class at the show.

Brood Bitch For brood bitches and at least two progeny, of which only the progeny have to be entered and exhibited in a breed class at the show.

Progeny For a dog or bitch, accompanied by at least three of its registered progeny. The dog or bitch does not necessarily have to be entered in another class, but all progeny must have been entered and exhibited in another class. The dog or bitch and the progeny need not be registered in the same ownership.

Brace For two exhibits (either sex or mixed) of one breed belonging to the same exhibitor, each exhibit having been entered in some class other than brace or team.

Team For three or more exhibits (either sex or mixed) of one breed belonging to the same exhibitor, each exhibit having been entered in some class other than brace or team.

Breeder For dogs bred by the exhibitor.

Imported Register For breeds whose registration is confined to the Imported Register, and which consequently may only be entered in this class and where an Interim Breed Standard has been approved by The Kennel Club.

Any Variety Not Separately Classified For breeds of dog for which no separate breed classes are scheduled.

Kennel Club Junior Organisation Stakes For Any Variety dog or bitch exhibited and handled by a member of The Kennel Club Junior Organisation and registered, either solely or jointly, in member's name or in the name of a member of the family, resident at the member's address.

Not for Competition Societies may at their discretion, accept Not for Competition entries. Societies may accept such entries from breeds of dogs not included within the title of the Society and at shows held over more than one day, such entries may be accepted on any day from any breed.

The Show Basset

Registration
Bassets intended for exhibition at dog shows must be registered by The Kennel Club. If the litter has been bred by the exhibitor, no doubt the whole litter has been registered a few days after birth.

When a puppy is sold, the registration certificate is given to the new owner, who should complete the back of the certificate and send it with the fee to The Kennel Club to have the puppy transferred into the new owner's name. The pup becomes eligible for showing at six months.

Should a puppy over six months, or an adult, be entered for a show prior to the transfer arriving from The Kennel Club, the new owner must write *TAF (Transfer Applied For)* after the Basset's name on the entry form.

Show Potential
If an eight-week-old Basset puppy has been bought with 'show potential', Lady Luck must still be on the side of the purchaser. Although the sire and dam may be show winners with many champions in their pedigrees, this does not guarantee the pup will be a good show hound. It will certainly have a far higher chance of inheriting quality because of its background but, between the age of three months and eight months, either it will improve considerably or faults will appear that will ruin it for the show ring.

If the puppy does not make the grade, the breeder really cannot be condemned. When selling an eight-week-old pup, the breeder can only point out the most promising pups in the litter. After the puppy leaves the breeder, it is entirely up to the new owner to carry out the breeder's instructions in detail. If the breeder has kept a puppy from the litter and, when the two puppies are compared six months later, the breeder's is larger, has more bone, and so on, do not think the breeder knew he or she was keeping the best. Most probably the one retained had no stress placed upon it, was kept on a routine diet, allowed the correct amount of exercise, had other Bassets around to compete for food, and so maintained a healthy appetite, and, above all, benefited from the long experience of the breeder.

It is quite likely that the pup the new owner bought had no competition for food and so became a picky eater, not really maintaining the food intake to give the good bone essential for a show Basset. Maybe the owner thought the breeder a bit paranoid about exercise, so had been over exercising the pup. Many factors could have taken place during the period the pup had been with the new owner – it may even have had an illness, which would have pegged back the pup's growth. There could be many reasons for the difference between the two puppies. There is no gratification for the breeder in selling a promising puppy, only to see it looking like a weed six months later. It is far more satisfactory for the breeder to see the pup blossom into a really beautiful show quality exhibit, maybe competing with his or her own pup and sometimes beating it in the show ring. Many novice owners cannot believe this but, rest assured, it is true.

Off to a good start: Brackenacre Yolanda winning Best Puppy in Breed at Crufts 1997.
Photo: J Clark

Show Training

Training a puppy for show should begin at an early age, eight weeks or even younger, beginning with the basic show stance. It is a good idea to practise this in front of a large mirror, so that you can see how the overall picture of Basset and handler appears to the judge. The Basset must be taught to walk at a controlled pace on the left hand side of the handler. If the pup tends to 'crab', that is, to walk with its hind legs out of sequence with its front legs, its body at an angle instead of straight, walk the pup very close to a wall or fence. This will help to train it to walk straight.

None of this training must subdue the pup's spirit. It should be a fun time, with much praise, so that, when the pup eventually enters the show ring, it will be full of confidence and enjoying itself.

It is sensible to get the pup used to a car when it is very young, prior to its vaccinations. If the youngster develops into a good show dog, hundreds of miles will be travelled by car to various shows all over the country, so the pup must learn from an early age to relax and sleep on a journey. A Basset who is being sick constantly on a journey can lose body condition and become dehydrated. Herbal car sickness tablets for dogs can help, but it is far better to have the pup trained to relax with the motion of the car.

Show Training and Sensitivity

Intelligence varies in Basset Hounds just as much as it does in humans. The ability to learn and to perform is limited by intelligence. Various facts such as sensitivity, aggression, stubbornness and willingness make each Basset an individual to train. In my own kennel, sensitivity and intelligence vary considerably between the hounds. The most sensitive bitch reacts instantly to a harsh word, whereas the dominant male virtually dares you to make him do what you want. Therefore, I have had to use different methods to train these hounds, being very gentle with the bitch and more domineering with the male. It is up to the owner training the Basset for show to decide how far to go in praising or scolding the youngster. Basset puppies are full of fun and nothing is further from their minds than to stand perfectly still for a few moments while their heads are held up and then their sterns held aloft. It may seem to the owner that the pup is being deliberately obstinate. The trick is short sessions, two or three times a day, rather than one long session of training. If tempers are rising, forget it for a while, have a cup of tea, and try again an hour later.

Basset Stance

Most breeds are handled in a manner that shows their various good points to advantage and conveys to the judge an impression of correct balance. A Basset is *set up* (presented to the judge to be assessed) in the following way. The handler holds the Basset in the standing position, ensuring that the front legs and feet and hind legs and feet are placed so that the body automatically assumes the correct balance and presents a pleasing outline to the judge. Front legs should be placed well under the body, with the feet beneath the lowest part of the ribs and parallel with each other. The elbows should rest easily alongside the rib cage. The hind legs are placed to show the bend of stifle, and the hind feet so placed that the legs between the hock joints and feet are perpendicular. The head is held up to show the arched neck and, in profile, the occiput, depth of lip and fine curling leathers. Take care not to detract from the dewlap, lip, or wrinkling by inadvertently holding the muzzle too tightly. Lift your hound's stern and hold it in the natural scimitar fashion. If the hound is well balanced and trained it will stand easily, as no one particular joint or muscle is being pulled or strained.

Keeping the Head Up

The Basset, being a hunting dog, finds the ground incredibly interesting; various scents must be wafting up all the time, especially if the show ring has been used by other breeds before the Bassets. The natural instinct will be to lower its head to inhale all these scents. I think stallion hounds are worse than females for this trait. Unfortunately, it can be most disconcerting for a judge trying to ascertain the front movement of a Basset to find the whole front assembly hidden by the exhibit's head and neck as it sniffs the ground. A head held well up, complemented by a long arched neck and a raised, scimitar-shaped stern, immediately alters the whole picture. It gives the Basset an air of elegance and keenness.

It is very difficult to train a Basset to walk with its head up all the time; it just goes against all natural instincts. However, the exhibit is only required to do this for a relatively short period while the judge is assessing its movement and style in the show ring.

When training the youngster to hold its head up, bait it with titbits. A piece of cheese, or liver that has been dried out in the oven or microwave, is an effective way of keeping its nose away from the ground. Hold liver or cheese and the lead in the left hand and, while moving the Basset, hold the left hand in front, but close enough to its head for it to locate the smell. The knack is to keep the head up without the hound jumping up to get the liver. After much patience and training the Basset will walk freely and naturally with its head held proudly. When using bait in the show ring, make sure you do not impede your fellow exhibitors' chances by attracting their exhibits.

I have also found that, on a dominant male, a Halti head collar is very good; each time he lowers his head, lift it up with the Halti and repeat the command, 'Head up'. I have never had to use a Halti on a female. In my experience, bitch hounds are far more biddable.

Presentation of a Show Dog

Presentation is extremely important for a show dog, bearing in mind that a dog show is a beauty show for dogs. The Kennel Clubs rules and regulations should be observed in connection with the preparation. These are far too lengthy to reiterate here but include directions that there should be no artificial colouring, no operation which could deceive, no chalk or whitener to remain in the coat, no lacquer, no re-setting of teeth, and so on.

Grooming

Fortunately, the Basset is a very easy animal to prepare for a show, provided that it is in good health. I normally bath my Bassets 24 hours before a show, making sure the shampoo is rinsed out of the coat thoroughly. Combing through the coat with a round-tooth comb removes old hair and helps to smooth the coat. Brushing every day with a hound glove will remove any loose hair and dry skin and tone up the muscles and texture of coat and skin.

Always ensure your hound's nails are clipped short. This cannot be done just by clipping them immediately before a show, but has to be a regular occurrence, especially if the hound is exercised over fields and moors. Road walking helps to wear its nails down. If a Basset has perfect feet and walks correctly the nails will wear away evenly, but in this world not everything is perfect, so a little human help and a pair of nail clippers are essential. Always trim the nail in front of the nerve. If the nerve is cut it will bleed profusely; should this happen, put some crystals of Potassium Permanganate on a ball of cotton wool and hold it against the nail for a few moments to stop the bleeding. No other trimming is carried out in Great Britain, but I think the whiskers are removed in the United States of America.

Ensure that the teeth are clean. Regular brushing with a dog toothpaste will help. Dog teeth scalers also can be obtained and, with care and practice, any tartar on the teeth can be removed. Check the Basset's ear canals each day, so that any problems can be nipped in the bud. A little benzel benzolate put in the ear and rubbed gently, the excess being removed by cotton wool balls, will keep the ear canals clean. I normally do this about twice a week. Never probe the ear canal; if there is a problem the vet can deal with it.

Exercise and Feeding

Exercise is very important for a show Basset. It is no good having a beautiful, sleek coat if the muscles underneath are soft and flabby. To ensure good muscling, both road walking and free running are necessary, but *never over exercise a young Basset puppy*. An adult Basset will enjoy controlled road walking plus plenty of free running every day.

In conjunction with exercising, feeding is vitally important. A well balanced diet is essential. The Basset's coat will indicate whether it is being fed correctly. The beautiful shine and bloom on the coat of a Basset is the result of good feeding and grooming, but no amount of bathing and grooming will give the satin finish to the coat if the diet is incorrect.

It is up to the exhibitor to enhance the Basset's appearance and therefore its chances in the show ring. All things being equal, a well muscled Basset, in A1 condition, moving happily and easily with its handler and presented in the correct stance with no fuss or bother, must have a chance of catching the judge's eye.

The Day of the Show

A Basset puppy that has been fed on a good, well balanced diet, so is looking in good condition, and has been patiently trained at home and at training classes will be ready to enter the show ring at six months. It would be best to seek a local show so that the puppy doesn't have a long distance to travel for the first outing. Most towns and cities have a local dog society. To find the address of the Secretary, contact The Kennel Club (see **Useful Addresses**). The weekly dog papers *Dog World* and *Our Dogs* advertise dog shows every week in their advertisement columns. The Secretary will forward a schedule and entry forms when requested. To a novice, this may look a bit overwhelming, but the entry form is self-explanatory, requiring details of registered name of dog, breed, sex, date of birth, breeder, sire, dam, and which classes you want to enter the dog in. The entry form is signed by the owner and the owner's name and address printed in the allocated space.

The schedule will give the list of classes and their definitions. As you will see from the list starting on page 121, minor puppy, puppy, junior and veteran are classes based on age only. Most of the others are based on prizes won previously. There will be a closing date on the schedule. Try to post the entry early as this will help the Secretary, and enclose a stamped, self-addressed postcard, which will be posted back to you as evidence that the entry has been received.

The best classes in which to enter a six-month-old puppy are minor puppy, puppy and perhaps a maiden class. Do not push the youngster hard at the first show; allow it to adjust and get accustomed to all the various breeds and sounds around. The object of the first show is enjoyment for the puppy, and any thought of a prize should be secondary.

Prior to attending the first show, it is advisable to find out its exact location and write the directions down. Plenty of time must be allowed to reach the venue, in case of road repairs or traffic hold-ups.

The Show Bag

Keep a bag especially for taking to shows. This should contain the following:

- Show lead
- Bench chain and collar
- Blanket for Basset to lie on
- Towel
- Chamois leather or velvet square
- Some plastic bags, in case the Basset leaves a deposit – it has to be cleaned up
- Bottle of disinfectant with some cotton wool balls
- Ring number clip
- Small box of titbits for baiting in the ring
- A paper kitchen roll always comes in handy
- A pen
- Schedule for the show
- Water bottle
- Water bowl
- Food for Basset
- A thermos of tea and a few sandwiches for the owner

If showing your Basset is going to be a regular occurrence it would be advisable to invest in a folding cage. These can be invaluable at venues where there is nowhere safe to leave the Basset. It is also extremely good for carrying the Basset in a car, as it is so easily erected.

At the Show

At the show there will be someone at the door to sell a catalogue and perhaps give out ring numbers to the exhibitors. This varies with shows; sometimes the ring numbers are given out by the stewards in the ring. If it is a small limited show, the Bassets remain with their owners; if it is a large open or championship show the Bassets will have benches in which they have to remain chained all day, except when they are in the show ring or being groomed or exercised. The exhibitors' ring numbers are usually on the benches.

If there is benching at the show and the exhibit has to remain on its bench most of the day, keep checking to make sure it is comfortable and always exercise it prior to benching or entering the ring. Make sure the bench chain is short enough to stop the Basset from jumping off the bench and damaging itself.

In the Ring
Ring Etiquette

No doubt, if a first-time exhibitor is keen, he or she will have been to shows before and seen the routine. There are several taboos in the show ring when you are showing a Basset – or any other breed, for that matter. Never strike up a conversation with the judge. Do not crowd the Basset in front. Do not tread on any Basset. Do not attract the attention of other exhibits. Make sure any previous first prize card is kept out of the way. Do not tear up a prize card in the ring, show dissent or unsporting conduct, or wear rosettes that have been won, unless it is for Best of Show. Keep your Basset on a reasonable length of lead and do not allow it to sniff at other Bassets in the ring. Do not make loud disparaging remarks about the judging.

Early in the day, locate the show ring and check the time of judging. When in the show ring, allow the Basset to relax a little when not being judged. Remember to be a good loser and gracious winner. Always be courteous to the judge and stewards. The latter give their services voluntarily and, without them, shows could not function efficiently.

Going Over the Exhibits

The Bassets will line up in the show ring and the judge will look at them, then ask the exhibitors to move their exhibits around the ring. Always keep the Basset on the left hand side, so that your body does not obscure the hound. No doubt, the judge will be in the centre of the ring and, after one circle of the ring, he or she will ask the leading handler to bring the hound out for examination.

The process will be the same for all the exhibits. The judge will allow the handler to set up the hound, then go over it in detail. He or she will ask the age of the exhibit, then look at the head, taking note of the colour and shape of eye and the ear placement, length and texture of leathers. The mouth will be examined by lifting the lips to check the set of teeth and formation of the jaw. The length and arch of neck is noted. The judge will feel the shoulder placement, and note the rib cage, depth of chest, the length and strength of loin, and the set of the stern. The judge will then feel the muscle tone on the hindquarters, note the bend of stifle and angle and let down of hock. If the Basset is male, he will be checked for entirety. Examination will be made of the bone structure, the shape of feet and depth of pads and the texture of the coat and the suppleness and looseness of the skin. The judge will be looking for soundness, quality, temperament, type, balance and condition, and will also be paying special attention to breed characteristics. This seemingly complex procedure takes about two minutes. Most judges will make allowances for inexperienced puppies misbehaving, but will expect older hounds to conduct themselves properly.

Once the judge has finished the examination, he or she will ask the handler to move the exhibit, normally in a triangle and straight up and down so that the Basset's action can be assessed from the front, the side and then the rear. Some hound judges, especially those with a hunting background, will ask for the hound to be 'stood free' for an assessment of balance and 'houndiness'.

When all the exhibits have been examined, the judge will ask for all the exhibits to be set up, take another look at them all, then pick out his first, second, third and very highly commended and line them up in the centre of the ring. He will inform the steward that he has finished with the rest, who will leave the ring in an orderly fashion.

How to Become a Judge

In Great Britain a person will probably be asked to judge only after some considerable success and experience with a particular breed. The first assignment will normally be a limited or open show of the breed that has been exhibited by this person. The invitation will come from the Secretary of the club holding the show, after consultation with the breed club committee. This may be the start of more judging invitations.

A person may be interested in judging only one breed, several breeds within a group, or perhaps eventually several breeds in all groups. It is a case of testing the ground slowly to start with, judging the breed you know best several times, and getting accustomed to the feel of judging and of being in charge of the ring. Judge match meetings if possible; these are invaluable for practice in officiating and for handling a variety of breeds.

Stewarding in a variety of breeds under expert judges can also help, especially if the judge is willing to impart some of his or her knowledge. A Judging Diploma Course can be attended, and very interesting and educational this is, as I can say from personal experience. The course is advertised in the weekly dog press under the heading *Canine Studies Institute*.

There are several requisites for a successful judge. First and foremost, the candidate must have an eye for a dog; this is an instinctive ability to see the true quality in an animal. This instinct must be tuned by constantly watching various breeds at championship shows, seeing them hunt or work, reading breed standards, attending seminars, and learning about the characteristics of various breeds: type, construction and movement. A dog show judge should be self-confident, strong-minded, poised and calm, and always courteous to the exhibitors. He or she should never be afraid of offending friends by placing them in a lower position than they would have liked, or risking criticism should a friend's exhibit win.

A judge's attitude towards judging is of the utmost importance. A sincere interest in dogs in general should be the motivating force behind a successful judge, coupled with a desire to obtain a record for ability and integrity.

The Judging Diploma

This is to certify that

Marianne Nixon

obtained a .... **Credit** .... Diploma having

satisfactorily completed the Judging Diploma Course.

(signed) .... *David Cavill*

David Cavill, M.C.C.Ed – Studies Coordinator

The Judging Diploma.

Chapter nine
The Hunting Basset

Kindly contributed by Michael Errey, MH

Having received, out of the blue, a letter from Marianne Nixon asking me, as someone dedicated to hunting, to write a chapter on that subject for a new book about the Basset Hound, I was initially rather proud to be described in such a manner. However, having taken down from my library shelves all the books that I have collected over the last 35 years containing any reference to the hunting of the hare with the Basset Hound, I soon found that I had to compete with some very famous predecessors, and any egotistic thought on my part was quickly replaced by humility and the realisation that I would have to attempt a totally different approach.

As I write this, right at the end of the second millennium, I see a way of life that has survived throughout that thousand years in this country, and for longer in Europe and Asia, coming under threat. I am not a countryman by birth; I was born in Hastings, East Sussex, a seaside town, with an urban population at that time of approximately 65,000. So how on earth did I become a dedicated hunting man?

In fact, it probably started with my genes. My forefathers were country folk whose diverse range of occupations were all involved with the land: corn-milling, dairy products, chicken fattening, bacon production, sheep and beef rearing. And it was the purchase of a Basset Hound in 1963 that brought me back to my grass roots.

Eminent Packs

The Burgonets

That first hound, Kitebrook Franklin, was bought for my wife, Avril. We had not the slightest intention of going hunting but, after entering him in a few shows, Avril met a lady called Winifred Burgess who informed her that, apart from showing, she had a pack which hunted in and around the village of Ringmer, only 10 miles from our home at Cowbeech. Avril was invited to take Franklin the following Saturday to see if he would *enter* (a hunting term that indicates whether a hound has the ability to hunt in the correct and appropriate manner).

On her return that fateful day – might I add not until about 8.00 pm – she informed me that she had met a nice crowd of people. She and Franklin had enjoyed themselves immensely. They had stopped for tea and Avril had been informed that, if she had a husband, he would be welcome the next time.

The following week was my introduction to the Burgonet Basset Hounds and to hunting the hare. My first impression was that many of the *field* (the followers of the hunt in the field that day) were 20 years or more older than I and, surprisingly, a great deal fitter; a point that was painfully obvious to me when I was trying to follow them up what was, at times, a four-in-one escarpment of the Sussex Downs. The second impression was that Avril had been right; they were a very nice bunch of people.

The Burgonet had been started in the late 1950s and was a *private pack* – in other words, followers could attend only at the Master's invitation. Mrs Winifred Burgess was Master, Mr Norman Burgess was Huntsman, Mr Tom Riley Secretary, and the *Whippers-In* (huntsmen's assistants who manage the hounds) were Jack Henshaw, Tom Riley, Kenneth Baden-Powell and, a few years later, Roger Gambell. I became thoroughly intrigued with the sport of hunting the wild hare with hounds and, as my fitness improved, so did my enjoyment. The following season I was delighted to be invited to become a uniformed Whipper-In and I remained with the Burgonet for something like 15 seasons. These were very happy years with a grand bunch of folks. Quite large fields were the order of the day with many well-known Basset fanciers in the South, such as Tony and Heather Freeman, Wally and Margaret Lines, and Ken and Joan Izard, in attendance.

The Albany Pack at an Essex meet, 1968–1969. Centre, John Evans, with hunt staff.

The Burgonet was not a registered pack, in that no *country* (in hunting parlance, an area in which a named pack is registered as having permission to hunt) in the heavily-populated South East was vacant for them to register in their own right. However, there were 30 locations in East Sussex where they could hold meets, in country registered by the Brighton and Storrington Foot Beagles and the Southdown Foxhounds. Only once was there a conflict of interest, when the Burgonet and the Brighton found themselves on the same stretch of disused railway line at Barcombe near Lewes. Winifred and Norman Burgess ran their pack in a very efficient and proper manner, with all due regards to hunting etiquette. Sadly, after their death, the Burgonet disbanded.

The Albany

The Burgesses were probably influenced in starting a working pack by the existence of the Basset Hound Club Working Branch, which started a few years after the Basset Hound Club was reformed in 1954. The Club's Chairman, Mr Alex McDonald, hunted hounds belonging to Miss Peggy Keevil, ably assisted by Mr John Evans and other followers. I did not attend one of their meets, being totally involved at that time with the Burgonet. However, within a few years, the Basset Hound Club had acquired its own pack, which was kennelled at Arkley on the outskirts of North London at the home of Mr and Mrs John Evans, where John was already kennelling the West Lodge Hare Hounds. John had a natural rapport with hounds and personnel and, during his Mastership from 1965 to 1980, a very professional pack was built up. His organisation of meets and of every detail of the pack's affairs was of the highest standard.

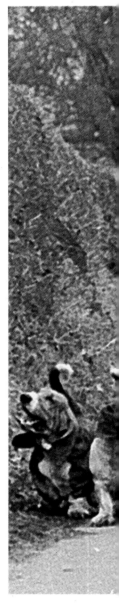

Without any doubt, my friendship with John was one of the greatest beneficial influences on me as a Master of Hounds. He was fortunate to have as his kennel assistant Carol Vickary, who came to Arkley direct from school to work at the kennel and stayed with John after his retirement. Carol is still among our friends and we spend many occasions reminiscing over the happy times spent with John and his supportive wife, Vi. John was the best huntsman with Basset Hounds I have ever seen, even allowing for the fact that it is easier for the hand that feeds the hounds to carry the horn. He was extremely fit, as you have to be to run perhaps half a mile, simultaneously blowing a hunting horn. Once when I was whipping in to him at a meet at Luton in South Devon before the clocks had changed in early October, to my great discomfort he carried on until nearly eight o'clock in the evening. I was thinking, 'When the hell is that old "begger" going to blow for home?' At that time, he must have been nearer 60 than 50. I did notice that, after dinner that evening, he quickly fell asleep in the armchair with a glass of rum, his favourite after-dinner tipple.

In 1972, John was joined in the Mastership by Mr Tim Thomas, who was instrumental in obtaining registered country for the Pack, now known as the Albany, in the County of Rutland near his home. The change of name was at the insistence of the Master of Basset Hounds Association, the name *Albany* being appropriate because it was the age-old name for Britain. This fairly represents the distance the pack travels to provide sport for members of the Basset Hound Club. The Club still owns the hounds in spite of the change of name.

Mr Arthur Tucker from Derbyshire joined the Mastership with John and Tim in 1975, and hunted hounds on many occasions until John retired in 1980, when the hounds were moved to the Westerby Kennels at South Kilworth in Leicestershire. This was the commencement of the 'Hipkins' era.

Graham Browne, huntsman, with the Melancthon Bassets, a private pack. Photo: Roger Tebbutt

Mr L S Hipkins, a very long-standing supporter and *Field Master* (someone who controls the followers in the field, not necessarily a Master), was appointed for the 1981 season and later joined by his wife Stella, who was also Secretary of the Basset Hound Club. 'Hippy', as he was affectionately known, died prematurely in 1986. Stella continued with no small measure of success, and her name was synonymous with that of the Albany throughout the country. Mr Peter Baker was a Master and Huntsman for a period, along with Mrs Hipkins. Other non-master huntsmen over the years have been Michael Dennis, Charles Buckland (a great East Anglian character), Jack Henshaw (after the Burgonet disbanded), Dr Mark Thomas (now Master of the Bolebrook Beagles) and, more recently, Mr Anthony Ringe as Master and a very effective huntsman for three seasons, the current Master, Mr David Money, and Mr Keith Deacon, who returned the hounds to South Kilworth after a short period of being kennelled in Essex. Keith Deacon hunted hounds for his first complete season in 1996, and had a very respectable tally of two-and-a-half brace – quite creditable with pure-bred Basset Hounds. I like Keith's style and wish him well.

Many people have played a part in the Albany story. I regret that I shall offend many good friends by not mentioning them all, but I must recall the names of Miss Jane Blois, Secretary of the Albany since its inception and still in office, Michael and Ricky Faulkner, Ray and Lana Johnson, John and Vera Wigmore, Sally Money, Joan Scott-Goldstone, Carol Smith and, from the very early days, Dennis de St Croix, who died prematurely in the 1970s. In the North, Don Bayes has arranged meets in Yorkshire and was also instrumental in the funding of the Albany Hunt Buttons. To these I would add all staunch supporters and fund raisers supreme who have kept the Albany on the road for many years.

It has been my pleasure, over the last 20 years, to arrange a series of meets for the Albany in my own country in Kent and Sussex. Most of them have been over a long New Year weekend but, in 1996, I had the pleasure of having their hounds once again in my kennels for a week in October, when they enjoyed meets on the South Downs and Romney Marsh. One meet that has become traditional is at the Cricketers at Berwick; this regularly draws a field in excess of 100 followers.

Unfortunately, John Evans passed away at the end of 1996. A measure of his esteem was the vast number of hunting folk who came to Greens Norton Parish Church in Northampton that day to celebrate his life and friendship. It must have been a comfort on a sad occasion to his wife Vi. It is said that behind every great man there is even a greater woman, and I thank her for the support she gave him and the manner in which she made us all welcome in their home.

To end this section about the Albany: I regard John Evans as the father of the child, and thank Stella and her husband Hippy for bringing the teenager to maturity but, with the approach of the new millennium, I wish their successors well in the current political climate.

The Melancthon

Having hunted in most counties in England and Wales, I have always regretted that, so far, I have not had the opportunity for a day with the Melancthon Basset Hounds in the North West. This pack of mainly tri-colour pure-bred hounds belongs to Mrs Winifred Aspin of Knutsford, Cheshire. Mrs Aspin acquired her first hound, Brockhampton Restless, from Mr Gerald Dakin in the late 1950s and commenced hunting with the Grims Hounds in the early 1960s. She started her own pack in 1968 with the help of a few *trencher-fed hounds* to augment those of her own. (Trencher-fed hounds are not necessarily owned by the Hunt and living in hunt kennels but, by invitation of the Master, they are brought from outside sources to augment the pack.) This pack has now been in existence for 30 seasons, hunting in Anglesey, Cheshire and Shropshire – a truly wonderful country of which I could be jealous. Former huntsmen have been the late Mr Bob Dixon and Dr Anton Aspin. The pack currently consists of about eight couples of hounds and is hunted by Mr Graham Browne. Mrs Aspin keeps the flag flying in that part of the country by showing a very good standard of sport in the hunting field and by some very polished performances parading at country shows.

The Two Types of British Basset Hound

Some readers may realise that two distinct types of smooth-coated Basset Hounds hunt hares in the British Isles. George Johnston in the chapter 'The Working Bassets' in his book *The Basset Hound,* published in 1968, admirably explains how the situation came about as a result of a split between the hunting and showing fraternities in 1911. A confusing situation for the layman

An English Basset: Westerby General. Photo: V Beard

immediately arose when the original type of hound that had been imported from France to this country in the latter part of the 19th century continued to be called the Basset Hound and, from early in the 20th century, a breed fairly dissimilar as a result of crossing to Harriers and other more long-legged scent hounds became known as the English Basset. This type of hound is not recognised by The Kennel Club even today, and the only place where they can be seen in the show ring is once a year at the Peterborough Hound Show, when they are in competition with pure-bred Basset Hounds, but only if both types are entered for competition by hunts registered by the Master of the Basset Hound Association.

The reason given for the original outcrossing was the critically small gene pool available to the Masters. Although I acknowledge that this was a serious problem, I have always had a sneaking feeling that the principal consideration was to breed a faster hound. They certainly have achieved this and, to this day, a pack of English Bassets will account for four or five times as many hares in a season as their pure-bred cousins, who suffer a serious problem where speed is concerned. However, it has always been the manner in which they overcome this disadvantage with their wonderful noses and pure perseverance that makes a splendid day's hunting with them. The tenacity of the Basset Hound is put into perspective when you consider that a fresh-found hare moves off at about 25 miles per hour, pursued by the hounds at half that speed. After about a quarter of a mile, the hare begins to slow, but it has built up an impressive lead – so much so that, within a few minutes, it can afford to stop and rest until the pack arrives in close proximity. The exercise is then repeated. At each check, the quarry goes away a little slower than before, while the pursuing hounds lose little pace, dropping back to about 10 miles an hour or, on a long run, to not less than 8 miles an hour. I must admit that these indications of speed are an estimation arrived at by my own experience, as I am not aware that any scientific measurement of speed has been taken in the hunting field. As regards the English Basset, I must admit a personal bias against any type of hound which is not pure-bred and I have always regarded them as reminiscent of small cars with high suspension and a turbo-charged engine – but then, beauty has always been in the eye of the beholder. To avoid appearing too dogmatic in my views, I must add that one of my memorable days was with the Westerby, an English Basset pack, at the Alston Hare week about six years ago, at Wintershields near Bewcastle, close to the Scottish Border. They hunted a single hare for about an hour and a half, before the hare ran to a safe haven away from the hounds.

Having perhaps given a false impression that Basset Hounds hunt at a leisurely pace, I must say I have never met anyone in the hunting field who could keep pace with Bassets in full flight. It's not an easy job for the huntsmen; within five minutes the pack can be a mile away, and perhaps out of sight. When they stop 'speaking' you start to worry; it seems an age before they return to the call of the horn, whereas Foxhounds are gone twice as fast but seem to be back in an instance.

The Quarry

It would be inappropriate not to mention the worthy quarry of the hounds, without which no hunting would be possible. Hares have been hunted by man and hounds since records were recorded on tablets of stone. In Asia they used sighthounds, but scenthounds in Europe, Beagles or Harriers being the most usual choice in the British Isles. Since the start of the 20th century, the Basset has pitted its wits against one of nature's most mysterious and wily creatures. After all these thousands of years, very little is known about *puss*, as the huntsman sometimes refers to the hare; *she* is always spoken of in the feminine gender. Most people in the South of England will have seen only the Brown Hare, but in the North, where the country rises generally to more than 500m, the Blue or Mountain Hare is the common species, although both can live side by side in the higher domain. The Blue Hare is never blue, but brown in the summer, changing to a patchy white in the winter – presumably nature's way of providing camouflage in the snow. The Blue Hare is generally only half the size of her southern cousin. In Ireland (Ulster and Eire) a subspecies of Brown Hare exists, which is between the other two in size.

The hare lives on the ground summer and winter. The female raises a small number of leverets in a scrape on the bare earth and sometimes separates them for safety. The only concession they make to comfort is to keep away from damp, water-logged areas and out of a bitter, cold wind. When pursued by hounds, the hare's intelligence is phenomenal. She is no doubt aware that she is being hunted by scent and will take a route that involves back-tracking, running walls, intricate figures, jumping rivers and streams 6m wide or more, swimming if necessary, and passing through sheep and cattle to provide a foil to its scent.

One of the most remarkable exhibitions I ever witnessed was at a meet of the Pevensey Marsh Beagles at The Royal Oak, Tandridge in Surrey. I was there at the invitation of the Surrey and North Sussex Beagles. Mr Ian Cunningham, Joint Master, was hunting hounds and, towards the end of the day, as I was about to go home to feed my own pack, a hare crept into the field, did a figure-of-eight some 20m long, then moved to one side and produced an almost identical manoeuvre adjacent to it, and then headed out of sight to the bottom of the field. I stood wondering what on earth was going on. This careful operation was carried out at a slow, deliberate pace, with no sight or sound of hounds. Five minutes later, the pack came into the field, and followed this pattern exactly – except that it took about four circuits of each figure-of-eight to unravel the manoeuvre before they moved to the bottom of the field!

This is the most spectacular display by hare and hounds I have ever seen. Ian Cunningham, like most good huntsmen, did not interfere with his hounds; they worked it out for themselves. This was hound work, and the reason that people follow hounds out hunting, in spite of the fact that I heard next day that *puss* got away. As I had then left the field to go back to my own kennel, I could not congratulate the Master on such a first-class display of hounds and hunting, and I have never since mentioned it to him.

Scent

The question of scent is a difficult and complex problem. After my first season as a huntsman, I thought I knew quite a lot about it. Many years later, I now admit I know very little. I wish the hounds could tell me, as they are the only experts.

In the early 1900s a firm manufactured an instrument that was supposed to define a good scenting day from a bad one. It had two thermometers, one that telling you the ground temperature and the other the air temperature, and, by sticking it in the ground, you could deduce how strong the scent would be that day. What you did when the ground was frozen I don't quite know and, as the manufacturers quickly went into liquidation, I will never know. I have listened to many self-appointed experts explaining about poor scent, catchy scent, breast-high scent, the effects of rain and fog, frost going in and coming out of the ground – all very interesting, but it does not explain why hounds are quite likely to go well on one of these experts' poor scenting days. My advice is, if you are a follower, don't be put off by the forecast of poor scent and, if you are the huntsman on a poor day, blame the scent.

Hunting Hospitality and Hostelries

Long-lasting friendships develop quite easily among the hunting fraternity, as they all seem to be very sociable people. As a result, many events are organised when they congregate for a real old 'knees-up'. The Albany's visits to the West Country used to come in this category. The first part of the week hounds were kennelled and hunting staff boarded at a fabulous farm, Fossefell, about three miles from Hartland, where the owners were hunting fanatics and the hospitality to us, as a visiting pack, was more than generous. Tea after the meet was ample – the problem being that, about an hour later, you were expected to sit down to a roast dinner and then get down to the Anchor Inn for the rest of the evening. Some of the antics that took place in this worthy hostelry defy belief. The same applied to the West Country Inn, where some of our party stayed. The local vicar would lay a challenge to drink a 'yard of ale'. Some of our followers, by the latter part of the evening or the early hours of the morning, were foolish enough to take him on. Needless to say, I never saw him beaten. They were halcyon days and I treasure the friendship of great characters like Tom Green and Terry Cartledge and three elderly ladies, Betty Dobson, Jane Stewart and Irene Gore-Curtis, who unfortunately are no longer with us. Later in the week, the show moved on, via North Devon Meats at Great Torrington to pick up bullock tripes to feed the hounds, to the home of Hugh and Wynne Hedley at Christow. Here hounds were kennelled in their garage. I do not recall the name of the inn at Christow, though I see it clearly in my mind's eye, but I do remember the Nobody Inn at Doddiscombsleigh.

In September 1968 a unique event occurred – regrettably the one and only time it was held. The Four Packs Meet was hosted by Mr and Mrs David Gandy at their home Lower Bottom Farm, Hartley Wintney, in Hampshire. The occasion was a competition between the four pure-bred Basset packs in existence at that time in the South: The Basset Hound Club Pack, The Burgonet, The Four Shires and the Leadenvale. The judges for the show, very eminent hound judges at that time, were the late Miss L Burns-Hartupp and Mr Rex Hudson, Secretary of the Master of Basset Hound Association. Four classes were held for un-entered and entered dogs and bitches. I do not recall the ultimate champion, but do remember that the Burgonet were more than delighted to win the class for un-entered dogs with their Burgonet Virgil 68. The jollifications included a horn-blowing competition, with classes for hunt staff, lady and gentlemen followers and children, and a foot point-to-point for hunt staff. John Evans finished second in the latter against competitors many of whom were half his age. On completion of the course, John was introduced to David Gandy's duck pond. The day ended with what in those days was an innovation: a barbecue. It all goes to show that we hunting folk are highly sociable.

This sociability exists just the same in the United States. I have not had the good fortune to hunt with any of the Basset packs operating in the eastern states, but have attended field trials at two of their Nationals in the fall during the 1980s: one at Lebanon, Pennsylvania and the other at Ann Arbour, Michigan. These trials take place in an enclosed, wired-in area several hectares in size. The quarry is generally the cotton-tailed rabbit, and proceedings are similar to hare coursing in this country, where the object is not to kill, but to score points awarded by two judges. Hounds compete in pairs against each other and, after two days of competition, a winner emerges. Experience has taught me that there are no better hosts than the Americans, especially when you share a common interest in the working Basset Hound. Winning at these trials leads to a very coveted award: that of Field Trial Champion. We have no similar title for Bassets in this country, but it is possible to hunt a privately-owned hound with the express permission of the Master of the Albany Bassets, which could lead to the award of a Working Certificate if the hound is competent. Classes for working hounds are available at the Basset Hound Club Championship and Open Show. What better than to own or breed a champion hound with a Working Certificate: a feat last achieved in this country by Mr and Mrs Gilberthorpe's Ch Blaby Hal.

Miss Peggy Keevil

In conclusion, I must remind readers that we have one person in particular to thank for the fact that we have Basset Hounds to show and hunt with today: Miss Peggy Keevil. She founded her kennel in 1935, when generally the breed was at a low ebb, keeping it going throughout the Second World War and introducing new bloodlines from France. When the Basset Hound Club was reformed in 1954, with her enthusiasm for the breed and its working ability, she was instrumental in the formation of the Working Branch, predecessor to the Albany, with her Grims Hounds.

Michael Errey MH

Hound Names

Traditional hound names are usually of two syllables, 'rolling off' the tongue easily and enabling the huntsman (or owner) to give a great degree of carrying power to his or her voice.

George Washington's Hounds

Bowler, Bumper, Damsel, Dido, Dinah, Doxy, Droner, Drummer, Duchess, Ringwood, Romeo, Rover, Ruler, Singwell, Slipper, Sweetlips, Tanner, Thisbe, Tippler, Toper, Tuneall, Venus, Vineyard, Vulcan.

John Peel's Hounds

Bellman, Briton, Champion, Cruel, Dancer, Glory, Jingler, Melody, Mopsy, Ranter, Rattler, Rockwood, Royal, Ruby, Ruler, Shifty, Towler.

Westerby Basset Hound Names

1957–1958 season Clinker, Crofter, Crolus, Cromwell, Crystal, Delta, Democrat, Decoy, Descant, Dewdrop, Gaelic, Gainful, Gladly, Glamour, Gothic, Graceful, Gracious, Graphic, Graying, Grecian, Ladybird, Lamport, Landlord, Lascar, Lavish, Legend, Levity, Napier, Nightshade, Noontide, Racket, Rambler, Ranger, Sable, Sabre, Sacrifice, Salient, Trespass, Trivial, Viceroy, Victory, Vigil, Visage.
1959 season Actor, Actress, Agent, Alibi, Ragtime, Rapid, Reader, Reason, Redman, Relish, Remedy, Reveller, Slider, Slightly, Spartan, Sportsman, Spotlight, Sprightly.

Rodney of Aberthin.

Breeding Basset Hounds

Six generations of Brackenacre Bassets.

Reasons for Breeding Bassets

Breeding Basset Hounds can be an absorbing, frustrating, exciting, but extremely interesting challenge. I consider that there are six types of people who breed them:

1 *The dedicated breeder* has bred Bassets for years and, after surviving all the pitfalls, has established a line that can be recognised in the show ring. This person can breed champion after champion but is ever striving for perfection, and abides by The Kennel Club's Code of Ethics and the Basset Hound Club's Code of Ethics.

2 *The novice breeder* has bought a reasonably good Basset bitch and is told that she is worthy of being shown. She is shown and possibly wins a few prizes at local open shows, which inspires the owner, who then decides to breed a litter. This person will probably ask advice from an experienced breeder regarding Basset Hound breed stud dogs and will possibly travel a few miles to use a reasonable stud dog on the bitch. By going to a few shows and talking to other exhibitors the novice will have some idea of what having a litter will entail and will probably be prepared for the event. Should a nice puppy from this litter be picked and proceed to win further afield, particularly at championship shows, the bug will have bitten. This type of breeder will probably become a serious breeder and exhibitor.

3 *The beginner,* having checked on various breeds and decided that the Basset Hound is his or her ideal, will go to some top championship shows and watch the judging. Having decided who is breeding the particular points in a Basset that are preferable, he or she will approach this breeder and be willing to wait for a promising bitch puppy or two. Next, he or she will study pedigrees and keep watching the show ring for the best stud dog for the bitch and be prepared for when the litter arrives, having read various books on the subject, and spoken to several breeders. This person will probably keep a couple of puppies from the litter for a future in the show ring, and do the very best to place the rest of the litter in kind, loving homes. This type of person will be the back-bone of the Basset breed in the future.

4 *The pet owner* has a bitch and feels it would do her good to have a litter (although this is not necessarily true). If the owner has not really thought of the consequences the family may end up with one of the following scenarios: (a) An uneventful whelping of five or six puppies by

the Basset stud down the road. The puppies will be thoroughly pampered by the family and grow up delightful companions for other people. (b) On the down side, the bitch may have complications, require a caesarean, have 13 puppies whom she rejects and/or for whom she has no milk. The 13 puppies will then need to be hand fed – not easy for a beginner. If there is no outside kennel, the mess 13 six-week-old puppies can make in someone's living room is unbelievable. This is the type of litter that, though advertised, cannot be sold. When the owner is at his or her wits' end and about to mortgage the home to pay food bills, an advertisement appears in a newspaper from a multiple-breed kennel, actually advertising for puppies. A quick telephone call – and, yes, they will take all the puppies that have not been sold. The litter will be transported to a multi-breed, commercial kennel and sold on to goodness-knows-where. Hopefully, this type of owner will never wish to repeat the experience.

5   *Multi-breed kennels* regularly advertise in a variety of papers, sometimes breeding their own puppies but mostly buying in unwanted litters of puppies, regardless of the standard, often when the puppies are very young, and re-selling at a much higher price than has been paid.

6   *The puppy farmer* has various breeds, usually kept in sub-standard conditions, breeding from bitches every season and crating the young puppies off to the continent, pet shops – in fact to anyone who will buy them with no questions asked. I leave the reader to decide what to think of this type of breeder.

The Breeding of Dogs Act 1973

According to the Breeding of Dogs Act 1973, a licence must be obtained if two or more breeding bitches are owned. Prior to the licence being issued, inspection of the premises is carried out by a member of the local authority, possibly from a representative of the Environmental Health Department, or by the local Dog Warden. They ensure that the accommodation is appropriate for the welfare of dogs. This licence is obtainable from the Local Council, and the criteria for granting a licence may vary between Councils, as does the cost.

The Perfect Basset

Trying to breed the perfect Basset Hound is a time-consuming and expensive hobby, with constant striving to produce the perfect specimen. There have been many great Bassets but every one has had faults, no matter how minor. I doubt if the perfect Basset will ever be bred because we all interpret the Breed Standard in different ways.

Before acquiring a foundation bitch, do a lot of homework on the breed, read the books written about Bassets, attend some of the principal championship shows and watch the judging, and talk to owners on the benches (*after* their hound has been judged, not before it is due to go into the ring). Try to attend seminars on the breed. Always remember that soundness is one of the most important aspects to look for. At this point, colour should not come into the calculation, as tri-colours can produce lemon-and-white, and lemon-and-white can produce tri-colours.

I was very fortunate when I obtained my first Basset. The breeder, Mrs Sheila Goldie from Milton of Campsie, near Glasgow, had a litter by Int Ch Crochmaid Bold Turpin of Blackheath out of Grims Flimsy. She informed me that two bitches were available, both tri-colours. One bitch had a very sound front but was rather straight in stifle, and the second bitch wasn't so good in front but had reasonable hindquarters. Having read how important it was to maintain the correct fronts I decided to have the bitch with the good front: Brackenacre Kierhill Oonagh. It was a decision I never regretted. Oonagh had very good shoulder placement, giving a sound front complemented by super feet and rib cage. She had a sweet head, though rather plain by today's standard, and she could have had a better bend of stifle. Mated to Hardacre Sungarth Eager (Sungarth Trumpeter ex Hardacre Sungarth Plover), a dog with a superb head, heavy wrinkling and excellent hindquarters, she produced a lovely litter of seven. The bitch I retained became Ch Brackenacre Annabella, thus proving a champion can be bred in the first litter if the quality breeding is behind the sire and dam – and, of course, if Lady Luck smiles down.

Although most Bassets are now bred as companions or for the show ring, the Basset Hound was originally bred to hunt small game. This should not be forgotten, and everything in the Breed Standard pertaining to their ability to do this work must be considered of prime importance.

The potential brood bitch should be sound, true to breed type and with no outstanding faults. She may have a good pedigree but, if she has not inherited all the good qualities from her forebears, she should not be bred from. No matter how hard a breeder can try to produce sound typical stock, in some cases faults appear in the offspring that can be traced back many generations, and what appears to be a promising litter will end up a dismal failure. Do not attempt to breed from these puppies at a later date, despite the pedigree.

Always remember the saying, *The finest seed will yield a poor crop if sown in indifferent soil.* If the brood bitch is of indifferent quality it doesn't matter if the finest dog hound is used; the chances are she will produce a mediocre litter. Not only must the proposed brood be of good quality; she must also be in very good condition, active, happy and carefree, with good muscle tone, and erring to leanness rather than to fat. Temperament is extremely important; the Basset has such a wonderful record for being good-natured that every endeavour must be made to retain the sweetness of its character. Shy or nervous bitches should not be bred from; it is a trait that could be passed on to their progeny.

The Breeding Programme

Starting out on a breeding programme can be a veritable minefield. Some potential breeders get confused by the various terms and what is actually meant by them. In-breeding, line-breeding or outcross: which is the best?

Three male champions in direct line: Ch Brackenacre Fino de Paris, Ch Brackenacre James Bond and Ch Brackenacre The Viking. From a life-size oil painting by Beryl Chapple.

In-breeding should only be carried out when the breeder has intimate knowledge of *all* the hounds in the pedigrees and knows that *none* had any outstanding faults and all were extremely sound with ultra-good temperaments. This is the mating of father to daughter, mother to son, or brother to sister. In-breeding can produce fabulous results – and it can also produce disasters. The breeder will not only be doubling up on all the good points of the pair, but also the bad points as well.

Line-breeding is similar to in-breeding, involving mating relatives, but further away in the relationship; for example, a half-brother to half-sister or grandsire to granddaughter. Line-breeding goes a long way towards establishing a line. Several of my Brackenacre champions have resulted from line-breeding.

Outcrossing is the mating of unrelated partners.This too can produce very good offspring, especially if the stud dog is compensating for some small weakness in the female. The offspring kept from an outcross can be mated back to either a close relation of the sire or of dam in an endeavour to perpetuate a particular good point.

In all cases write down the pedigrees of the various stud dogs that are being considered and compare them with the bitch that is to be mated. Try to double up on stud dogs that are known to produce good stock.

Choosing the Stud Dog

The next problem confronting the breeder is to decide which stallion hound to use. I can only reiterate what I have already written: watch the show ring and look carefully at all the male Basset Hounds being shown, noting which seem to win the most under both types of judge – breed specialist and all rounder. Check the show catalogues and note which stud dogs are predominant at siring quality offspring both to line-bred and outcross bitches. Sometimes it is safer to choose an older stud dog who has a good success rate of winning offspring, examining his particular merits carefully. He

Ch Brackenacre Fino de Paris. Photo: Diane Pearce

should excel in soundness, have an excellent character, have all the breed points that are particularly admired and, preferably, have some line-breeding behind him that will tie in with your bitch.

No matter how careful one is in choosing the correct pair, and even if both bitch and dog are handsome to look at, nature has a way of interfering with the best laid plans, and the genes of the pair play a great part in the ensuing litter. Dominant genes usually mask or dominate over recessive genes but, should both the male and female have these recessive genes in their make-up, the recessive trait will show up in the offspring. It is apparent that light eyes are recessive to dark eyes, thick flat leathers to the fine in-curling leather, and so on. The worst folly is to mate a male and female with the same faults, doubling up on recessives so that the fault will appear in possibly all the offspring. Do not be 'kennel blind': acknowledge a fault in the bitch to be mated, if only to yourself, and find a suitable stud that excels and dominates in that particular point. Good points

Life with the pack.

and faults vary in degree. There are plain heads, good heads, and outstanding heads, excelling in all breed points; the same applies to fronts, rib cages, hindquarters, and all other parts. To obtain the best results, try to pick the pedigree with as many of the desirable points as possible, developed to the highest degree, manageable without going to extremes. Unless the very best hounds are used, the progeny will fall below the standard of the very best. It has always been my policy to use the best stud dogs available, to keep the best bitch from the ensuing litter, then line-breed the bitch back to the best male progeny of the sire or dam for good results. Perhaps I have been fortunate in building my kennel on the foundation of the great stud dogs: Ch Fredwell Varon Vandal, Ch Fredwell Ideal, Ch Wingjays Ptolemy, Bezel Action Man, Ch Brackenacre Fino de Paris, Ch Langpool Carries Lad and Ch Brackenacre The Viking.

It does not always follow that champions are the best sires. There have been several champions who have never sired anything noteworthy, while some hounds who have not been

shown very much are producing some very worthwhile, sound, typical stock. If one of those hounds is of a suitable bloodline, use him. A Basset who comes to mind is Bezel Action Man, bred by Mrs Thorley of Derbyshire. He never attained the title of champion, but he certainly stamped his type on his offspring, giving beautiful, dark eyes, substance and excellent forequarters.

Keeping a Stud

I would advise any first-time breeder to think very carefully before keeping a male from their first litter with the hope that he will become a great stud hound. It is far better to keep a female. Should she inherit a few minor faults, she can be mated to a dominant male who excels in these points and, probably, have a reasonably good litter. If a male is kept and inherits faults, he will not win in the show ring or be wanted at stud, and it is far more difficult to find a good home for an older male puppy.

It is easy to say this, but in a litter the males always look better, being more robust and outgoing. Believe me, after over 30 years in the breed, I have fallen into this trap a few times and speak from experience. If you are lucky enough (and I do mean *lucky*, however many hours are spent checking pedigrees) to breed a good stallion hound, a considerable amount of hard work lies ahead. To begin with, he must be campaigned to keep him in the eyes of the public. Many thousands of miles can be covered in taking him to most of the championship shows. He must be fed on the best and exercised well to keep him in the shining condition needed. He must have great character and show charisma to hold his place at championship shows.

No matter how much winning your hound has done, look at him objectively when enquiries arise for stud work. If he is winning well he may be required to be used at stud many times, so he could influence the breed for some considerable time. When looking at him – without rose-tinted glasses – remember that the primary consideration is whether he will be of value to the gene pool of his breed. Does he have all the breed requisites? Has he outstanding features worthy to be perpetuated? Is he sound, healthy and robust? Is he an outstanding representative of the breed? There should be no compromise in the areas of health, temperament and soundness. When it can honestly be said he meets all these criteria, then, and only then, should he be offered at stud.

Checking the Bitch

The owner of the stud dog should check the bitch's pedigree to ensure there is nothing in the background of the bitch that will not complement the dog. Ascertain that the owner of the intended bitch has ensured that the bitch has no uterine infection that can be passed on to the stud dog and make his sperm infertile. I know of a large kennel of brood bitches and stud dogs (not Basset Hounds) that had problems getting the bitches to conceive. Eventually a vet swabbed all the bitches, and tests revealed an infection in the bitches' vaginas. There was no outward sign of any

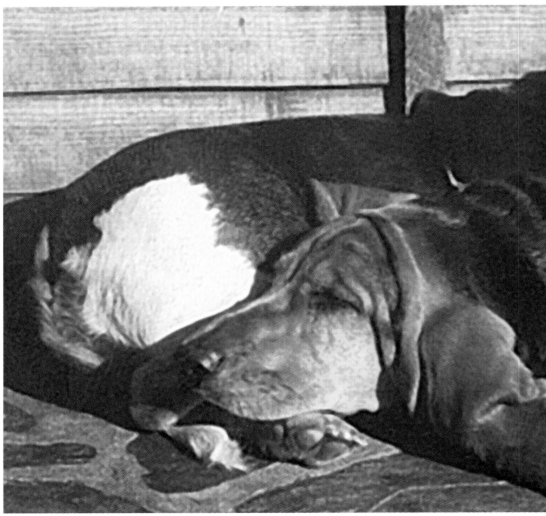

infection, and all the bitches seemed in perfect health, but the germ killed the sperm. All the dogs on the premises were given a course of a broad-spectrum antibiotic and thereafter, whenever a bitch was to be mated, she was given antibiotics. All the bitches conceived when next mated.

If I have a bitch who has travelled the country being shown for a couple of years and is therefore much more likely to pick up infections, when I wish to mate her I always remember that kennel and ask the vet to give her a course of antibiotics at the onset of her season. Of course, any advice regarding the giving of antibiotics must be up to the vet, and his or her advice must always be respected.

Make sure from the owners of the bitch that her vaccinations are up to date, that she is registered by The Kennel Club and that the registration is in the owner's name, and also that she has been wormed.

Paperwork and Agreements

Prior to the bitch coming to be mated, the stud dog owner should have The Kennel Club form completed and ready to pass over to the owner of the bitch once mating has been accomplished, together with the pedigree of the stud dog and receipt for the stud fee.

Nose to tail heating – Bassets love to touch each other.

In some cases agreements are drawn up between the stud dog owner and the owner of the bitch for the stud owner to have a puppy back in lieu of a stud fee. I never think this is very satisfactory; the puppies cannot be sold until the stud dog owner has seen them and picked whichever one is required, and it may be the very pup the bitch's owner has picked as the one to keep. It is far better to save up and pay a stud fee.

The Mating

Before the actual mating, allow both male and female a little exercise and time to relieve themselves. Always have a sturdy collar on both dog and bitch for something to hold onto should either get over-excited.

It helps the stud dog if the same area is used for mating each time; perhaps a shed or empty garage. He will come to view the area with anticipation. The Basset is not the easiest hound to mate, especially if it is his first time. For a young stud it is better to use an older bitch who has been mated before as, quite often, he will get very excited and try to mount everywhere other than where he should. The older matron will probably swing her hindquarters around and present herself to him, whereas a young maiden bitch may get frightened by all his friskiness and attack him, putting him off the business altogether.

Never discourage a young hound if he shows sexually orientated behaviour when a puppy, mating his siblings or kennel mates. This is normal behaviour; in fact it is better to encourage it in a moderate way. If a youngster is scolded for this behaviour he may not cooperate when he is required to mate a bitch, thinking it is wrong.

Help is often needed when Bassets are mated. It is easier to have two people attending a mating: one to hold the bitch's head and to be ready to slip a muzzle on her if she is inclined to snap at the stud dog, and the other to attend to the business end. In most cases support is needed under the stomach and rib cage of the bitch. This helps her to remain standing when the 31.7–36.3kg (70–80lb) male mounts her. Some people prefer to sit on the floor and put the bitch over their knees, so that she can be kept standing by the knees being lifted slightly under her body. The only trouble I have found with this is that, after a few moments, with the combined weight of dog and bitch (easily over 50kg), the helper's legs tend to collapse and, like a pack of cards, all comes tumbling down! It is far easier to construct a very simple platform approximately 25cm wide by 45cm long by 12cm high (10in x 18in x 5in), tack a piece of carpet over the platform and stand the bitch over the platform so that she cannot sit down or collapse when mated. I have found that the stud dog will soon perform very easily with the platform, even placing his hind feet on the parts of it that protrude either side of the bitch to help him when thrusting.

The preliminary approach of the stud dog is characterised by sniffing, licking and perhaps pawing the bitch, obviously trying to test her reaction. Always be ready to muzzle the bitch, as it is amazing how quickly a Basset bitch can attack the stud dog if she is not quite ready for mating. I have never known a male retaliate and defend himself with a bitch on heat, so she could damage both him and perhaps someone's hand if it gets in the way.

As soon as the bitch is willing to stand, the male will clasp her around the flanks with his front legs and thrust until his penis enters the vulva. I have found it easier at this stage to help the male enter the bitch rather than let him exhaust himself by continually thrusting and missing. Once he has entered her the thrusting increases as the penis engorges and enters the vagina. Now the male rides higher over her back and, after hopping on one hind leg then the other, his back legs can leave the floor altogether. This is when the platform is useful to place his hind feet on, rather than the person at the business end holding his hindquarters on their arm. The intense thrusting is known as *intense ejaculatory response*, and this is when the bulb of the penis enlarges and ejaculation begins. The fluid the male ejaculates can be divided roughly into three parts:

- the first part is colourless and relatively sperm free.
- the second part should be rich in sperm and is cloudy in colour.
- the third amount is a colourless fluid from the prostate gland, ejected to help the sperm flow up to fertilise the eggs. It is virtually sperm free.

The Tie

The enlargement of the bulb within the vagina causes the penis to be locked in the vagina, and the tie begins. When the tie is completed the male will look to slide to one side of the bitch by lifting one of his back legs over her. The tie is then spent, with the dog and bitch standing tail to tail. It is easier if they can be encouraged to lay down as the tie can last anything up to an hour. Nearly all of my stud dogs go to sleep until the tie is broken. Never leave a male and female alone when they are tied as the bitch may get nervous and try to get away, dragging the male behind her, and in so doing damage him.

When the tie is broken the male will withdraw his penis into the sheath. Some of the prostatic fluid may drain from the bitch but, as stated, this does not contain sperm. I usually sponge my stud dog with a light disinfectant (which he does not like) but, after a dish of milk and a biscuit, he will return to the kennel and kennel mates quite happily. The owner of the bitch should return her to the car, making sure she doesn't urinate outside the gate or premises and thus alert all the wandering Romeos in the area.

'Atten-*shun!*'

Head study of a lovely tri-colour bitch.

Free Return Stud

It is polite for the bitch's owner to contact the stud dog's owner nine weeks later about the outcome of the mating. If the bitch has not conceived, most stud dog owners will give a free mating next time the bitch is in season. This is not compulsory, as the fee is for the actual mating, but I have never known anyone refuse a free return stud.

Whelping and Rearing Puppies

The Start of Life

The period when a bitch can be mated occurs approximately every seven or eight months. This varies with different bitches; some may come into heat every five months, while others may go as long as twelve months. It is my personal opinion that Basset bitches should never be mated before two years of age; they are slow to mature, and I do not think a bitch should be required to carry, whelp and rear a litter until she is fully mature.

It is traditional for the period of pro-oestrus and oestrus to be referred to as *heat*, and sometimes a bitch may be referred to as being *in season*. The stages of the cycle are as follows:

- *Pro-oestrus* (1–8 days) is the beginning of being *in season*. The vulva becomes swollen and the bitch has a blood-stained discharge.
- *Oestrus* (9–15 days) is when the bitch will accept a stud dog and actually encourage him. The vulva is enlarged and soft and the bitch will switch her tail to one side and posture in front of the male. The blood-stained discharge is paler in colour.
- *Ovulation* occurs two days after oestrus.
- From 15–21 days the vulva returns to normal, the discharge ceases altogether, and the bitch is no longer attractive to males.

There can be no hard and fast rules as to the exact number of days bitches will be in pro-oestrus and oestrus. Some have been mated successfully on day 18–20 and some on day 4–5, but it is safe to say that the majority of bitches will fall in the 1–8- and 9–15-day category. The favoured days for mating are 11–13. It must be remembered that sperm from an active, fit stud dog can live in the bitch's reproductive tract for at least three days, perhaps longer, so, if a bitch is mated, her eggs still may be fertilised.

After fertilisation, two nuclei appear in each egg, one from the sire and one from the dam, each carrying half the chromosomes. When these two nuclei fuse, a whole new entity, carrying the full complement of 78 chromosomes, comes into being. Each puppy is programmed by these chromosomes for all the inherited characteristics it will have. Once fertilised, the egg goes through a process of very rapid division.

It can be seen from this that the puppy carries 50% of inherited characteristics from the sire and 50% from the dam. I always think it very strange that, when abnormalities or faults appear in the offspring, the first question always asked is, 'Who was the sire?', as if the dam had no part in the make-up of the pup.

Care of the Pregnant Bitch

From the time the bitch is mated extra care must be taken of her – though not to the extent of pampering or overfeeding her, as good, regular exercise is important and normal food intake should be maintained for the first three weeks. It is best to be advised by a veterinary surgeon regarding worming during this period. Various new worming products are continually being advertised, but the vet will know which product is the best for an in-whelp Basset bitch. It is courteous at this period to tell the vet when the bitch is expected to whelp. For the first three weeks the fertilised egg remains free in the uterus; at 21 days the forming embryo attaches itself to the walls of the uterine horns. This is when the vet can feel the budding foetuses and, in some cases, tell how many are forming. Once the foetuses are attached to the walls of the uterine horns by way of the placenta and umbilical cord they are very susceptible to any infection the dam may catch. After her season and for the following three weeks it is important to keep her away from any area with a high risk of infection and consequent damage to the foetuses.

Bassets can produce large litters: Brackenacre Mary Rose with a itter of 13.

Food and Supplements

After your bitch's season, carry on with her normal routine regarding food and exercise. The better condition she is in, the easier her whelping. Some people make the mistake of treating the in-whelp bitch as an invalid, but mating and pregnancy in an animal are perfectly natural functions.

At three weeks some bitches start refusing food. This only seems to last for two or three days and afterwards they eat normally. At 21 days I start feeding raspberry leaf tablets, an old-fashioned birth aid but one which I believe is very good. Also at this time the diet should be supplemented with extra calcium and Vitamin D. Many products on the market contain calcium and vitamin D in the correct proportions, but be sure you read the labels for the correct amounts. If the bitch is being fed solely on home-prepared food such as raw tripe, beef or fish, give extra vitamins. Check the labels for the contents of manufactured food; there is no point in doubling up on vitamins and minerals already included.

The Scan

If at 28 days it is imperative to know if the bitch is in whelp she can be given a scan. Ascertain whether your vet has the required equipment, as not all vets have a scanning machine available. No anaesthetic is required; just the bitch lying on her back while a jelly is rubbed over her tummy. The few times I have had a bitch scanned she has seemed to enjoy the experience. Normally her chest is smoothed or scratched by her owner, which all Bassets love, and this allows her to

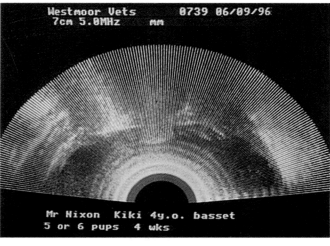

A scan taken at four weeks.

154

become very relaxed. In some cases she can stand up. The probe is gently moved over her stomach and the scanning machine can pick up the puppies, if any; these can be seen as small white blobs on the screen. A photograph of the image on the scanning machine is then given to the owner, stating the number of puppies the bitch could be expected to have. These numbers can only be approximate but at least it will be confirmed whether the bitch is in whelp or has missed.

The Later Stages

At 28–35 days it is rare to actually see any difference in the shape of the bitch, although at about five weeks the mammary glands begin to enlarge and the teats become a little bigger, pinker and more noticeable. I have found after the fifth week the bitch tends to look after herself more, refusing to play with her kennel companions and finding a quiet corner to relax in. She should be allowed as much exercise as she requires. If she is taken out on a lead, allow her to go at her own pace and do not over-tire her. From about the fifth week an opaque discharge may be noticed from the vagina, rather like egg white. This is perfectly natural and a good indication of pregnancy. By the sixth week she should be requiring more food, preferably divided into two meals: one morning and one in the evening. She will now probably start to increase in girth. As the foetuses are growing and the uterine horns fold back on themselves and drop lower in the abdomen, she will look very full from beneath the ribs. As she grows larger and the foetuses are taking up more room, she will probably be able to eat only small amounts, so small meals at more frequent intervals are imperative. Plenty of fresh water must always be available to her. It is at this stage that I introduce her to her whelping room, although I never force her to remain on her own. I have found that Basset bitches prefer to stay with kennel companions, but by this time I have removed any playful youngsters and leave her with a couple of old matrons who are happy eating, sleeping and quietly plodding about. During the last few days of pregnancy foetal movement may be detected after she has eaten or when she is lying asleep.

The Whelping Room

A room in your house is a far better place in which to whelp your bitch, regardless of how well appointed your kennel. You and your bitch will be spending a lot of time together in this room, so prepare well in advance for your mutual comfort.

Bedding

Whelping is a messy business, so have plenty of newspapers, preferably unused, as these should not have been contaminated by other animals. I always have plenty of blankets cut up into reasonable sizes. It may be thought that blankets are rather expensive to use but I normally tour the charity shops and pick them up very cheaply, then make a quick visit to the launderette to give them a good wash. These are then put in a bin liner to keep them clean.

The Whelping Box

The whelping box should now be put in the room. If it has been used before, make sure it is well and truly scrubbed with disinfectant and left in the sunlight to dry. If it is the first litter I would recommend that the whelping box be made of wood, with sides approximately 45cm (18in) high. On one side there should be a door with hinges to allow the bitch access. Laminated wood is excellent for the sides as this can easily be cleaned. Lay your bitch on her side and measure half-way up her back, which will be approximately 10cm (4in), and then screw a piece of wood 5cm x 5cm (2in x 2in) around the inside of the box 10cm from the base. This will enable the pups to get behind the mother without being crushed against the sides when she lies down. The size of the whelping box is determined by the length of the bitch lying relaxed on her side. Measure the length from the base of her tail to the tip of her nose when she is lying fully extended, then allow at least 30cm (12in) more. This enables her to lay relaxed with her whelps without being cramped in any way. I always have a wooden floor in my whelping box as some bitches dig a terrific amount, even when the pups are several days old. With a wooden floor, polyester fur can be tacked into the base. This prevents the bitch from digging the bedding into a heap and then lying on it with probably one or two puppies buried in the heap – a sure way of suffocating them. I use blue tacks with large, flat heads that can easily be removed at a later date.

Heat and Light

For light and warmth I use heated bulbs: the clear variety for the actual whelping, as this gives a very bright light, and a red bulb for when the litter is born and the bitch settles. The heating bulbs are usually on a flex that can be adjusted in height over the bitch – the higher the bulb the greater area the heat is spread over, the lower the bulb the more concentrated the heat on a particular spot.

Other Furnishings and Equipment

A reading lamp is useful, enabling one to read whilst waiting for the bitch to produce, a good book and a comfortable chair are essential, and a portable radio can also be an advantage.

A strong table covered with a non-slip cloth so that the bitch can be examined by a vet should the need arise is another essential. I also recommend two strong cardboard boxes, each containing a hot-water-bottle covered with a blanket. Use some of the blanket pieces to make a large envelope shape and put the bottle in this with the flap on the blanket envelope tucked well around; it is surprising how new born pups can wriggle into and under pieces of blanket. I have even known a breeder lose a puppy this way when it got stuck in the corner of the box under the blanket and suffocated, so pad the cardboard box and make sure there are no corners the pup can wriggle into. You will also need scales and pen and paper, to note the time each pup is born and its weight.

Other essentials in the whelping room are:

- A bowl for warm water, soap, nail brush and disinfectant – it's amazing how many times you need to wash your hands and scrub your finger nails during whelping.
- A bowl for fresh water for your bitch and a packet of glucose. A tablespoon of glucose in a pint of water will give her a little more energy and nourishment.
- Several packets of paper kitchen towels and some old towelling that can be discarded after use. These will help dry the pups quickly after birth.
- A couple of plastic bin-liners in which to place the soiled paper.
- A digital thermometer – the one that I like bleeps when the correct temperature is reached.
- Blunt-ended scissors (at the time of whelping these remain in a vessel of antiseptic).
- Surgical thread. In certain circumstances the umbilical cord may have to be tied to avert excessive bleeding.
- A camp bed or sleeping bag. Bassets are notorious for lying on puppies, so it is essential to have someone on hand 24 hours a day for the first two weeks.
- Always have the vet's telephone number at hand.
- If you have a mobile phone it would be useful to have it at your side.

The Birth

Gestation is nine weeks or 63 days, and I start taking the temperature of the in-whelp bitch once a day from the 56th day onwards. In my experience, when the temperature drops to 37.2°C (99°F) she will whelp within 24 hours. The normal temperature of a dog is 38.6°C (101.5°F), and it will be noticed the temperature will drop approximately 0.3°C (0.5°F) a day for the 4–5 days prior to

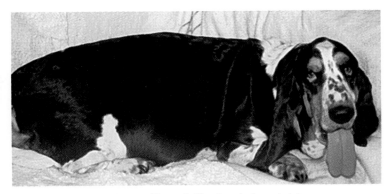

Ch Brackenacre Navan, half an hour before whelping.

whelping. Most of my Bassets have whelped on the 61st or 62nd day; should one go over the 63rd day the vet must be consulted.

Once the temperature has dropped to 37.2°F the bitch is brought indoors. My Basset bitches wish to be as close to me as possible at this period.

The First Stage

At the beginning of the first stage of whelping the bitch starts to shiver and pant, her eyes appear glassy and she will probably be sick a few times. This is when I put her in her whelping box with plenty of newspapers and blanket pieces. She will spend hours digging and shredding the newspapers and making innumerable beds with the blankets.

The Second Stage

At the onset of the second stage she will become quieter, pushing her hindquarters against the side of the whelping box as the abdominal contractions begin. This is when she needs someone with her all the time, preferably her owner. I have found over many whelpings that the bitch requires plenty of encouragement, affection and sympathy, especially if it is her first litter. The contractions may be spaced well apart – just two or three, then 10 minutes or more before she starts again. When the contractions are coming regularly (approximately one every 2 minutes) the birth will be imminent. Make sure there are plenty of newspapers and a piece of blanket under her hindquarters.

The membrane sack may appear filled with black fluid, and will probably break, spilling the fluid. This is not the puppy, but the water bag which has surrounded the foetus during gestation. Shortly afterwards the puppy's head or hind legs will appear, hopefully enclosed in its allantoic membrane. A few contractions, and the puppy should slide out. The bitch may neglect the puppy at first; she will be in a state of shock and does not appear to know what to do. This is when the owner must act quickly, removing the membrane from the puppy's head and wiping the nose and mouth with a cloth to clear away the fluid. The puppy will probably still be attached by the umbilical cord with the placenta inside the mother. Do not pull; hold the umbilical cord against the puppy's stomach and wait for a few moments. Once the bitch contracts again the placenta will slide out. Cut the cord about 5cm (2in) from the puppy's stomach. Should it bleed profusely, tie the cord with surgical thread. Once the puppy has been shown to the bitch and accepted by her, licked and cleaned, place the pup on a teat.

Ch Brackenacre Navan four hours after whelping started.

The Third Stage

Shortly after the puppy, the placenta should appear, and the bitch will probably try to eat it. Allow the bitch to eat two or three placentas, as it is thought that consumption of the placenta assists the flow of milk and contractions of the uterus. I do not let my bitches eat more than this as they usually get very loose bowel movements if they do.

Accepting the New Puppy

Should the bitch reject her first puppy, do not be alarmed; she is probably worried and shocked. Give the puppy a good rub with towelling and put it on a well wrapped hot-water-bottle. Heat is most essential for the pup at this time. Allow the bitch to clean herself while you clear away the wet newspapers and pieces of blanket and

A healthy litter of ten at four days.

The finished product: two of Navan's litter at six weeks.

insert fresh under her. This must be done after each puppy is born, so that the bitch is kept as clean, comfortable and dry as possible. Soothe and reassure her and, after she has settled, put the pup on the teat again, still reassuring her. In most cases she will investigate the puppy, lick it a few times, and the maternal instincts will take over; she will curl around the puppy and clean it again and again. Be careful that she does not get over excited; she may try to chew the umbilical cord really short, damaging the pup's stomach.

Contractions may start again within an hour. This time the bitch will most likely do all the business herself. Make sure the first puppy does not get crushed under her. I usually take the first puppy away and place it on the hot-water-bottle during the birth of the next pup. Provided that the bitch is resting between puppies and not having continuous contractions with nothing appearing, allow her to sleep as much as she likes. It is not unusual for a Basset to start whelping at midnight and perhaps produce her seventh puppy at 6.00 pm the following day. There is nothing more rewarding than seeing a Basset bitch with several puppies feeding contentedly.

When to Call the Vet

Occasionally a whelping may go wrong. A dead puppy may be the problem, or a puppy that is very large and cannot be passed. Alternatively, the bitch may be over-tired or succumb to uterine inertia. It is up to the owner to decide when the bitch requires veterinary attention. Never allow a bitch who is contracting evenly every two minutes to continue for a long period – you will have seen how long it took to expel a pup. Contact the vet immediately.

If the bitch appears to be in difficulty, contact the vet immediately, and be prepared to transport her to the surgery for examination and probably a caesarean. Always be advised by the vet. Should the bitch be given oxytocin (a drug which helps the uterus to contract) before being taken home, make sure there is someone else in the car; she can expel a puppy very quickly after these injections, possibly on the back seat of a car!

After Whelping

Once the whelping is over, allow the bitch to sleep as long as she wishes; this may be for several hours if she is exhausted. Once she is awake, I put all the puppies on the hot-water-bottles and take the bitch outside to relieve herself, then thoroughly wash her hindquarters in warm water and mild disinfectant. She will probably try to rush back to her puppies and normally, for the first few days, she will have to be taken out to the garden on a collar and lead, as she will not wish to leave her litter. When the bitch has been washed and dried, ensure that plenty of clean newspapers and a blanket are again placed in the whelping box so that she returns to a clean, dry box ready for her puppies.

This exercise is repeated every day for the next 10 days. At 10 days I place a thick pad of newspapers on the base of the whelping box, and then tack polyester fur securely over the paper; this is changed every four days until the pups are four weeks of age. I never allow young puppies to scrabble on newspapers; they are either on blankets or polyester fur. I find that on newspapers their legs are constantly slipping away from them and I do not think this helps either their shoulders or their hindquarters.

After the bitch's hindquarters have been washed and dried and she has returned to the litter, offer her some food. I always have some chicken ready for my bitches. They usually accept this and may eat a whole plateful or just a little. It often takes a couple of days for a bitch to get her full appetite back. Just keep offering her small meals of chicken or fish, as this is tasty and appetising. For the first few days after whelping, keep an eye on her temperature, which should return to normal (38.6°C) within 48 hours and remain fairly steady. Should it suddenly start to rise, consult the vet.

Rearing the Litter

By the time the puppies are two weeks old their eyes will be open and they will also be able to hear. The eyes will be blue, but they will gradually turn brown. The mother will be eating three good meals a day plus 1/2 pint of milk, two calcium and vitamin D tablets and some multi-vitamin tablets. Between the second and fourth week after whelping the bitch will eat an enormous amount of food. As well as feeding herself she is having to produce enough milk to help keep seven or eight puppies content. If the bitch has a litter of 10 or more, the puppies will have to be rotated on a two-hourly basis; otherwise the largest, strongest pups will force the smaller ones away from the teats and source of milk. Supplementary feeding may also be needed. There are several substitute milk products on the market for puppies, but nothing is as good as the dam's milk.

By two weeks the puppies should have had their nails cut twice. Always keep the nails short from the very beginning as it is kinder for the bitch. She will not want sharp claws on her teats, and it will prevent any scratching and injury to the eyes of the puppies.

Once the puppies can see and are up on their legs moving freely, the constant vigilance can cease. The puppies will be strong enough to move away from the bitch when she flops down.

Weaning

At three weeks the puppies are offered finely minced beef, and they are also wormed for the first time. I have found over the years that if I start weaning on goat's milk the puppies get loose bowel movements but if I start them with beef for a few days, and then introduce milk, this does not occur.

For the first few days I hand feed them with the very fine mince, but the time soon arrives to set a dish down with minced beef and gravy. After the first session the mother will spend about an hour cleaning them. It has to be seen to be believed; the pups will walk through it, sit in it and lie in it. No matter how many times they are pulled out, they go straight back in. Luckily, they soon get the message and stand around the dish, eating properly.

After they have had three days on the beef I start introducing milk: either warmed goat's milk or proprietary powdered milk. The quantities required will be printed on the label. Between the milk and meat meals they will still be feeding from their mother.

Once the puppies are on milk and beef meals and are about a month old, I remove the whelping box, allowing more space and freedom to move around. The mother will probably decide to remove herself from their presence for an hour or two at a time. I never force a bitch to stay with her litter all the time, but nor do

Like mother, like daughter.

LITTER OF 5 BORN
3 FEMALES   2 MALES

SIRE. BRACKENACRE HUGUENOT OF BEWMAY   DAM. CHAMPION BRACKENACRE MARY ANNE.

	WEEK 1	WEEK 2	WEEK 3	WEEK 4	WEEK 5	WEEK 6	WEEK 7	WEEK 8
WEIGHT BORN LEMON AND WHITE FEMALE, A LOT OF LEMON MARKINGS. **17 OZ**	1lb 10oz	2lb 10oz CUT NAILS	4lb 9oz WORMED STARTED TO FEED MINCED BEEF	5lb 1oz CUT NAILS INTRODUCED GOATS MILK	6lb 8oz eating 3 meals a day 2 mince 1 milk	7lb 15oz WORMED CUT NAILS REG: WITH KC	8lb 15oz 4 meals a day 2 thickened milk 2 meat + biscuits	10lb WORMED CUT NAILS INSURED
WEIGHT BORN TRI FEMALE **15 OZ**	1lb 12oz	2lb 8oz CUT NAILS	4lb 6oz WORMED STARTED TO FEED MINCED BEEF	5lb 7oz CUT NAILS INTRODUCED GOATS MILK	6lb 6oz eating 3 meals a day 2 mince 1 milk	7lb 10oz WORMED CUT NAILS REG: WITH KC	8lb 14oz 4 meals a day 2 thickened milk 2 meat biscuits	9lb 14oz WORMED CUT NAILS INSURED
WEIGHT BORN TRI FEMALE. **16 OZ**	1lb 13oz	2lb 9oz CUT NAILS	4lb 8oz WORMED STARTED TO FEED MINCED BEEF	5lb 6oz CUT NAILS INTRODUCED GOATS MILK	6lb 7oz 3 meals a day 2 mince 1 milk	7lb 11oz WORMED CUT NAILS REG: WITH KC	8lb 13oz 4 meals a day thickened milk 2 meat + biscuits	9lb 12oz WORMED CUT NAILS INSURED
WEIGHT BORN BLACK BLANKET MALE. **17 OZ**	1lb 13oz	2lb 10oz CUT NAILS	4lb 9oz WORMED STARTED TO FEED MINCED BEEF	5lb 7oz CUT NAILS INTRODUCED GOATS MILK	6lb 9oz eating 3 meals a day 2 mince 1 milk	7lb 14oz WORMED CUT NAILS REG: WITH KC	9lb 00 4 meals a day 2 meat + biscuits thickened milk	10. 0 WORMED CUT NAILS INSURED
WEIGHT BORN 18 OZ LEMON AND WHITE MALE NEARLY ALL WHITE. **18 OZ**	1lb 15oz	2lb 15oz CUT NAILS	4lb 1oz WORMED STARTED TO FEED MINCED BEEF	5lb 9oz CUT NAILS INTRODUCED GOATS MILK	6lb 12oz eating 3 meals a day 2 mince 1 milk	8lb 00 WORMED CUT NAILS REG: WITH KC	9lb 8oz 4 meals a day 2 meat + biscuits 2 thickened milk	11lb 00 WORMED CUT NAILS INSURED

A development chart for a litter. It doesn't have to be a work of art to be a great help in identification.

I remove her after a few weeks and never let her back with them. I know some breeders who cannot wait to remove the bitch from her litter so that her milk will dry up and and they can get her back into the show ring, but I think that this must be very distressing for the bitch and her litter. I let the dam decide when she wishes to be with them or when she wants to leave them. At about a month I put a raised bench in the room so that she can get up out of the way of her pups if she wishes.

At six weeks the litter is moved to an outdoor kennel, with access to an outside run. A wireless is installed, letting the pups get used to various noises. At six weeks the puppies will be wormed again, and at this time various other food products will be introduced to them, such as tinned puppy food, tripe, and a little all-in-one puppy food. I like to think they can eat a variety of food by the time they leave at eight weeks.

When the pups are about four weeks old the mother will cease to clean up after them, and the owner must then ensure that the puppies and their immediate surroundings are kept clean and fresh. From four to six weeks my pups' area is cleaned out about three or four times a day but, after six weeks, it seems never ending. If it is a summer litter and the weather is good the pups can get out in the run and they seem to get the message to urinate and defecate outside. However, a winter litter is difficult, as young puppies cannot be put out in the cold or rain, so plenty of newspapers have to be used in the kennel. The puppies will naturally go away from the bed with the polyester fur and use the newspaper, but this has to be cleaned up several times a day and replaced with fresh.

From about six weeks the puppies love to have toys to play with; an old cardboard box will occupy them for hours, and they also enjoy a plastic milk bottle to chase after, a large marrow bone that has been boiled clean, hard rubber bones and all sorts of things. Be vigilant with them; if they should chew the plastic, take it away from them. However, they must have their play time for mental and physical exercise and stimulation.

From the time the puppies can lap, their milk is thickened with baby rusks (Farleys or Boots, for example). These are for human babies, but puppies love them, and they also enjoy cereals such as Ready Brek and Shredded Wheat. Their meat will have a gravy made from Bovril poured over it and soaked puppy biscuits. As they get a little older they tend to prefer more solid food with less gravy, and pieces of meat they can pick up rather than the mushy mincemeat they had at four to six weeks. They also like to be able to pick up small biscuits and crunch them. At eight weeks the puppies should be wormed again.

Keeping Records

When the puppies were born their sex and markings should have been noted to differentiate between them. They should be weighed each week, to make sure they are all gaining weight as they should. An easy way to mark the progress is to cut out a small outline of a Basset in cardboard and trace as many outlines as there are puppies onto a sheet of paper, then roughly shade in a pup's markings on each silhouette. This is fairly easy with Bassets as they come in a variety of markings. As the pups grow it is easy to pick them out individually and use their chosen names. Even young puppies quickly recognise their names, but when they are very young it can be difficult. While I was writing this book my champion bitch Annie had a litter, and opposite you will find the chart of the litter (Brackenacre Huguenot of Bewmay ex Ch Brackenacre Mary Anne).

Selling the Puppies
Questions for Prospective Buyers

When the breeder of a Basset Hound litter receives enquiries from prospective buyers, the breeder should try to vet them. My first questions are as follows:

- *Will someone be at home for most of the day?* Bassets hate being left on their own for long periods of time.
- *Is there an enclosed garden?* The very nature of a Basset is to explore and hunt, so it would be useless to let a Basset pup out into an open-plan garden – the pup certainly wouldn't be there two minutes later!
- *Have you had a Basset Hound before?* I'm always glad if the reply is, 'Yes'.
- *Why do you want a Basset Hound?* If someone is thinking of owning a Basset Hound, they should have checked on the nature and characteristics of their chosen breed.

Paperwork

The breeder, prior to selling a puppy, should always have following available

- The pedigree.
- A feeding chart with a little advice on the breed.
- Any insurance papers for the puppies: I always insure my Basset puppies for the first month.
- The Kennel Club Registration must be included. The breeder can ensure that various endorsements are added to this, such as *Progeny Not Eligible For Registration* or *Not Eligible for the Issue of an Export Pedigree*. I feel that, before selling the puppy, the breeder should point out to the prospective buyer that these endorsements may only be removed by the breeder.

Sample Feeding Chart

[The feeding chart I give to prospective puppy owners]

The Basset Hound for its size has more bone than any other breed. To obtain this heavy bone the sire and dam must come of good, sound, heathy stock, but nature must be assisted by good feeding. The puppy that you have obtained from us has been bred from some of the finest blood lines in England, and from the time the dam was mated, she and her puppies have been fed on good quality meat, biscuits, milk, with calcium and vitamins added.

Food

Brackenacre....................is at present eating four meals per day as follows:

08.00 am	milk meal
12.00 noon	meat meal with vitamins and calcium.
04.00 pm	meat meal
10.00 pm	milk meal

The milk meal consist of:
190ml ($^1/_3$ pint) cow's or goat's milk with two Farley's rusks
or $^1/_2$ tin rice pudding + 190ml milk
or 190ml cow's or goat's milk thickened with Ready Brek

The meat meal consist of:
230g ($^1/_2$lb) meat cut into small pieces plus a handful of biscuits. Moisten the whole with gravy made from Bovril or Marmite.

Vitamins and calcium per day:
2 Canovel Tablets + 2 Calcidee Tablets   }
or 2 Pet Tabs + 2 Calcidee Tablets   } From your vet
or SA 37 Powder + Extra Calcium and Vitamin D   }

Canoval Tablets and Calcidee Tablets are for animals and are also obtainable from pet shops.

A large marrow bone is beneficial for the puppy to chew, but *do not* give small bones. A Basset has a very strong jaw and can easily crunch small bones into splinters.

These meals can continue until the puppy is three months. Then drop one of the milk meals. At nine months the puppy will probably only require one milk meal and one meat meal, and by twelve months 280ml ($^{1}/_{2}$ pint) milk per day plus 450g (1lb) meat and biscuits should be sufficient.

Do not cut out the puppy's vitamins and calcium until it is at least 18 months to 2 years, and even then you could carry on giving them.

Should you wish to transfer the puppy to an all-in-one food product, start introducing it gradually into the meat meal, reducing the meat and biscuit and increasing the all-in-one product each day. Once the puppy is eating the all-in-one product, cut out all the other food. The instructions on the packet must be adhered to and no extra vitamins or calcium added.

Another product which is good for a Basset is Vetzyme tablets.

Worming and Vaccinations

Brackenacre....................was wormed at the age of six weeks and eight weeks, and should be wormed again at 12 weeks. He/she should also be taken to the veterinary surgeon to be epivaxed (vaccinated) at 12 weeks.

Sleeping Quarters

Brackenacre ....has been living with the rest of the litter in a warm room for the last eight weeks, and no doubt it will be very strange for him to be alone with new owners. It will take a few days for him to adjust. He will, of course, miss the warmth and company. It will probably help to put a hot water bottle (well wrapped) in his bed, and a ticking clock seems to comfort a young pup. As he is used to sleeping in a draught-proof box on a blanket, it would help if this practice could be continued. If he has his own bed, kept in the same place, he will soon learn this is his particular corner of the room and will retire to it whenever he wishes to sleep or be quiet.

Exercise

A Basset should *never* be allowed to walk in the street before he has been epivaxed (fully vaccinated) at the age of three months. Also, because of the terrific growth rate of the Basset, he should *not* be taken for any long walks before the age of six months. Playing in the garden and short walks of about 180m (200yd) will be sufficient. *Do not* allow your pup to jump up and down steps or on furniture, as this could easily produce loose shoulders and unsound front.

Training

The Basset takes a long time to learn simple rules of obedience but, once a lesson has been learnt, it will take heaven and earth to remove it from his head, so please be patient and firm.

Grooming

The Basset needs very little grooming; one good brush a day will be enough. A couple of points to watch: if the ears drop in the food, just sponge them with warm water and soap to prevent them from smelling and stop food clogging the ends. Also, keep his nails clipped short.

Any Further Problems...

If you should have any problems with your puppy, please do not hesitate to ring us. The telephone number is Plymouth (01752) 361201 and the best time to ring is 5.30–6.30 pm.

Basset Hound Champions

Name	Sex	DOB	Sire	Dam	Breeder
1904					
Queen of the Geisha	b	30.03.1898	Ch Paris	Fairstar	J Stark
1906					
Loo Loo Loo	d	17.06.01	Ch Louis Le Beau	Sibella	Mrs M Tottie
1907					
Sandringham Dido	b	13.09.04	Tarquin	Viola (*unregistered*)	Col J H Amand
1909					
Waverer	d	12.07.04	Major (*unregistered*)	Daisy (*unregistered*)	A Croxton-Smith
1913					
Mentor	d	03.07.10	Ch Waverer	Ch Melanie	J P & W Roberts
Melanie	b	25.07.07	Ch Loo Loo Loo	Mirette	Miss E Wright
1915					
Warrender	b	26.07.10	Ch Waverer	Sandringham Pamela	Queen Alexandra
1925					
Walhampton Andrew	d	20.06.22	Walhampton Ferryman	Walhampton Actress (*unregistered*)	Maj G Heseltine
1926					
Walhampton Gratitude	b	23.06.24	Walhampton Linguist	Walhampton Grizel	Maj G Heseltine
1931					
Patience	b	09.02.29	Walhampton Lingerer	Walhampton Pardon	Maj G Heseltine
Walhampton Ambassador	d	07.05.28	Walhampton Lymington	Walhampton Amber	Maj G Heseltine
1932					
Walhampton Lynnewood	d	22.05.28	Walhampton Musket	Walhampton Lyric (*unregistered*)	Maj G Heseltine
1933					
Walhampton Nightshade	b	28.06.30	Walhampton Grazier	Walhampton Nicknack	Maj G Heseltine
1935					
Orpheus of Reynalton	d	09.12.33	Ch Walhampton Lynnewood	Ch Walhampton Nightshade	Mrs N Elms
1936					
Pigeon	b	09.10.33	Walhampton Grazier	Walhampton Nicknack	Mrs E Grew
Plover	d	09.10.33	Walhampton Grazier	Walhampton Nicknack	Mrs E Grew
Venus of Reynalton	b	09.12.33	Ch Walhampton Lynnewood	Ch Walhampton Nightshade	Mrs N Elms
1937					
Minerva of Reynalton	b	09.12.33	Ch Walhampton Lynnewood	Ch Walhampton Nightshade	Mrs N Elms
Monkshood of Reynalton	d	01.05.35	Loyalty of Reynalton	Ch Walhampton Nightshade	Mrs N Elms
1938					
Narcissus of Reynalton	b	09.12.33	Ch Walhampton Lynnewood	Ch Walhampton Nightshade	Mrs N Elms
1950					
Grims Warlock	d	26.09.46	Grims Worship	Grims Waspish	Miss M Keevil
Grims Wishful	b	14.05.40	Marquis	Wick Welcome	Miss M Keevil
Grims Waterwagtail	b	30.04.49	Grims Doughnut	Grims Watercress	Miss M Keevil

Year / Name	Sex	Date	Sire	Dam	Owner
1952					
Grims Doughnut	d	11.08.47	Westerby Rennet	Grims Daisy	Miss M Keevil
Grims Useful	b	09.07.50	Grims Ulema de Barly	Grims Wallflower	Miss M Keevil
1954					
Grims Wideawake	d	01.11.51	Grims Ulema de Barly	Grims Waterlily	Miss M Keevil
Grims Willow	b	01.11.51	Grims Ulema de Barly	Grims Waterlily	Miss M Keevil
Songster of Reynalton	d	01.01.48	Sovereign of Reynalton	Miranda of Reynalton	Mrs E Elms
1956					
Grims Whirlwind	d	05.05.54	Grims Ulema de Barly	Grims Wanda	Miss M Keevil
Grims Gracious	b	18.07.54	Ch Grims Wideawake	Grims Garrulous	Miss M Keevil
1957					
Grims Westward	d	05.05.54	Grims Ulema de Barly	Grims Wanda	Miss M Keevil
Rossingham Amber	b	01.07.53	Ch Grims Warlock	Ch Grims Willow	Mrs A Hodson
Rossingham Anxious	b	01.07.53	Ch Grims Warlock	Ch Grims Willow	Mrs A Hodson
Rossingham Badger	d	20.02.55	Ch Grims Doughnut	Ch Grims Willow	Mrs A Hodson
Grims Vapid	b	19.06.56	Grims Emblem	Ch Grims Useful	Miss M Keevil
1958					
Fochno Trinket	b	29.04.57	Ch Grims Whirlwind	Sykemoor Gossip	Mrs J Lorton
1959					
Barnspark Rakish	d	07.07.57	Ch Grims Westward	Ch Grims Gracious	Mrs M Rawle
Brockhampton Soloman	d	08.08.56	Ch Grims Westward	Grims Minx	G W Dakin
Rossingham Cosy	b	07.08.56	Ch Grims Doughnut	Ch Rossingham Anxious	Mrs A Hodson
Mariseni Rarnee	b	12.04.58	Ch Rossingham Badger	Barnspark Rustic	Mrs P Warren
1960					
Jamestown Generous	b	22.07.55	Rossingham Ambassador	Grims Gainful	Mrs J Eisenman
Fochno Trooper	d	29.04.57	Ch Grims Whirlwind	Sykemoor Gossip	Mrs J Lorton
1961					
Sungarth Sykemoor Aimwell	d	03.06.59	Ch Grims Whirlwind	Ch Rossingham Amber	G J Johnston
Sykemoor Wiza	b	05.06.58	Sykemoor Garnet	Sykemoor Jealousy	G J Johnston
Bashful Bert	d	24.06.58	Grims Charlie	Lucy of Morcombelake	Countess of Craven
Kelperland Baneful	b	07.06.59	Grims Emblem	Kelperland Amanda	Mrs J Townson
Barnspark Vanity	b	23.04.59	Ch Grims Westward	Ch Grims Vapid	Mrs M Rawle
1962					
Breightmet Chimer	d	15.03.58	Grims Charlie	Grims Vanish	Mrs E Baynes
Kelperland Artful	d	11.11.57	Ch Rossingham Badger	Rossingham Amorous	Mrs J Townson
Crochmaid Bold Turpin of Blackheath	d	12.07.57	Santana Hounslow Highwayman	Santana Kate Hardcastle	Mrs C Babson (USA)
Stalwart Debbie	b	02.06.59	Grims Varlet	Stalwart Thoughtful	E J Evans
Mariseni Breightmet Wessex	d	05.05.59	Ch Grims Westward	Grims Vanish	Mrs M E Baynes
Dreynin Appeline Coral	b	08.09.61	Grims Lager	Appeline Dawn	Mr & Mrs D Appleton
Fredwell Varon Vandal	d	21.11.60	Ch Fochno Trooper	Rollick of Fredwell	E Roberts

Name	Sex	DOB	Sire	Dam	Breeder
1963					
Appeline Rochester	d	29.05.61	Ch Grims Westward	Solemn Melody	Mrs J M Milne
Hooksway Cheeky Checkmate	b	08.10.61	Ch Sungarth Sykemoor Aimwell	Peardrop Princess	Mrs B Symonds
Sungarth Phoebe	b	30.09.60	Ch Sungarth Sykemoor Aimwell	Aesops Able	Mrs B Prior
1964					
Sykemoor Emma	b	16.05.62	Fochno Trumpeter	Sykemoor Jealousy	G I Johnston
Wingjays Fanciful	d	22.11.61	Ch Sungarth Sykemoor Aimwell	Sungarth Jasmin	Mrs J Rowett-Johns
Avenwood Dulcis	b	04.04.63	Ch Breightmet Chimer	Wingjays Beautiful	Mrs M Ashton
Barnspark Clarion	d	05.11.60	Ch Breightmet Chimer	Ch Grims Gracious	Mrs M Rawle
Pointgrey Suss's Folly	d	24.01.62	Lyn-Mar Acres Dauntless	Julie of Aldbury	Mrs A Reed
Chantinghall Flaxen	b	19.03.62	Grims Lager	Mariseni Goodness Gracious	Mrs B Greensmith-Downes
Chantinghall Jemima of Maycombe	b	13.11.62	Grims Lager	Chantinghall Bramble	Mrs R McKnight
1965					
Wingjays Fabulous	b	22.10.63	Ch Fredwell Varon Vandal	Ch Sungarth Phoebe	Mrs J Rowett-Johns
Chantinghall Ancestor	d	24.06.64	Ch Pointgrey Suss's Folly	Chantinghall Harmony	Mrs R McKnight
Fredwell Ideal	d	01.12.61	Ch Mariseni Breightmet Wessex	Fredwell Rennet	Mrs J Wells
Chantinghall Harmony	b	15.09.63	Chantinghall Cognac	Mariseni Goodness Gracious	Mrs R McKnight
Chantinghall Kitebrook Barley	b	19.06.63	Ch Breightmet Chimer	Kitebrook Lilliesleaf Helen	Mr & Mrs M McDermott
Chantinghall Fredwell Amber	b	01.04.64	Ch Fredwell Varon Vandal	Musical Melodies	Mrs Bowen
1966					
Mapleroyal Avenwood Atalanta	b	18.04.64	Kitebrook Actor	Wingjays Lovable	Mrs M Ashton
Fredwell Charmer	b	12.08.64	Ch Fredwell Ideal	Fredwell Annuk	Mrs J Wells
Grims Fochno Charming	b	03.05.63	Ch Breightmet Chimer	Ch Fochno Trinket	Mrs W Jagger
Maycombe Vaisya	b	17.08.65	Ch Fredwell Varon Vandal	Ch Chantinghall Jemima of Maycombe	Mrs M Seiffert
Bactona Jupiter	d	01.08.63	Ch Fredwell Varon Vandal	Narrabri Andromeda	Mrs J Lacey
Wingjays Ptolemy	d	13.07.64	Ch Breightmet Chimer	Ch Sungarth Phoebe	Mrs J Rowett-Johns
1967					
Fredwell Maitri	d	16.07.63	Ch Fredwell Varon Vandal	Treasure of Fredwell	Mrs J Wells
Vescou Phoebe Jane	b	18.04.64	Ch Fredwell Varon Vandal	Justice of Cherryrock	Mr & Mrs Tilley
Brackenacre Annabella	b	04.07.64	Hardacre Sungarth Eager	Brackenacre Kierhill Oonagh	Mr & Mrs J F C Nixon
Wingjays Polygamy of Maycombe	d	06.12.65	Ch Wingjays Ptolemy	Mapleroyal Zelma	Mrs R Rowett-Johns
Fredwell Perfect	b	31.05.64	Fredwell Maestro	Blairgold Venture	Mrs J Wells
1968					
Huckworthy Tankard	d	22.02.64	Sungarth Token	Goldie's Dorothy	Mrs J Kynoch
Rowynan Lark	b	27.07.65	Rowynan Chantinghall Legacy	Rowynan Cindy	Mrs R Goodyear
Foyewyn Stroller	d	02.12.65	Ch Breightmet Chimer	Rosudgeon Dido	Mrs S Goodwin
Bargriff Eden	d	18.12.65	Ch Fredwell Ideal	B argriff Rowynan Gigi	Mrs B Griffiths
Manory Craton Gretel	b	21.12.65	Ch Fredwell Varon Vandal	Doles Cleopatra	M Crabbe
Tintally Dubonnet	b	06.06.66	Ch Wingjays Ptolemy	Tintally Anisette	Mrs S Blackler
Framlands Clover	b	22.06.66	Ch Fredwell Varon Vandal	Framlands Blossom	Mmes Guthrie-Reed & Taylor
Hardacre Valorous	d	21.10.66	Ch Fredwell Varon Vandal	Chantinghall Quality of Maycombe	Mrs A Matthews

Name	Sex	Date	Sire	Dam	Owner
Balleroy Chestnut	d	24.03.67	Ch Chantinghall Ancestor	Ch Chantinghall Beatrice	Mrs P Moncur
Rollinhills Wingjays Fabric	b	17.05.67	Ch Wingjays Ptolemy	Ch Wingjays Fabulous	Mrs J Rowett-Johns
1969					
Chantinghall Beatrice	b	10.05.65	Ch Wingjays Fanciful	Chantinghall Airs 'n' Graces	Mrs J Rowett-Johns
Wingjays Polonaise	b	12.12.65	Ch Wingjays Ptolemy	Maploroyal Zelma	Mrs J Rowett-Johns
Charford Hurtwood Grisette	b	13.10.66	Kitebrook Banner	Weirwater Grizelle	Mrs F Bridger
Fredwell Varon Fawkes	d	24.02.67	It/Swiss Ch Fredwell Dimber	Fredwell Pickle	E Roberts
Fredwell Varon Fichle	b	24.02.67	It/Swiss Ch Fredwell Dimber	Fredwell Pickle	E Roberts
Fredwell Symon	d	05.03.67	It/Swiss Ch Fredwell Dimber	Axters Jezabel	Mrs Galley
Foyewyn Berenice	b	13.10.67	Rowynan Chantinghall Legacy	Foyewyn Diamond	Mrs S Goodwin
Verwood Mirus	d	25.04.68	It/Swiss Ch Dreymin Duskie Knight	Verwood Chinook	Mrs V Ross
1970					
Ballymaconnel Forester	d	13.09.65	Ch Chantinghall Ancestor	Ballymaconnel Boule de Suif	Mr & Mrs Bridgham
Huckworthy Leader	d	19.10.66	Hellidon Lager	Huckworthy Hopeful	Mrs Hall-Parlby
Huckworthy Lyric	b	19.10.66	Hellidon Lager	Huckworthy Hopeful	Mrs Hall-Parlby
Fredwell Tolly	b	22.10.66	Ch Wingjays Ptolemy	Fredwell Dreamer	Mrs J Wells
Saxonsprings Bargriff Kimble	d	09.09.67	Ch Fredwell Ideal	Bargriff Rowynan Gigi	Mrs B Griffins
Maycombe Victoria	b	28.10.67	Ch Hardacre Valorous	Ch Chantinghall Kitebrook Barley	Mrs M Seiffert
Dowerwood Soames	d	20.11.67	Chantinghall Dynasty	Breedmore Mirabelle	Mrs D Heslewood
Rowynan Taro	d	31.12.67	Rowynan Chantinghall Ancestor	Rowynan Chantinghall Marcasite	Mrs R Goodyear
Fredwell Balleroy Faithful	b	29.04.68	Ch Chantinghall Ancestor	Ch Chantinghall Beatrice	Mrs P Moncur
Wingjays Parthenon	d	03.09.68	Ch Wingjays Ptolemy	Wingjays Vanilla	Mrs J Rowett-Johns
Langstone Pearl	b	03.09.68	Ch Chantinghall Ancestor	Ch Hooksway Cheeky Checkmate	Mrs J Thompson
1971					
Barnspark Frolic	b	19.08.64	Ch Pointgrey Suss's Folly	Barnspark Charity	Mrs M Rawle
Barrabooka Apple Pie	b	17.10.67	Ch Fredwell Ideal	Grims Ready	Mrs J Wilson
Turberville Amaryllis	b	21.07.68	Ch Wingjays Ptolemy	Turberville Kelperland Necessity	Mrs D Shemeld
Rollinhills Wingjays Phoebe	b	03.09.68	Ch Wingjays Ptolemy	Wingjays Vanilla	Mrs J Rowett-Johns
Coastal Winston	d	18.11.68	Montague of Aberthin	Coastal Agnes	Miss W Thomas
Hobcote Folly	b	20.06.69	Balleroy Fanfare of Twobridge	Chantinghall Promise	Mrs A Hainsworth
Brackenacre Daisy Belle	b	11.10.69	Ch Fredwell Varon Vandal	Ch Brackenacre Annabella	Mr & Mrs J Nixon
Rollinhills Camilline Cuckoo	b	16.12.69	Wingjays Prometheus	Bargriff Camille	Mrs J Lawther
1972					
Coastal Weaver of Aberthin	d	18.11.68	Montague of Aberthin	Coastal Agnes	Miss W Thomas
Balleroy Nero	d	25.10.69	Ch Balleroy Chestnut	Ch Balleroy Elegant	Mrs P Moncur
Lymewoods Finesse	b	07.11.69	Watercrest Solo	Lymewood Elegance	A Wood
Wellshim Cruiser	d	26.07.70	Dalewell Rambler	Stationhouse Honey	Mrs A Shimwell
Maycombe Merryman	d	30.08.70	Ch Chantinghall Ancestor	Maycombe Merrylass	Mrs Gurney

Name	Sex	DOB	Sire	Dam	Breeder
Fredwell Flick	d	04.10.70	Ch Fredwell Ideal	Ch Fredwell Balleroy Faithful	Mrs J Wells- Meacham
Tamsmorna Heinekin	d	09.10.70	Croswolla John Peel	Tamsmorna Cleopatra	Mrs Trezona
Balleroy Yasmin	b	16.11.71	Ch Balleroy Chestnut	Balleroy Toffee	Mrs P Moncur
Balleroy Elegant	b	03.02.68	Ch Wingjays Polygamy of Maycombe	Balleroy Chantinghall Dreamer	Mrs P Moncur
1973					
Chalkridge Francine	b	27.04.68	Ch Fredwell Varon Fawkes	Varon Eleonore	Mrs P Stevens
Beacontree Vanessa	b	10.07.69	Ch Hardacre Valorous	Beacontree Emotion	Mrs B Golding
Wingjays Pippin	b	29.07.70	Wingjays Prometheus	Wingjays Peonie	Mrs J Rowett-Johns
Stormfield Hugo	d	10.10.70	Ch Ballymaconnel Forester	Stormfield Tansey	Mrs W Burgis
Wingjays Polygon	d	13.04.71	Wingjays Prometheus	Ch Wingjays Polonaise	Mrs J Rowett-Johns
Rollinhills The Swan	d	24.06.71	Wingjays Prometheus	Rollinhill Rollick	Mmes White & Lawther
Tintally Deborah	b	31.07.71	Ch Wingjays Parthenon	Ch Tintally Dubonnet	Mrs S Blackler
Tintally Dubotante	b	31.07.71	Ch Wingjays Parthenon	Ch Tintally Dubonnet	Mrs S Blackler
Brackenacre Fino de Paris	d	18.09.71	Ch Fredwell Ideal	Brackenacre Chime of Bells	Mr & Mrs J Nixon
Langpool Miss America Pie	b	18.03.72	Am Ch Longview Acres Bonza	Balleroy Barshaw Caprice	Dr E Andrews
Cwmdale Kynaston of Aberthin	d	17.10.70	Badger of Cwmdale	Monklow Aphrodite of Aberthin	Mrs J Hallett
Lymewoods Howard	d	15.11.71	Brigantium Fredwell Flipacoin	Lymewoods Elegance	A Wood
1974					
Woodland Amber	b	22.02.69	Ch Wingjays Ptolemy	Woodland Beauty	Mrs S Phillips
Boarfield Cassius	d	20.11.70	Ch Wingjays Parthenon	Boarfield Bonnie	Miss C Freeman
Trevayler Thomas John	d	18.03.71	Croswolla John Peel	Goeland Mambo	Mrs M Williams
Wingjays Opinion	d	24.06.71	Wingjays Optimistic	Wingjays Penelope	Mrs F Morgan
Akerwood Pollyanna	d	27.07.71	Ch Wingjays Parthenon	Akerwood Echelle	Mrs J Walker
Bevois Anna-Marie	b	06.11.71	Ch Maycombe Merryman	Langstone Epona of Bevois	Mrs L Bright
Gaymel Gay Tamarisk of Drawdell	b	28.02.72	Gaymell Marcus	Framberleys Bellisima of Gaymell	Mrs M Travis
Hobcote Portrait	b	16.06.72	Badger of Cwmdale	Ch Hobcote Folly	Mrs A Hainsworth
Akerwood Tweedledum	d	27.08.72	Ch Tamsmorna Heinekin	Akerwood Echelle	Mrs J Walker
Langpool Carrie Anne	b	23.03.73	Am Ch Longview Acres Bonza	Balleroy Barshaw Caprice	Dr E Andrews
1975					
Ballymaconnel Ravish	b	06.04.70	Ir Ch Ballymaconnel Orator	Ballymaconnel Happy	Mr & Mrs G Bridgham
Medgoed Sensation of Aberthin	b	19.04.70	Ch Coastal Weaver of Aberthin	Mineva of Aberthin	Mrs J Hallett
Turberville Akerwood Jester	d	15.08.70	Turberville Acanthus	Akerwood Garland	Mrs J Walker
Maycombe Mignon	b	20.02.72	Ch Wingjays Ptolemy	Wentworth Mystic	Mrs M Seiffert
Abbeyacres Pippa	b	13.05.72	Fredwell Destrie	Foyewyn Erica	Miss C Montjambert
Gaymel Saffron Dehazebury	b	01.01.73	Gaymel Indigo Pippin	Gaymel Selena	Mrs M Travis
Balleroy Luther	d	22.09.73	Balleroy Bacchus	Balleroy Hoo-Ha	Mrs P Moncur
Rollinhills Silver Wings	b	16.10.73	Ch Rollinhills The Swan	Rollinhills Peppermint	Mrs B White
1976					
Riverton Pepperpot	b	09.04.73	Rollinhills Wingjays Polo	Riverton Rollinhills Gabrielle	R Proctor
Beacontree Teazel	d	22.05.73	Langpool Friar Tuck U The Beacontree	Beacontree Chervil	Mrs B Golding
Brackenacre Jessica	b	16.09.73	Ch Brackenacre Fino de Paris	Ch Brackenacre Daisy Belle	Mr & Mrs J Nixon
Blaby Hal	d	25.02.74	Ch Lymewood Howard	Blaby Biddy	Mrs D Gilberthorpe

Name	DOB	Sex	Sire	Dam	Owner
Bezel Sweety Pie	30.05.74	b	Bezel Banner Man	Ireton Charity Sweet	Mrs M Thorley
Red Baron of Ide	27.10.74	d	Chesterfield Simon	Bassbar Flareout Contralto	W O'Loughlin
Wingjays Pania	15.04.75	b	Wingjays Prometheus	Wigjays Mimi	Mrs J Rowett-Johns
Stormfield Russet of Merreybeech	05.09.75	b	Ch Stormfield Hugo	Beacontree Ember	Mrs S McHardy- Young
1977					
Dibbypooh Premiere	13.03.72	b	Ch Winjays Polygon	Wingjays Parapet	Mrs Tiplady
Balleroy Fiddler	28.07.72	d	Ch Cwmdale Kynaston of Aberthin	Balleroy Sapphire	Mrs P Moncur
Golden Boy of Jeffrone	03.07.74	d	Ch Rollinhills The Swan	Blaby Starlit	Mrs Rice
Bassbar Victoria Plumb	02.11.74	b	Ch Hardacre Valorous	Temerloh's Sundays Child	W O'Loughlin
Meddgoed Mary Poppins	27.03.75	b	Ch Trevayler Thomas John	Meddgoed Cedarglen Diomed	A Reed
1978					
Langpool William	23.03.73	d	Am Ch Longview Acres Bonza	Balleroy Barshaw Caprice	Dr E Andrews
Brackenacre Jingle Bell	16.09.73	b	Ch Brackenacre Fino de Paris	Ch Brackenacre Daisy Belle	Mr & Mrs J Nixon
Rollinhills Sailing By	16.10.73	d	Ch Rollinhills The Swan	Rollinhills Peppermint	Mrs B White
Bevois Bordeaux	26.11.73	d	Ch Stormfield Hugo	Langstone Epona of Bevois	L Bright & K Vincent
Turberville Easter Rose	17.04.74	b	Tamsmorna Heinekin	Turberville Duchess	Mrs D Shemeld
Lyndthorpe Bashful	24.08.75	b	Ch Brackenacre Fino de Paris	Fredwell Puffball	Mrs J Stewart
Tintally D'Arcy	25.08.75	d	Ch Brackenacre Fino de Paris	Ch Tintally Deborah	Mrs S Blackler
Wynsell Bumble	27.07.76	b	Ch Rollinhills Sailing By	Lockridge Brocade	Mrs D Selwyn
Franshaw War Cry	16.10.76	d	Ch Red Baron of Ide	Franshaw Rennet	Mrs F Shaw
1979					
Brackenacre James Bond	08.05.74	d	Ch Brackenacre Fino de Paris	Brackenacre Emma Peel	Mr & Mrs J Nixon
Stormfield Diana of Lelaurin	05.09.75	b	Ch Stormfield Hugo	Beacontree Ember	Mrs S McHardy-Young
Bezel Genevieve of Tamsmorna	15.10.75	b	Akerwood Pegasus	Bezel Penny Piece	Mrs Thorley
Jeffrone Guillemot	12.05.76	b	Ch Rollinhills Sailing By	Jeffrone Replica of Clancy	F Horsley
Jeffrone Red Admiral	21.07.76	d	Tonegar Kestrel of Jeffrone	Jeffrone Sugar and Spice	F Horsley
Harecroft Magnus of Balleroy	27.07.76	d	Ch Balleroy Luther	Gaymel Moray	Mr & Mrs R Price
Maycombe Ali Baba	24.04.77	d	Verwood Varne	Minerva of Maycombe	Mrs M Seiffert
Sykemoor Ruby	17.06.77	b	Ch Balleroy Luther	Sykemoor Urfa	G Johnston
Sykemoor Rosebud	17.06.77	b	Ch Balleroy Luther	Sykemoor Urfa	G Johnston
Langpool Scrumpy	29.08.77	d	Ch Rollinhills Sailing By	Ch Langpool Carrie Anne	Dr E Andrews
Harecroft Lydia	03.10.77	b	Ch Balleroy Luther	Gaymel Moray	Mr & Mrs R Price
Langpool Carries Lad of Islwyn	22.09.78	d	Verwood Wabash	Ch Langpool Carrie Anne	Dr E Andrews
1980					
Witchacre Tom Tom	15.12.75	d	Ch Trevayler Thomas John	Trevayler Tambourine	Mr & Mrs J Ryan
Mayflower of Langpool	26.03.76	b	Ch Langpool William	Dubrova Hanky Panky	Mrs Whitmarch
Zonda's I'm A Muddy Girl of Verwood	23.05.76	b	Nord Ch Verwood Dado	Nord Ch Roosters Muddy Girl	Mr & Mrs Samuelsson (Swe)
Sykemoor Ruthie	17.06.77	b	Ch Balleroy Luther	Sykemoor Urfa	G Johnston
Bezel Isabella	13.11.77	b	Bezel Action Man	Ireton Charity Sweet	Mrs M Thorley
Tanneron Staffa	12.12.77	d	Ch Beacontree Teazel	Tanneron Jinty	Mrs F Luxmoore-Ball
Ledline White Apache	22.02.78	b	Inov The Red at Beacontree	Tonegar Warbler of Ledline	T Ledbury
Eastville King of Swing	14.05.78	d	Bassbar Jimmy Ruffin	Stormfield Caprice	Mrs M Wood

Name	Sex	DOB	Sire	Dam	Breeder
Yeldersley Geminesse	b	06.07.78	Ch Langpool William	Yeldersley Age of Aquarius	Mrs R Leaf
Bezel Jolligolly Man	d	30.09.78	Bezel Action Man	Ch Bezel Sweety Pie	Mrs M Thorley
1981					
Harecroft Lucretia of Balleroy	b	03.10.77	Ch Balleroy Luther	Gaymel Moray	Mr & Mrs R Price
Mayacre Mr Magoo	d	01.11.77	Beacontree Virgil	Witchacre Tympano	Mrs M Mayling
Maycombe Mirontine	b	28.08.78	Verwood Varne	Maycombe Medina	Mrs M Seiffert
Sykemoor Birdsong	b	17.11.78	Ch Balleroy Luther	Sykemoor Urfa	G Johnston
Beacontree Gelarista Gold Blend	d	16.12.78	Beacontree Dogdays	Beacontree Coffee Bean	Mrs I Crawford
Lelaurin Jaffa	d	14.03.79	Ch Langpool William	Ch Stormfield Diana of Lelaurin	Mrs J Laurie
Knockfinn Isaac of Lymewoods	d	09.01.80	Ch Rollinhills The Swan	Ir Ch Cilfoyle Franchesca	Mr & Mrs McDowell
Blaby Marrygolde	b	02.02.80	Ch Harecroft Magnus of Balleroy	Jussland Fancy Free of Blaby	Mrs D Gilberthorpe
1982					
Metesford Blazer	d	30.05.77	Ch Lymewoods Howard	Fredwell Sharon of Metesford	Mrs Halstead
Mevacombe Suki	b	06.03.78	Ch Tamsmoma Heinekin	Birchacre Lyric	Mr & Mrs B Carslake
Sykemoor Bugle Ann	b	17.11.78	Ch Balleroy Luther	Sykemoor Urfa	G Johnston
Bassbarr Dutch Bonnet	b	16.04.79	Nl Ch Beacontree Whynot	Bassbarr Chanteuse	Mrs J Walker
Lodway Lancer of Islwyn	d	16.09.80	Ch Langpool Carries Lad of Islwyn	Ch Mayflower of Langpool	Miss P Flynn
Brackenacre The Viking	d	22.12.80	Ch Brackenacre James Bond	Witchacre Magpie of Brackenacre	Mr & Mrs J Nixon
Vinell Antimony	b	24.10.80	Ch Beacontree Gelarista Gold Blend	Tanneron Eriskay of Vinell	Mrs L Ellrich
1983					
Galants Etcetera of Maycombe	b	12.03.81	Verwood Royal Swede	Maycombe Scheherazade of Galant	Mrs I Mosebery
Rossfell Long John Silver	d	03.11.80	Ch Jeffrone Red Admiral	Drawdell Kalamity Kate	Mr & Mrs R Parker
Hartlake Twilight	b	15.07.80	Ledline Why Not Me	Hartlake Black Magic	Mr & Mrs Bursey
Kuntree Rhodes at Belvere	d	13.08.81	Ch Langpool Carries Lad of Islwyn	Belvere Gemima	Mrs A Ventrella
Brackenacre Primrose	b	11.08.78	Witchacre Jimlad	Brackenacre Diamond Lil	Mr & Mrs J Nixon
Vinell Adorable of Tanneron	b	24.10.80	Ch Beacontree Gelarista Gold Blend	Tanneron Eriskay of Vinell	Mrs L Ellrich
Knockfinn Isabel of Rollinhills	b	09.01.80	Ch Rollinhills The Swan	Ir Ch Cilfoyle Franchesca	Mrs G McDowell
Carresmar Legend	d	22.07.79	Ch Mayacre Mr Magoo	Birchacre Laurel of Carresmar	Mrs E Watson
Lingross Debonair	b	13.07.80	Kirbyparks Born Free	Lingross Bo-Peep	Mr & Mrs K Grosse
Langpool Wishing Star	b	12.06.81	Ch Langpool William	Meddgoed Moonbeam of Langpool	Dr E Andrews
1984					
Biscovey Robert-E-Lee	d	11.11.81	Ch Harecroft Magnus of Balleroy	Drawdell Magnolia Blossom	P Rooney
Badgerbrook Tokyo Joe	d	09.03.79	Ch Harecroft Magnus of Balleroy	Gaymel Miss Smarty Pants of Badgerbrook	Master J Williamson
Rossfell Crazy Horse	d	14.08.81	Ch Harecroft Magnus of Balleroy	Drawdell Weeping Willow	Mr & Mrs R Parker
Siouxline Matthew	d	25.12.79	Ch Langpool Scrumpy	Siouxline Kelly	Mrs S Ergis
Waldo of Akerwood	d	25.03.80	Ch Mayacre Mr Magoo	Ch Turberville Easter Rose	Mrs D Shemeld
Bezel Lorna Doon	b	28.12.79	Bezel Action Man	Ch Bezel Sweety Pie	Mrs M Thorley
Jeffrone Gypsy	b	10.12.81	Bassbarr Roving Reporter	Ch Jeffrone Guillemot of Jeffrone	Mr & Mrs F Horsley
Norendo Amazing Grace	b	05.05.82	Ch Langpool William	Mevacombe Perlita	Mr & Mrs J Green
Badgerbrook Casablanca	b	09.03.79	Ch Harecroft Magnus of Balleroy	Gaymel Miss Smarty Pants of Badgerbrook	Mr & Mrs M Williamson

Name		DOB	Sire	Dam	Owner
Biscovey Sweet Caroline	b	11.11.81	Ch Harecroft Magnus of Balleroy	Drawdell Magnolia Blossom	P Rooney
Karipat Spring Mist	b	21.03.83	Merrybeech Wellington of Balmacara	Karipat Sharoween Pride	Mrs P Wedgewood
Harecroft Regina of Helmsdown	b	07.11.80	Bassbarr Dutch Courage	Harecroft Mistletoe	Mr & Mrs R Price

1985

Name		DOB	Sire	Dam	Owner
Belvere Maggie May at Frome Bank	b	19.07.82	Ch Kuntree Rhodes at Belvere	Belvere Tiffany	Mrs M Gray
Gladsomes Harvest Gold	d	24.05.83	Ch Biscovey Robert-E-Lee	Windwell Hanky Panky	Mrs G Douglas
Gladsomes Hisper	d	24.05.83	Ch Biscovey Robert-E-Lee	Windwell Hanky Panky	Mrs G Douglas
Verwood Raphia	b	09.05.83	Ch Kuntree Rhodes at Belvere	Ch Zondas I'm A Muddy Girl of Verwood	Mrs V Ross
Barrengers Queen's Indian	b	08.03.83	Verwood Royal Swede	Verwood Brimstone of Barrenger	Miss S Thexton
Sykemoor Rosamund of Rollinhills	b	24.08.83	Ch Brackenacre The Viking	Ch Sykemoor Rosebud	G Johnston / Bascor Quarell
Vinell Dapper Dandy	b	14.08.83	Bascor Royal Nugget	Langpool Dolly Daydream	Mmes M Powell & H Jones
The Senator of Siouxline	d	08.09.83	Ch Brackenacre The Viking	Ch Vinell Antimony	Mrs L Ellrich
	d	19.04.82	Verwood Varne	Siouxline Miriam	Mmes S Ergis & A Billows

1986

Name		DOB	Sire	Dam	Owner
Ledline Lady Chatterley	b	28.09.82	Ch Waldo of Akerwood	Ch Ledline White Apache	T Ledbury
Fredwell Finesse	b	25.05.83	Balmacara Puddles	Fredwell Freedom	Mrs J Wells-Meacham
Fresh Lettuce of Verwood	b	30.12.84	Verwood Royal Swede	Prudence of Romney March	Mrs M Austin
Fredwell Freebie	d	29.05.83	Ch Beacontree Gelarista Gold Blend	Fredwell Friendly	Mrs J Wells-Meacham
Ledline Drucilla Penny	b	14.05.84	Beacontree Widgeon	Ledline Foolish Maid	Mrs T Ledbury
Elkington Felicity	b	01.06.83	Swiss Ch Fauntleroy v d Hoeve	Swiss Ch Elkington Dear Me	Mrs C Roch
Brackenacre The Witch	b	19.12.81	Ch Brackenacre James Bond	Pendlewitch of Brackenacre	Mr & Mrs J Nixon
Badgerbrook Dirty Harry	d	09.01.81	Ch Badgerbrook Tokyo Joe	Franshaw Rosie of Badgerbrook	Mr & Mrs M Williamson
Bashur Zorba The Greek	d	17.11.84	Ch Lodway Lancer of Islwyn	Verwood I'm A Hustler of Bashur	Mrs K Barr
Brackenacre The Challenger	d	15.11.83	Ch Brackenacre The Viking	Pendlewitch of Brackenacre	Mr & Mrs J Nixon

1987

Name		DOB	Sire	Dam	Owner
Vinell Hooray Henry	d	14.01.85	Lodway Mickey Finn	Ch Vinell Antimony	Mrs L Ness
Fredwell Fiasco	d	31.10.85	Ch Gladsomes Harvest Gold	Fredwell Fleur	N Frost & Mrs J Wells-Meacham
Langpool Wandering Star	d	05.07.83	Ch Langpool William	Meddgool Moonbeam of Langpool	Dr E Andrews
Charford Ceilidh	b	13.04.85	Ch Carresmar Legend	Leirum Chrysanthemum	Mrs A Charman
Whiteland Cassandra	b	06.03.83	Bassbarr Dutch Courage of Jeffrone	Eastville Rhythm	Mrs E Johnson
Dahenol Diamond	b	07.08.85	Wenceslas of Langpool	Bascor Ola of Dahenol	Mr & Mrs J Savory
Helmsdown Daphne	b	23.10.84	Ch Lodway Lancer of Islwyn	Ch Harecroft Regina of Helmsdown	C Gillanders

1988

Name		DOB	Sire	Dam	Owner
Rittyrig Wallis	b	28.08.85	Merrybeech Wellington	Rittyrig Xitta of Balmacara	Mr & Mrs A Campbell
Brackenacre Jasmine	b	19.11.85	Ch Brackenacre The Viking	Brackenacre Zero Zero	Mr & Mrs J Nixon
Bascor Sorel	b	31.07.85	Bascor Royal Nugget	Langpool Dolly Daydream	Mrs M Powell & H Jones
Vinell Digeri Doo	b	08.09.83	Ch Brackenacre The Viking	Ch Vinall Antimony	Mrs L Ness
Karipat Sweetbriyne of Switherland	b	03.09.86	Karipat Olympic Banner	Ch Karipat Spring Mist	Mrs P Wedgwood
Wellboy Lucky Lady	b	03.06.85	Ch Lodway Lancer of Islwyn	Wellboy Val-N-Teena	Mrs L Hogarth
Balmacara Gunfire	d	27.10.85	Merrybeech Wellington of Balmacara	Balleroy Buxom	Mrs F Meredith

Name	Sex	DOB	Sire	Dam	Breeder
Lelaurin Lennox	d	30.04.85	Ch Vinell Dapper Dandy	Beacontree Whooper of Lelaurin	Mrs J Laurie
Brackenacre Katie Mia	b	28.11.85	Ch Brackenacre The Viking	Brackenacre Zinnia	Mr & Mrs J Nixon
Sykemoor Gilder	d	25.10.85	Ch Gladsomes Harvest Gold	Sykemoor Raven	Mrs G Johnston
Vinell Double Diamond	d	08.09.83	Ch Brackenacre The Viking	Ch Vinell Antimony	Mrs L Ellrich
1989					
Tal-e-ho's Upstart of Verwood	b	12.09.83	Tal-e-ho's Trooper George	Am Ch Tal-e-ho's Pistachio	Mrs A Jerman & P Campanella
Maquisard Woeful Wogan	d	02.11.84	Gelarista Ebonite	Maquisard Heylook That's Me	Mr & Mrs D Dunbar
Mooroolbark Land of Song	b	23.10.86	Ch Lodway Lancer of Islwyn	Jussland Ophelia at Mooroolbark	Mr & Mrs A Salusbury
Taormina January Gem	b	26.01.87	Siouxline Reuben	Bassmass Right As Rain	Mr & Mrs G Taor
Brackenacre Top Class	b	13.01.88	Brackenacre Black Knight	Brackenacre Mary Rose	Mr & Mrs J Nixon
Locketwhite Inspiration of Khabaray	b	19.04.88	Ch Langpool Wandering Star	Wellshim Posie	Mrs Whitehead
Gladsomes Gold Ranson	d	04.12.86	Ch Gladsomes Harvest Gold	Gladsomes Davina	Mr & Mrs G Douglas
Ledline Rosie Glow at Castlebrook	b	22.11.86	Ch Lelaurin Lennox	Ch Ledline Drucilla Penny	T Ledbury
Eastport Classic Gold Lace	d	31.08.86	Ch Beacontree Gelarista Gold Blend	Eastport Paper Lace	Mr & Mrs E Mayne
Stookewood Tigerlily	b	27.12.85	Ch Lodway Lancer of Islwyn	Mevacombe Modesty of Stookewood	Mr & Mrs I & P McLean
Suzanna of Siouxline	b	26.01.87	Siouxline Reuben	Bassmass Right As Rain	Mr & Mrs G Taor
Eastport Black Coffee	d	31.08.86	Ch Beacontree Gelarista Gold Blend	Eastport Paper Lace	Mr J & Mrs E Mayne
Brackenacre Fancy and Free of Tancegems	b	14.07.84	Ch Brackenacre The Viking	Brackenacre Zero Zero	Mr & Mrs J Nixon
1990					
Viness Vinell Whoops-a-Daisy	b	14.10.88	Ch Vinell Hooray Henry	Ch Vinell Digeri Doo	Mr & Mrs M Ness
Switherland Wild Rose	b	21.03.88	Karipat Olimpic Banner	Karipat Penelope of Switherland	Mr & Mrs P Freer
Highchart Evening Primrose of Galant	b	09.02.87	Watermead Chestnut of Cayuga	Highchart Blonde Bomb Shell	Miss M Swanson
Balmacara Gunshot	d	27.10.85	Merrybeech Wellington of Balmacara	Balleroy Buxom	Mrs F Meredith
Witchacre Stroller	d	01.06.87	Ch Gladsomes Harvest Gold	Witchacre That's My Girl	Mr & Mrs J Ryan
Kortina Big-Bad-Dom	d	06.11.87	Lodway Private Benjamin of Kortina	Kortina Dark Crystal	Mrs C Cornell
Carresmar Lawrence	d	07.04.88	Ch Lodway Lancer of Islwyn	Carresmar Look At Me	Mrs E Watson
Brandydale Royal Gold	d	09.01.85	Ch Gladsomes Harvest Gold	Brandydale Dulcie	Mr & Mrs J Coopey
Brandydale Equerry For Barratini	d	14.10.88	Ch Brandydale Royal Gold	Brandydale Joanna	Mr & Mrs J Coopey
Karipat Wildair of Switherland	d	22.02.86	Bascor Royal Nugget	Karipat Shooting Star	Mrs P Wedgwood
1991					
Limgoning April	b	20.06.89	Lowaters Lottery	Balleroy Kersey	J Wilson
Verulam Morgan Le Fay	b	24.12.87	Can Ch Sand-Dell's Sanko	Can Ch Verulam Harriet	Mr & Mrs R Albon
Helmsdown Gertrude	b	02.06.88	Ch Balmacara Gunfire	Ch Helmsdown Daphne	C Gillanders
Barrenger Demon King	d	18.12.88	Siouxline Reuben	Ch Barrengers Queen's Indian	Ms S Thexton
1992					
Kentley Marmalade of Verwood	b	16.01.90	Verwood Hyper-Hyper	Kentley Honey Suckle	Mrs J Humphery
Hollysend Ghostbuster	d	23.09.88	Ch Eastport Black Coffee	Fieldsman Mistletoe	Mrs J Bartley
Karipat Lawrence	d	10.01.90	Ch Karipat Wildair of Switherland	Karipat Lizzie	Mrs P Wedgwood
Limgoning Avril	b	20.06.89	Lowaters Lottery	Basseroy Kersey	J Wilson
Charford Claudia at Puckaman	b	07.11.89	Ch Carresmar Lindsay	Charford Carriad	Mrs A Charman
Locketwhite Magic Merl	d	20.09.90	Ch White Gold of Andyne	Locketwhite Lydia	Mr & Mrs D Whitehead

Name	Sex	DOB	Sire	Dam	Owner/Breeder
Switherland Wild Orchid	b	25.02.91	Ch Karipat Lawrence	Ch Switherland Wild Rose	Mr & Mrs J Freer
White Gold of Andyne	d	15.06.89	Balleroy Jazzman at Andyne	Freckles Golden Sunset	Mrs Jerram
Bassbarr O'Sullivan	d	21.01.91	Ch White Gold of Andyne	Ch O'Hara van Hollandheim	W O'Loughlin
1993					
Viness Vinell Yum Yum of Lelaurin	b	15.04.1991	It Ch Bassbarr Fred Astaire	Ch Viness Vinell Whoops-a-Daisy	Mr & Mrs L Ness
Fredwell Faldo	d	16.09.90	Fredwell Fidelio	Chantalle's Nuisance	N Frost & Mrs J Wells-Meacham
Maghefeld Defender of Bassbarr	d	25.05.91	Verwood Hyper-Hyper	Lady Emma of Maghefeld	Mrs Raeburn
Switherland Camilla	b	25.11.90	Fredwell Fidelio	Switherland Ruby	Mr & Mrs Freer
Viness Vinell Vice Versa	b	07.06.87	Ch Lodway Lancer of Islwyn	Ch Vinell Digeri Doo	Mr & Mrs I Ness
Bassbarr O'Shea	b	21.01.91	Ch White Gold of Andyne	Ch O'Hara van Hollandeim	W O'Loughlin
Barrenger Devil Snuffbox	b	01.09.91	Ch/Ir Ch Barrenger Demon King	Barrenger Indian Summer	Mmes Thexton & Martin
Bassbarr Oh Clare	b	21.01.91	Ch White Gold of Andyne	Ch O'Hara van Hollandheim	W O'Loughlin
1994					
Brackenacre My April Fool	b	01.04.92	Ch Hollysend Ghostbuster	Ch Brackenacre Top Class	Mr & Mrs J Nixon
Five Valleys Aurora	b	16.02.91	Kortina's Patrolman	Kortina's Madonna	Mrs S Allen
White Mischief of Moragden	b	20.09.93	Lowaters Lottery	Moragden Magnolia	Carter & Gray
Viness Vinell Bizzy Lizzie	b	16.09.92	Verwood Hyper-Hyper	Ch Viness Vinell Vice Versa	Mr & Mrs L Ness
O'Hara van Hollandheim	b	13.06.89	Nl/Int/B Ch Lonesome Lover v Hollandheim	Nl/Int Ch Sensation v Hollandheim	Mrs C Gerber
Andyne Milky Way	b	09.11.92	Bassbarr On Parade at Andyne	Andyne Over The Moon	Mrs A Dynes
Bassbarr Obsession with Bronia	b	16.07.93	Ch Bassbarr O'Sullivan	Andyne Chanel for Bassbarr	W O'Loughlin
1995					
Brackenacre Navan	b	14.10.92	Ch Hollysend Ghostbuster	Brackenacre Victoria	Mr & Mrs J Nixon
Switherland Sage	d	23.01.93	Bassbarr On Parade at Andyne	Ch Karipat Sweetbriyne of Switherland	Mr & Mrs P Freer
Viness Vinell Just William	d	16.09.92	Verwood Hyper-Hyper	Ch Viness Vinell Vice Versa	Mr & Mrs L Ness
Faburn Gypsy	b	23.05.93	Ch Bassbarr O'Sullivan	Faburn Folly	Mr & Mrs P Garry Arthurs
Islwyn Sophinee	b	14.06.93	Mooroolbark from The Master at Islwyn	Islwyn My Fanwy	Mr & Mrs J Roberts
Switherland Surprise	b	23.01.93	Bassbarr On Parade At Andyne	Ch Karipat Sweetbriyne of Switherland	Mr & Mrs P Freer
1996					
Brackenacre Mary Anne	b	01.04.92	Ch Hollysend Ghostbuster	Ch Brackenacre Top Class	Mr & Mrs J Nixon
Siouxline Daniella	b	04.10.92	Barratini Ambassador to Siouxline	Ch Suzana of Siouxline	Mrs S Ergis
Siouxline Doyle of Dereheath	d	04.10.92	Barratini Ambassador to Siouxline	Ch Suzana of Siouxline	Mrs S Ergis
Bassbarr Queen of Diamonds	b	25.09.94	Ch Bassbarr O'Sullivan	Andyne Chanel for Bassbarr	W O'Loughlin
Viness Vinell Ko-Ko	b	16.05.94	Viness Vinell Zoic	Ch Viness Vinell Yum Yum of Lelaurin	Mr & Mrs L Ness
Switherland Strudel	d	23.01.93	Bassbarr On Parade at Andyne	Ch Karipat Sweetbriyne of Switherland	Mr & Mrs P Freer
Switherland Desert Orchid	d	12.11.93	Bassbarr On Parade at Andyne	Ch Switherland Wild Orchid	Mr & Mrs P Freer
Switherland Blue Jeans	d	22.02.95	Ch Switherland Wild Orchid	Switherland Designer Jeans	Mr & Mrs P Freer
Switherland Betabuy Design	b	22.02.95	Ch Switherland Desert Orchid	Switherland Designer Jeans	Mr & Mrs P Freer
Dereheath Cuddles	b	15.10.94	Karipat Dicken	Barratini Almond of Dereheath	Mr & Mrs D Storton
Morkebergs It's Now Or Never at Balmacara (*import*)	d	10.01.95	Dk/Am Ch Scheels Excalibur	Dk Ch Morkebergs Ophelia	N Morkeberg-Smidt

	01	02	03	04	05	06	07	08	09	10	11	12	13	14	15	16	17	18	19	20	21	22	23	24	25	26	27	28	29	30	31
Served Jan	01	02	03	04	05	06	07	08	09	10	11	12	13	14	15	16	17	18	19	20	21	22	23	24	25	26	27	28	29	30	31
Due to whelp Mar/Apr	05	06	07	08	09	10	11	12	13	14	15	16	17	18	19	20	21	22	23	24	25	26	27	28	29	30	31	01	02	03	04
Served Feb	01	02	03	04	05	06	07	08	09	10	11	12	13	14	15	16	17	18	19	20	21	22	23	24	25	26	27	28	(29)		
Due to whelp Apr/May	05	06	07	08	09	10	11	12	13	14	15	16	17	18	19	20	21	22	23	24	25	26	27	28	29	30	01	02	(03)		
Served Mar	01	02	03	04	05	06	07	08	09	10	11	12	13	14	15	16	17	18	19	20	21	22	23	24	25	26	27	28	29	30	31
Due to whelp May/Jun	03	04	05	06	07	08	09	10	11	12	13	14	15	16	17	18	19	20	21	22	23	24	25	26	27	28	29	30	31	01	02
Served Apr	01	02	03	04	05	06	07	08	09	10	11	12	13	14	15	16	17	18	19	20	21	22	23	24	25	26	27	28	29	30	
Due to whelp Jun/Jul	03	04	05	06	07	08	09	10	11	12	13	14	15	16	17	18	19	20	21	22	23	24	25	26	27	28	29	30	01	02	
Served May	01	02	03	04	05	06	07	08	09	10	11	12	13	14	15	16	17	18	19	20	21	22	23	24	25	26	27	28	29	30	31
Due to whelp Jul/Aug	03	04	05	06	07	08	09	10	11	12	13	14	15	16	17	18	19	20	21	22	23	24	25	26	27	28	29	30	31	01	02
Served Jun	01	02	03	04	05	06	07	08	09	10	11	12	13	14	15	16	17	18	19	20	21	22	23	24	25	26	27	28	29	30	
Due to whelp Aug/Sep	03	04	05	06	07	08	09	10	11	12	13	14	15	16	17	18	19	20	21	22	23	24	25	26	27	28	29	30	31	01	
Served Jul	01	02	03	04	05	06	07	08	09	10	11	12	13	14	15	16	17	18	19	20	21	22	23	24	25	26	27	28	29	30	31
Due to whelp Sep/Oct	02	03	04	05	06	07	08	09	10	11	12	13	14	15	16	17	18	19	20	21	22	23	24	25	26	27	28	29	30	01	02
Served Aug	01	02	03	04	05	06	07	08	09	10	11	12	13	14	15	16	17	18	19	20	21	22	23	24	25	26	27	28	29	30	31
Due to whelp Oct/Nov	03	04	05	06	07	08	09	10	11	12	13	14	15	16	17	18	19	20	21	22	23	24	25	26	27	28	29	30	31	01	02
Served Sep	01	02	03	04	05	06	07	08	09	10	11	12	13	14	15	16	17	18	19	20	21	22	23	24	25	26	27	28	29	30	
Due to whelp Nov/Dec	03	04	05	06	07	08	09	10	11	12	13	14	15	16	17	18	19	20	21	22	23	24	25	26	27	28	29	01	01	...	
Served Oct	01	02	03	04	05	06	07	08	09	10	11	12	13	14	15	16	17	18	19	20	21	22	23	24	25	26	27	28	29	30	31
Due to whelp Dec/Jan	03	04	05	06	07	08	09	10	11	12	13	14	15	16	17	18	19	20	21	22	23	24	25	26	27	28	29	30	31	01	02
Served Nov	01	02	03	04	05	06	07	08	09	10	11	12	13	14	15	16	17	18	19	20	21	22	23	24	25	26	27	28	29	30	
Due to whelp Jan/Feb	03	04	05	06	07	08	09	10	11	12	13	14	15	16	17	18	19	20	21	22	23	24	25	26	27	28	29	30	31	01	
Served Dec	01	02	03	04	05	06	07	08	09	10	11	12	13	14	15	16	17	18	19	20	21	22	23	24	25	26	27	28	29	30	31
Due to whelp Feb/Mar	02	03	04	05	06	07	08	09	10	11	12	13	14	15	16	17	18	19	20	21	22	23	24	25	26	27	28	01	02	03	04

Important Pedigrees

Grims Ulema de Barly

An Artésien-Normand born in France 2 June 1946 and imported by Miss Keevil. Sire of 5 champions and grandsire of 13 champions.

Parents	Grandparents	Great-grandparents	Great-great-grandparents
Sire: Sans Souci de Bourceville	Sire: Néro de Bourceville	Sire: Gabelou de Bourceville	Enjoleur de Bourceville
			Delurée de Bourceville
		Dam: Javotte de Bourceville	Gabelou
			Belizaire de Barly
	Dam: Ravaude de Bourceville	Sire: Néro de Bourceville	Gabelou
			Javotte de Bourceville
		Dam: Missia (à M Huirel)	Fakir
			Jalouse
Dam: Querelle de Barly	Sire: Mireau de Barly	Sire: Turbulent de Barly	N/K
			N/K
		Dam: Élégante de Jaulzy	N/K
			N/K
	Dam: Mirabelle de Barly	Sire: Hitler de Barly	N/K
			N/K
		Dam: Luronne de Bourceville	N/K
			N/K

Ch Fredwell Varon Vandal   Born: 21 November 1960. Sire of 10 champions.

Parents	Grandparents	Great-grandparents	Great-great-grandparents
Sire: Ch Fochno Trooper	**Sire:** Ch Grims Whirlwind	**Sire:** Grims Ulema de Barly	Sans Souci de Bourceville
			Querelle de Barly
		Dam: Grims Wanda	Radium of Reynalton
			Ch Grims Wishful
	Dam: Sykemoor Gossip	**Sire:** Trumpeter of Reynalton	Sovereign of Reynalton
			Miranda of Reynalton
		Dam: Ch Rossingham Amber	Ch Grims Warlock
			Ch Grims Willow
Dam: Rollick of Fredwell	**Sire:** Ch Rossingham Badger	**Sire:** Ch Grims Doughnut	Westerby Rennet
			Grims Daisy
		Dam: Ch Grims Willow	Grims Ulema de Barly
			Grims Waterlily
	Dam: Barnspark Rollick	**Sire:** Ch Grims Westward	Grims Ulema de Barly
			Grims Wanda
		Dam: Ch Grims Gracious	Ch Grims Wideawake
			Grims Garrulous

Ch Wingjays Ptolemy Born 13 July 1964. Sire of 8 champions.

Parents	Grandparents	Great-grandparents	Great-great-grandparents
Sire: Ch Breightmet Chimer	Sire: Grims Charlie	Sire: Grims William	Grims Ulema de Barly
			Grims Waterlily
		Dam: Grims Chopette	Grims Chasseur
			Grims U Cornemeuse
	Dam: Grims Vanish	Sire: Grims Emblem	Envoy
			Ch Grims Waterwagtail
		Dam: Ch Grims Useful	Grims Ulema de Barly
			Grims Wanda
Dam: Ch Sungarth Phoebe	Sire: Ch Sykemoor Aimwell	Sire: Ch Grims Whirlwind	Grims Ulema de Barly
			Grims Wanda
		Dam: Ch Rossingham Amber	Ch Grims Warlock
			Ch Grims Willow
	Dam: Aesops Able	Sire: Ch Rossingham Badger	Ch Grims Doughnut
			Ch Grims Willow
		Dam: Rossingham Clover	Ch Grims Doughnut
			Ch Rossingham Anxious

Ch Harecroft Magnus of Balleroy   Born 27 July 1976. Sire of 6 champions.

Parents	Grandparents	Great-grandparents	Great-great-grandparents
Sire: Ch Balleroy Luther	Sire: Balleroy Bacchus	Sire: Aust Ch Balleroy Karl	Ch Balleroy Chestnut
			Stormfield Giselle
		Dam: Balleroy Rumba	Ch Balleroy Chestnut
			Balleroy Gypsy
	Dam: Balleroy Hoo-Ha	Sire: Am Ch Long View Acres Bonza	Am Ch Abbot Run Valley Brassy
			Am Ch Kazoo's Flora Tina
		Dam: Balleroy Scylla	Ch Balleroy Chestnut
			Chantinghall Dreamer
Dam: Gaymel Moray	Sire: Gaymel Marcus	Sire: Ch Verwood Mirus	It/Swiss Ch Dreymin Dusky Knight
			Verwood Chinook
		Dam: Bazelgette Felecie of Gaymel	Ch Fredwell Ideal
			Bazelgette Premery
	Dam: Bazelgette Felecie of Gaymel	Sire: Ch Fredwell Ideal	Int Ch Mariseni Breightmet Wessex
			Fredwell Renne
		Dam: Bazelgette Premery	Ch Fredwell Varon Vandal
			Bazelgette Arabella

Ch Fredwell Ideal   Born 1 December 1961. Sire of 6 champions.

Parents	Grandparents	Great-grandparents	Great-great-grandparents
Sire: Ch Brackenacre James Bond	**Sire:** Ch Brackenacre Fino de Paris	**Sire:** Ch Fredwell Ideal	Int Ch Mariseni Breightmet Wessex
			Fredwell Rennet
		Dam: Brackenacre Chime of Bells	Ch Winjays Ptolemy
			Ch Brackenacre Annabella
	Dam: Brackenacre Emma Peel	**Sire:** Ch Stormfield Hugo	Ch Chantinghall Ancestor
			Ballymaconnel Boule de Suif
		Dam: Brackenacre Chantress	Ch Wingjays Ptolemy
			Ch Brackenacre Annabella
Dam: Witchacre Magpie of Brackenacre	**Sire:** Bezel Action Man	**Sire:** Brackenacre Hopeful	Ch Fredwell Varon Fawkes
			Ch Brackenacre Daisy Belle
		Dam: Ireton Fashionable Fad	Ch Fredwell Varon Fawkes
			Ireton Fantasia
	Dam: Ch Brackenacre Jingle Bell	**Sire:** Ch Brackenacre Fino de Paris	Ch Fredwell Ideal
			Brackenacre Chime of Bells
		Dam: Ch Brackenacre Daisy Belle	Ch Fredwell Varon Vandal
			Ch Brackenacre Annabella

Ch Brackenacre The Viking Born: 22 December 1980. Sire of 8 champions.

Parents	Grandparents	Great-grandparents	Great-great-grandparents
Sire: Ch Brackenacre James Bond	**Sire:** Ch Brackenacre Fino de Paris	**Sire:** Ch Fredwell Ideal	Int Ch Mariseni Breightmet Wessex
			Fredwell Rennet
		Dam: Brackenacre Chime of Bells	Ch Winjays Ptolemy
			Ch Brackenacre Annabella
	Dam: Brackenacre Emma Peel	**Sire:** Ch Stormfield Hugo	Ch Chantinghall Ancestor
			Ballymaconnel Boule de Suif
		Dam: Brackenacre Chantress	Ch Wingjays Ptolemy
			Ch Brackenacre Annabella
Dam: Witchacre Magpie of Brackenacre	**Sire:** Bezel Action Man	**Sire:** Brackenacre Hopeful	Ch Fredwell Varon Fawkes
			Ch Brackenacre Daisy Belle
		Dam: Ireton Fashionable Fad	Ch Fredwell Varon Fawkes
			Ireton Fantasia
	Dam: Ch Brackenacre Jingle Bell	**Sire:** Ch Brackenacre Fino de Paris	Ch Fredwell Ideal
			Brackenacre Chime of Bells
		Dam: Ch Brackenacre Daisy Belle	Ch Fredwell Varon Vandal
			Ch Brackenacre Annabella

Ch Lodway Lancer of Islwyn   Born: 16 September 1980. Sire of 7 champions.

Parents	Grandparents	Great-grandparents	Great-great-grandparents
Sire: Ch Langpool Carries Lad of Islwyn	**Sire:** Verwood Wabash	**Sire:** Am Ch Lyn-Mar Acres Endman of Maycombe	Am Ch Lyn-Mar Acres M'Lord Batuff
			Lyn-Mar Acres Burl-Lee-Q
		Dam: Welshim Carmen	Dalewell Rambler
			Stationhouse Honey
	Dam: Ch Langpool Carrie Anne	**Sire:** Am Ch Long View Acres Bonza	Am Ch Abbot Run Valley Brassy
			Am Ch Kazoos Flora Tina
		Dam: Balleroy Barshaw Caprice	Ch Balleroy Chstnu
			Balleroy Dewdrop
Dam: Ch Mayflower of Langpool	**Sire:** Ch Langpool William	**Sire:** Am Ch Long View Acres Bonza	Am Ch Abbot Fun Valley Brassy
			Am Ch Kazoos Flora Tina
		Dam: Balleroy Barshaw Caprice	Ch Balleroy Chestnut
			Balleroy Dewdrop
	Dam: Dubrova Hanky Panky	**Sire:** Langpool Friar Tuck U The Beacontree	Am Ch Long View Acres Bonza
			Balleroy Barshaw Caprice
		Dam: Hathersall Princess	Dalewell Rambler
			Abbey Bathsheba

Bibliography

Great Britain

Appleton, Douglas *The Basset Hound Handbook* 1960

Fitch Daglish, E *The Basset Hound* 1964

Johnston, George *The Basset Hound* 1968

Millais, Sir Everett *Two Problems of Reproduction* 1895

Rowett Johns, Jeanne *All About the Basset Hound* 1973

Wells-Meacham, Joan *The Basset Hound* 1981

United States

Basset Hound Club of America *Field Trialing with a Basset Hound* 1978

Braun, Mercedes *The Complete Basset Hound* 1965

Leibers *and* **Hardy** *Raise and Train a Basset Hound* 1959

Look, M Travis *Pet Basset Hound* 1960

McCarty, Diane, ed *Basset Hounds* 1979

Smith, Carl *Training the Rabbit Hound, Basset and Beagle* 1926

Walton, Margaret *The New Basset Hound* 1993

France

Berton, Claude *Les Bassets Français* 1977

Bourbon, Alain *Nos Bassets Français* 1911

Leblanc, Maurice *Le Basset Artésien Normand* 1982

Leblanc *et* **Miller** *Les Bassets Courants* 1987

Leseble, L *Les Bassets*

Verrier, Léon *Les Bassets Français* 1921

Other countries

Christensen, I C *Basset Hound* 1976 Denmark

Gondrexon, A *De Franse Basset Artésien-Normand* 1976 Holland

Heinsius, Carmen *Der Basset* 1984 Germany

Johnston, George *El Basset Hound* 1982 Argentina

Johnston, George *Il Basset Hound* 1983 Italy

Taragano, R *Basset Hound* 1974 Argentina

A bbreviations

ABBREVIATIONS

Am Ch   : American (United States) Champion

Aust Ch   : Australian Champion

BHF Ch   : German Ch

BIS   : Best In Show

BOB   : Best Of Breed

CAC   : Challenge Certificate (FCI)

CACIB   : International Challenge Certificate (FCI)

Can Ch   : Canadian Champion

CC   : Challenge Certificate

Ch   : Champion (on its own, British Champion)

Dk Ch   : Danish Champion

FCI   : Fédération Cynologique Internationale

Fin Ch   : Finnish Champion

Int Ch   : International Champion

It Ch   : Italian Champion

Lux Ch   : Luxembourg Champion

Nu Ch   : Norwegian Champion

Nl Ch   : Netherlands (Dutch) Champion

Nor Du Ch : Nordic Champion (a dog with CCs from Sweden, Norway and/or Finland)

Su Ch   : Swedish Champion

VDH Ch   : German Champion (German Kennel Club)

W   : World Winner (an FCI award)

The Kennel Club:

The Kennel Club
1–5 Clarges Street
Piccadilly
London   WIY 8AB

Basset Hound clubs and organisations:

The Basset Hound Club
Hon Secretary: Mrs S Ergis
15 Scott Close
Wallisdown
Poole
Dorset   BH12 5AX

The Basset Hound Club of Northern Ireland
Hon Secretary: Mrs G McDowell
The Cottage
Portnoo
Co Donegal

The Basset Hound Club of Scotland
Hon Secretary: Mr D Sharpe
Four Winds
Greenloaning
Braco
Dunblane
Perthshire

The Basset Hound Club of Wales
Hon Secretary: Mrs A Roberts
2 Melin Street
Cwmfelinfach
Nr Newport
Gwent   NP1 7GZ

Basset Hound Rescue and Welfare
National Coordinator: Mrs Pat Green
32 Muswell Road
Derby   DE22 4HN

The Hadrian Basset Hound Club
Hon Secretary: Mr T Coddington
10 Lartington Gardens
South Gosforth
Newcastle-upon-Tyne   NE3 !SX

The Lancashire, Yorkshire and Cheshire
  Basset Hound Club
Hon Secretary: Mr M Ledward
909 Middleton Road West
Chadderton
Oldham
Lancs

The Midlands Basset Hound Club
Hon Secretary: Mrs J Horsley
Blythe Kennels
Dexter Lane
Hurley
Nr Atherstone
Warwicks

The South of England Basset Hound Club
Hon Secretary: Ms S Thexton
The Elms
West Yeo
Moorland
Bridgwater
Somerset   TA7 0AU

Other useful addresses:

Dog World Ltd
Somerfield
Wotton Road
Ashford   Kent   TN23 1BR

The Homoeopathic Society for Animal Welfare
(HSAW)
Co-Ordinator: Mrs N J Brook
New Parc
Llanthidrai
Gower
Glamorgan   SA3 H1A

Our Dogs Publishing Co Ltd
5 Oxford Road Station Approach
Manchester
M60 1SX

PAT Dogs
4–6 New Road
Ditton
Kent   ME20 6AD